HOW TO APPRAISE
COMMERCIAL PROPERTIES

How to APPRAISE COMMERCIAL PROPERTIES

PETER C. ROBINSON, A.S.A.

PRENTICE-HALL, INC. Englewood Cliffs, N. J.

PRENTICE-HALL INTERNATIONAL, INC., *London*
PRENTICE-HALL OF AUSTRALIA, PTY. LTD., *Sydney*
PRENTICE-HALL OF CANADA, LTD., *Toronto*
PRENTICE-HALL OF INDIA PRIVATE LTD., *New Delhi*
PRENTICE-HALL OF JAPAN, INC., *Tokyo*

LIBRARY OF CONGRESS
CATALOG CARD NUMBER: 73–158107

PRINTED IN THE UNITED STATES OF AMERICA

ISBN—0-13-401828-1
B & P

To *Joanne W. Robinson*

In grateful recognition
of her enduring patience
and faith, high humor,
hope and charity.

About the Author

Peter C. Robinson, A.S.A., is an independent real estate appraiser specializing in commercial and industrial properties. For twenty-five years he has been instrumental in erecting shopping centers, office buildings, and apartment houses in Connecticut, New York, and New Jersey. As agent for the Connecticut Development Commission, he maintains contacts with brokers and appraisers throughout the nation to find commercial prospects for his state. Mr. Robinson's professional memberships include: The American Industrial Council, The American Right of Way Association, and Senior Member and past Regional Governor of The American Society of Appraisers. He is a director of the Investment Corporation of America. He also holds state and federal accreditations as a fee appraiser.

A Word from the Author

This is the first book on commercial real estate appraising to emphasize *The Investment Analysis Method* as an applied science in determining value.

The Investment Analysis Method consists of making proper tests for most likely-profitable use; of setting up sensible techniques and procedure for market analysis and income capitalization; and finally determining value through the *combined* gristmill actions of the *Income Approach* and a *Comprehensive Market Study* of the property's magnetisms.

This book is a gateway to understanding why, how, where and when beneficial or deteriorating influences accrue to income property. It illuminates the appraisal of commercial property as a *process,* in terms of: (1) How to state the appraisal problem, purpose and function; (2) how to estimate Highest and Best (most likely-profitable) Use; (3) how to set about the Market Survey and the Property Analysis, i.e., how to distinguish between *Macro-market* and *Micro-market* factors; and (4) how to develop the *Investment Analysis Method* into a coherent statement.

The demand for a product or service in any locale rests, to some degree, on external (Macro-market) socio-economic forces acting in harmony with, or in conflict with, a smaller (Micro-market) area immediately surrounding the subject under appraisement. Invariably, the larger area is a dominant influence within which the smaller marketing area must adjust as part of an overall structured urban pattern. It is the melding of these influences that leads the appraiser to measurable qualities and sound judgment in his Market Survey; hence to proper determinations of rate in the Income Approach and a statement of Investment Worth.

I have made a comprehensive effort in this volume to "touch all the bases" in the appraisal of commercial realty, and concrete examples are used throughout, such as:

1. How to Analyze the Investment Property Site.
2. How to Equate Depreciation Factors in All Types of Commercial Structures.
3. How to Apply Capitalization Methods and Rates, and Residual Techniques Under the Income Approach.
4. How to Appraise for Condemnation—the Partial Take—the Total Take—and How to Use the Government's 49-Point Form.
5. How to Appraise for Mortgage Financing.
6. How to Appraise for a Tax Function.

7. How to Use a Tenant and Design Profile in Office Building and Apartment House Feasibility Studies and Appraisals.

This is the sum and substance, then, of the Investment Analysis Method of appraising commercial properties. There are no mystiques, word-bridges, methodologies or game elements to be encountered here.

Part One of this book will provide you with a special slant on the Appraisal Process, emphasizing the Income Approach; Part Two will demonstrate specific techniques and procedures of appraising, with Model Appraisals illustrating nearly every conceivable posture of investment value.

In the construction of this book, I am indebted to a number of master-appraisers for their thoughtful advice and suggestions as to major points of illustration, and for their warmth and friendship in extending to me the benefits of their wisdom and experience.

These gentlemen are: Arthur K. Beman, M.A.I.; Francis G. Brennan, A.S.A., AR/WA; Patrick A. Flynn, A.S.A ., AR/WA; Edward M. Freda, M.A.I.; Francis Gorka, A.S.A.; Edward F. Heberger, A.S.A., M.A.I.; Harry H. Kussner, A.S.A., AR/WA; Raymond Lesher, M.A.I.; William T. McCarthy, F.R.A., AR/WA; A. R. Parente, M.A.I., AR/WA; John Purdon, A.S.A.; Charles Randolph, M.A.I.; John Rowlson, M.A.I., S.R.E.A.; Ralph Sprague, M.A.I.; John Robert White, M.A.I.; and Miss Marie Louise Langdon of the American Right of Way Association.

As Members of the Appraisal Institute (M.A.I.), the American Society of Appraisers (A.S.A.), or the Society of Real Estate Appraisers (S.R.E.A.), these skillful eyes and ears belong to a corps of real estate experts who have, in the past fifty years, raised their job disciplines to professional accreditation in the highest courts of the nation—and recognized abroad as well.

This book actually owes its content to the entire profession, since it transmits only that input invested in the writer by good teachers and industrious companions from each of the appraisal societies, and more than several enlightening seminars conducted by the American Right of Way Association (AR/WA).

I am also indebted to master-builder, and author, William Zeckendorf, Sr., of New York; Adriel Harris, veteran broker and investor, of Greenwich, Connecticut; financier Richard J. Micheel, president of the Investment Corporation of America, Philadelphia; Samuel Pierson, president, Society of Industrial Realtors, Stamford, Connecticut: Richardson Wood, educator, of New College, Bradenton, Florida; and Attorney Alvin Arnold, assistant professor of Real Estate at New York University, and editor of *Real Estate Review* (Boston), for sage reflections, professional consultations and enthusiastic support in the development of this effort.

And last, but not least, I wish to express my deep appreciation for the educational and news information services of The National Association of Real Estate Boards, 36 South Wabash Avenue, Chicago, Illinois.

PETER C. ROBINSON

Contents

Part One

PRINCIPLES AND APPROACHES IN EVALUATING COMMERCIAL PROPERTIES

I

Defining the Problem

Market value may be described as an elastic band stretching and recoiling between oscillating poles of Supply on the one hand, and Demand on the other. Value is never constant. It is an elusive symbol of ideas which must be extruded through a fine tooth comb, so to speak, a suitable analogy for the term *Appraisal.*

An appraisal of commercial property is first a statement of the problem to be solved; second, working through the core of that problem; and third, the solution of that problem. The initial step in setting up the problem for analysis rests on your conception of commercial market value.

The value of commercial real estate in general is dependent upon certain dynamic forces created by human beings in their attempt to manipulate their environment. These dynamics are Social Standards, Economic Pressures and Government Regulations. They may be specifically broken down into the following factors:

Social Standards	*Economic Pressures*	*Government Regulations*
Demography, i.e. Statistical Study of Where People Go, and Why, and What They Do When There; Population Densities; Advertising Stimuli; Educational, Esthetic and Psychological Attitudes and Changes; Cultural Atmosphere.	Natural Resources, etc; Communications-Transportation; Labor Pools; Employment Trends; Flow of Money and Credit; Interest Rates and Taxes; Price and Wage Levels; Purchasing Power; the Securities Markets.	National Defense Acts; Interplanetary Space Programs; Government Loans; Urban Renewal; Police and Fire Ordinances; Zoning and Building Codes; Rent and Credit Controls; Federal Monetary Policy; Federal Housing Programs.

The cost, the price and the value of real property is determined by *people* and their activities, as factored above. Recognition of these factors is vital to an appraisal of commercial real property. The accuracy of the appraisal will be weighed by your knowledge, diligence, judgment and honesty as the appraiser, in accounting for the people and forces influencing your calculations.

It is impossible to evaluate commercial (income) property except by collection in writing of pertinent data, a written description of the property as of a specified date, and written arithmetical analysis in support of the value conclusion. There are just too many factors involved in evaluating commercial property to try to process them all in the head, or to rely on memory in attempting to articulate them.

At the beginning of the appraisal process, we must examine the Purpose of appraising. Purpose is paramount in preparing to write an appraisal of commercial property.

The fundamental purpose of an appraisal of commercial property is to form a considered opinion of value. The value most often sought and the value with which this book is concerned is *Fair Market Value.*

However, there are numerous other types of Value, contingent upon the Purpose for which an appraisal is made. These may be:

Amenity Value, Assessed Value, Book Value, Condemnation Value, Depreciated Value, Economic Value, Insurable Value, Going Concern Value, Leasehold Value, Liquidation Value, Mortgage Loan Value, Plottage Value, Potential Value, Rental Value, Replacement Value, Reproduction Value, Sound Value, Tax Value, Utility Value, and Value in Use, to name a few.

In preparing to write an appraisal of commercial property, it is most often found that more than one kind of value must be weighed and correlated to establish a Value Conclusion. In addition to Income or *Capitalized* Value, the Reproduction Cost or Depreciated Cost, and the Market Data or Comparative Approaches to value are brought into play.

This book will deal primarily with evaluation of commercial properties for the Purpose of estimating *Fair Market Value,* and it assumes the reader is not a newcomer to real property appraisal terminology.

Fair Market Value has been acceptably defined in the courts of the land as follows: "The price which a property will bring in a competitive market under all conditions requisite to a fair sale, which would result from negotiations between a buyer and a seller, each acting prudently, with knowledge and without undue pressure."

Requests for Market Value appraisals of commercial property arise from everyday needs such as these: (1) Toward Conveyance, Sale or Lease; (2) Toward Just Compensation in Condemnation; (3) Toward a Basis for Taxation; (4) Toward Mortgage Financing.

There are many other needs to be served in making an appraisal, and Purposes other than Market Value to be estimated. The *Function* of the appraisal is to serve the need. It is important to distinguish between the Purpose of an appraisal (to estimate a specified kind of value) and the Function which this evaluation will serve, i.e. *Why* the appraisal is being made.

The first page of every formal appraisal should state the Purpose of the appraisal, e.g. "To Estimate Fair Market Value," or "To Estimate Value in Use," or other Purpose.

It is also proper to state the Function, e.g.: "To Estimate Market Value for Mortgage Financing," or "To Estimate Value as a Fair Basis for Merger." However, the appraiser is sometimes given the Purpose of estimating Fair Market Value, without being told the Function, or the "Why." This should not deter him from going ahead with his estimate of Fair Market Value, the Purpose.

THE APPRAISAL PROCESS AS APPLIED TO INCOME PROPERTY

The appraisal process is an orderly procedure in making a value estimate of commercial property. It consists of defining the problem, making a market survey and property analysis, gathering all necessary basic data, applying the Income Approach, the Market Data Approach, and the Cost Approach, where possible; and, finally, forming an opinion of value. Appraising, being under the law of economics, is not a science producing findings of an exact nature. Values of real properties cannot be determined or established by an appraisal. They can only be estimated.

Begin the appraisal process by writing a clear definition of the problem. Any doubt about the Purpose of the appraisal should be resolved at once. Crystallization of the problem can be gained by taking five basic steps in defining it:

A. You identify the property to be evaluated.
B. You specify the rights inherent.
C. You state the Purpose of the appraisal and its functions: (to estimate market value, for instance, for just compensation in condemnation proceedings).
D. You fix the date as of which the estimate is to be made.
E. You define the value to be estimated.

(Figure 1 illustrates the appraisal process step-by-step.)

The Five Basic Steps Amplified In Definition of the Problem

A. *Identification of Property—First,* identify the property by a mailing address, so that your reader can go to the property to inspect it also. For instance: *955 Broad Street, New City, Connecticut, situated on the northwest corner of North and Good Streets. Land is 100 feet front by 150 feet deep, improved with a four-story and basement, brick office building with stores on the ground level.*

The correct legal description of the property is also necessary for positive identification. This description can be obtained from the existing deed, or from the public records.

B. *Property Rights Inherent*—The *second step* in defining the problem is to determine the rights inherent to the property. An appraisal is not only an evaluation of physical land and buildings; it also evaluates the rights which one or more individuals have to the ownership and use of the land and improvements. It may be that an appraisal of only a part interest in the property is wanted.

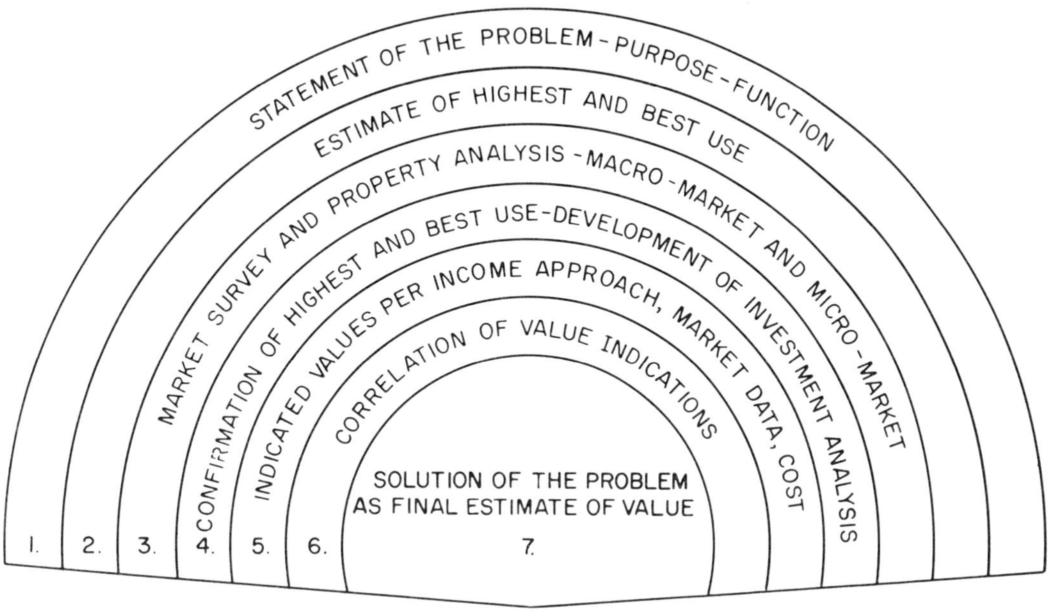

SIGHTING THE BULL'S EYE IN THE APPRAISAL PROCESS AS IT IS APPLIED TO INCOME PROPERTY
FIGURE 1.

The property rights or interests to be appraised may be the value of rents to be received plus a reversionary right at the end of a lease term. The air rights over a specified area, or designated subsurface rights, or the value of a tenant's interest in an existing lease, or an easement, or right of way, may have to be evaluated. *You cannot define your problem precisely until you know exactly what property rights are involved.*

You establish at the outset exactly which rights you are to evaluate. This enables you to estimate accurately the complexity of the assignment, the research required, the time necessary to write the appraisal, whether or not to call for specialized assistance, and the likely cost.

C. *Purpose and Function of the Appraisal*—A clear statement of the reasons for making the appraisal is the third step in defining the problem. The purpose of the appraisal and the function it is to serve indicates the data to be gathered, the methods to be employed, the type of data and factors likely to wield the most influence, and the type of report required. While the purpose of an appraisal may be to estimate market value, the function for which it is needed will vary. For example:

1. If the purpose is to estimate market value for mortgage financing, the stability of the commercial district is significant because the lender is concerned not only with present worth but with the stability of that value during the period the mortgage will be in force.

2. If the purpose is to estimate market value in connection with condemnation proceedings, current sales of comparable properties are of the first importance since the rule in most jurisdictions as to admissible evidence requires that opinion testimony be based on the reaction in the market of informed buyers and sellers of comparable property.
3. If the purpose is to estimate market value for possible purchase of a property, current sales of comparable properties, the rate of return the property is producing, and the availability of comparable substitute properties are probably the most pertinent and influencing factors to consider.

In each instance above, you would be reporting Fair Market Value. But the data with most weight in formulating your final estimate of value and the arrangement of your report would reflect the function for which appraisal would be used. Therefore, in defining the problem, you try to develop an exact statement of the appraisal's purpose and function so that it is clearly understood by and acceptable to your client and yourself. There are instances when a client will be clear about the purpose, but unwilling to divulge the function. This should not deter you from estimating Fair Market Value, if that is the purpose, but in this case you should explore *highest and best use* as an initial surrogate function.

D. *Date of Value Estimate*—The fourth step in defining the problem is the date of the value estimate. The specific date is important because the value of real property varies. The factors which create or destroy value are always in the process of change. An opinion of value is good only for that period in time when it was formulated. Usually an appraisal assignment is for a value estimate as of the present, or near future. But there are occasions when you will be asked to appraise a property as of some date in the past. Such a value estimate may be required for tax purposes, to settle an estate, or to adjust an insurance claim.

It is costly and time-consuming to research all conditions affecting a property in the distant past, and the client should be made aware of this at the outset.

E. *Definition of Value*—The fifth step in assaying the problem is to spell out the value to be estimated. A property has, of course, only one Market Value as of a given date. But there are times when value for a special purpose, such as *value in use,* is the question. If the value estimate is to be based upon special conditions, then the definition of value must be stated accordingly.

MARKET SURVEY AND PROPERTY ANALYSIS

Now that the problem is clearly stated, you are ready to make a market survey of the subject property in terms of its use, location, condition, and desirability. Attack the problem first by estimating its *highest and best (or most likely-profitable) use.*

The *highest and best use* of a property is often its present use and that utilization usually conforms to the use permitted under zoning regulations. There are instances where you will find that the existing use may not be its highest and best use.

In this event, you must judge the other factors which influence highest and best use. These factors are covered in the setup of the principle of *highest and best use* in Chapter II.

In your market survey and property analysis, the data likely to be required in the appraisal should be established, early. This will depend upon the type of property being appraised since a great deal more information would be required in the appraisal of an office building than of a frozen custard stand. Choice of an Approach which will develop the most rational value indication will also indicate the type of data required. In appraising income properties *Income Data* is most often paramount, but in some appraisals the application of all three approaches is important. Therefore, Cost Data and Market Data (comparable sales) may also be necessary.

For the purposes of this book, which will dwell on the *investment analysis method* of evaluating commercial, income-bearing properties, emphasis will usually be placed on the Income Approach, with Market Data and Cost Approaches in close support where possible. Exceptions to this rule, however, will be evidenced in the evaluation of shopping centers and gasoline service stations.

Macro-market vis-à-vis Micro-market Study

The demand for goods or services, housing, lodging or offices at a site in a given commercial district most often rests on far-flung, external economic and social forces working in sympathy, or in conflict, with the marketing magnetisms of the site. The interface relationships of such data, the one *general* (macro-market), and the other *specific* (micro-market), will be referred to and demonstrated in this book under the double label, in the interest of reminding the appraiser that in his market survey and property analysis he uses two instruments: first, a telescope applied to general data; then, a microscope to "zoom down" on the specific. Or vice versa.

How to Proceed

Programming the appraisal helps establish working tempo, both the appraiser's own and those of his assistants. A clear picture of the nature of the work to be done by the appraiser himself and by each person selected to assist him will smooth the handling of the assignment.

It is the appraiser himself who must estimate the final value conclusion, sign the report, and be ready to testify in court that he personally inspected the subject property and made the valuation. His assistants can be of no help in the end product. They can aid in the collection of data, take photographs, make measurements, check calculations, draw maps and do research, but the appraiser alone sums it all into coherence, and value estimate.

Thus, the appraiser, having established highest and best use in his mind, now proceeds to collect data which will document and support his conviction about subject property. (In the process, he may encounter surprise data which negates his first conviction, causing him to start again with highest and best use.)

He and his assistants proceed with two categories of data, as follows:

MACRO-MARKET ANALYSIS

1. *General Data* relating to conditions in the *nation, region, city,* and the *trade* area, or those elements outside the neighborhood which affect its value. (a) *Regional and city data* pertain to factors such as population trends, price levels, levels of employment, and other external influences. (b) The trade area embraces the greater metropolitan spread of a city to include suburbs within thirty minutes drive of the subject trade center. This area will be calculated in terms of number of households, median family income, and dollar volume of total retail sales per annum.

In appraisal practice you will accumulate a large volume of *general data,* especially about the region and city. Information about the trade area is also vital. It is well to set up a permanent filing system and an office procedure to maintain the system and keep it current. Thus, *general data* for any assignment will be readily available when called for.

MICRO-MARKET ANALYSIS

2. *Specific Data* concerns *the title, the site, the buildings,* and *the district:* (a) *Title history* will be secured in the course of identifying the property. It is vital to know who owns the property; the type of ownership deed; what easements and encroachments, if any, exist; zoning regulations; assessed value and taxes; and deed or other restrictions. (b) *Site data* would include a description of the size, shape, topographical nature of the land and the types of public improvements thereon, such as walks, curbs, water, sewers, gas, electricity and width and kind of street paving, and its traffic controls nearby. (c) *Building data* would include a complete description of the physical improvements and its condition together with an analysis of its layout, style and design. (d) *Commercial district* (or Micro-market) *data,* which is less broad in its scope than city, trade area, or regional data since it pertains to factors present in a smaller area. Commercial district data would point to typical land uses, zoning controls, public utilities, transportation facilities, shopping facilities, and the quality of the properties comprising the district. It would also include a record of the sales of comparable properties to be investigated and analyzed in the appraisal.

Data which the appraiser reaps eventually becomes a library. This includes the accumulated *general data* as well as *specific property data,* carded by location and type of property, making the collection progressively more useful. Your library should embrace the publications in Land Use, Construction Law, Mortgage Banking and Accounting related to your work; those reporting building costs, materials, and trend information; and, of course, those devoted to evaluation.

THE THREE APPROACHES TO MARKET VALUE

Years of experience in evaluating investment properties have crystallized for appraisers three main avenues of estimating Fair Market Value:

1. The value the property's net earning power will support, based upon a capitalization of net income, or *Income Approach.*
2. The value indicated by recent sales of comparable properties in the market, or *Market Data Approach.*
3. The current cost of reproducing a property less depreciation from all sources, that is, deterioration and functional and economic obsolescence, or *Cost Approach.*

In some assignments, the appraiser of commercial property utilizes all three approaches. Obviously there are appraisal problems in which market value cannot be obtained through the use of the *Cost Approach,* nor for a specialized property such as a federal court house by the *Market Data Approach.*

The use of all three approaches when possible is standard appraisal technique and acknowledged by the courts as fundamental procedure. In commercial properties, the *Income Approach* is usually the soundest indicator of Market Value.

The three approaches to Market Value will be treated in detail in Chapter V, following a discussion of principles and techniques weighing upon these approaches in Chapters II and IV.

CORRELATION, VALUE ESTIMATE, AND THE APPRAISAL REPORT

The last step in the appraisal process is the correlation of the indications of value derived by the Income, Market Data and Cost Approaches. In correlating these approaches into your *Final Estimate of Value,* you weigh the purpose of the appraisal, the type of property, and the strength of the data processed in each of the three approaches. These considerations will influence the strength to be accorded each approach.

For instance, in the case of an owner-occupied retail store, if the appraisal were being made for insurance purposes, the greatest weight might be assigned to the Cost Approach. In the case of an antiquated income-producing apartment house, greater weight would fall on the Market Data and Income Approaches. In the absence of conclusive Market Data in this case, your selection would be narrowed to the Income Approach, for Final Estimate of Value.

You gain your *Final Estimate of Value* by weighing two or three preliminary value estimates and considering the spread between the minimum and maximum figures. You place emphasis on the Approach which appears to be the most logical solution to the stated appraisal problem.

If this discipline is carefully pursued and the resulting Final Estimate of Value is logical, your report will reveal no inexplicable vagaries.

The documented development of the data considered and analyzed, the methods used, the opinions and conclusions reached in formulating your Final Estimate of Value, comprise your *Appraisal Report.* Your report is the palpable product of your service. It is the consummation of your contract with your client, for which you will receive a fee. The manner in which it is articulated, the rationale employed, and the neatness and order of the format in which it appears, will be respected by the client, his attorney and the court it may come before.

It is important at this point to turn back to some additional basic definitions necessary to an understanding of evaluation in general, and commercial properties in particular. They are as follows:

REAL ESTATE, REAL PROPERTY AND PERSONALTY

In order to be able to write an appraisal of commercial real estate, one must have a clear picture in mind of the differences existing in definitions of Real Estate, Real Property in Fee Simple, Escheat and Personal Property, as follows:

Real Estate: Physical land and structures affixed to it.

Real Property: This relates to rights of real estate ownership rather than to physical things such as land and buildings. It is a right, or interest, in land and improvements of a permanent nature thereon. It may be said to consist of the ownership of a "bundle of legal rights" to real estate including, in the case of fee simple ownership, rights to:

1. Enter upon or into.
2. Use or decline to use.
3. Sell or refuse to sell, all, or a part or any interest therein.
4. Lease or refuse to lease.
5. Peaceful possession.
6. Donate or grant as a gift.

When the owner of real estate has all the rights referred to, he is said to have a *fee simple* title. Frequently, however, such an owner has voluntarily given up or parceled out certain of these rights for a consideration. He may have leased the property to a user and therefore put limitations on his right of entry and of use. He may have voluntarily placed in the deed certain restrictions on the future use of the property. Thus, because of these restrictions in the deed, it is possible that in the future uses to which the property may be put are definitely limited. He may have sold certain rights to his property, such as the right to light and air, or the right to the minerals, or the right to put a pipeline through it, or a powerline over it. In all these cases, his title is *less than a fee simple title* and the rights which remain to him are less than the full "bundle of legal rights" that accrue to such a title.

In fact, fee simple ownerships are subject to basic powers and rights of government.

In addition to the ordinary police powers that are exercised under this power of government, you will find regulations regarding land use, building codes, regulations regarding traffic control, regulations regarding relaxation and enjoyment of natural resources, and many other matters affecting the relationship of one person with another.

Escheat refers to the process by which any interest in land or other property reverts to the state upon the death of the owner without a will for the disposition of the property and without heirs. Partnership and corporate property may also escheat under various state statutes now in effect. The right to escheat belongs only to the States. There is no such right in the federal government but a somewhat similar right to seize enemy alien property in the United States or its possessions is vested in the federal government by statute. The general theory is that title immediately passes to the State upon the death of the owner under the cited circumstances. Problems relating to escheat are legal in nature, pertain to title and are not for the appraiser to resolve.

Personal Property: Movable objects, not permanently built into the real estate. Examples: Brick kiln baker's ovens are built in and part of the bakery, whereas the ordinary ovens in a restaurant are likely to be movable. The vault in a bank is part of the steel and concrete of the bank, whereas an ordinary safe in a store, even a very large one, might be moved out with block-and-tackle rig. Anything that may be moved without damage to the real estate is to be considered personal property.

The Development of Value Theory

The word "value" means color, light or shading to an artist; tone to a musician; weight or density or other dimension to a scientist. To an investor, it means dollars, perhaps his life-savings.

Economists will undoubtedly continue to advance propositions of value, which have been evolving since the sixteenth century Mercantilists first developed the theory of a favorable balance of trade.

The eighteenth century Physiocrats, who first distinguished between Value in Use and Value in Exchange, and Adam Smith's emphasis on the Cost of Production as the basis of value in *The Wealth of Nations,* opened the way for refinements of definition by Malthus and Ricardo. Karl Marx introduced the theory that Labor is the only determinant of value. The nineteenth century Marginal Utility School (Austrian) considered the expanding Supply of a commodity as a limiting factor on its Use-Value, and the twentieth century Neoclassical School has attempted to reconcile the Cost of Production and Marginal Utility doctrines.

Value, as this capsuled history of value theory outlines, is a word of many meanings. Its abstruse qualities perhaps have been best expressed by the late John B. Spilker, Professor of Real Estate at the University of Cincinnati, who asserted:

> Commercial value is "*want productive power,*" that is, that seemingly elusive quality that an object has of producing, on the part of the buying public, so strong a want or desire to possess it that a buyer is willing to pay for it the price asked, measured in terms of money.

Evaluating Real Property

Because "value" has so many interpretations, it is necessary to define here the meaning used in the valuation of real property, point by point, as follows:

1. It is the relationship between a property desired and a potential purchaser. It varies from man to man and from time to time, as human desires vary.
2. A property has no value unless it has utility; it must arouse the desire (demand) for possession and have the power to give satisfaction to someone, somewhere.
3. Scarcity must be present before value exists.

4. Utility and scarcity do not alone create value; purchasing power must be present, the ability of the individual to trade in the market in order to satisfy his desire.

Estimation of the value of real property is further complicated by the element of longevity.

Unlike food and wine and tobacco which are quickly consumed and their utility with it, the benefits of real property are long-term.

Land and buildings have a useful life for many years.

The full value of real property, therefore, is equal to the present and all future utilities of land and buildings.

Estimating the value of all future uses is the most complex feature of real estate appraising. Your estimate of value must take into account social and economic trends which may bear heavily on the value of future utilities.

As an appraiser, you must understand the trends and forces affecting a property under appraisement and be able to forecast long-range conditions which may influence use of the property.

Value in Use vs. Value in Exchange

The distinction in this instance is that a property may have one value in use and a different value in exchange. For example:

You are called upon by your State Highway Department to estimate Fair Market Value (value in exchange for money) of a plumbing wholesaler's property in condemnation proceedings; location is at a five-way main artery intersection in the heart of an urban commercial district: land area is about 80,000 square feet.

The plumbing wholesaler's buildings are old, mill-type, three- and four-story brick, containing hundreds of bins for the assortment and storage of thousands of kinds of pipe, joints, connectors, threads and tools. His showroom and sales offices are antiquated. His yard (land) is arranged so that large metal storage tanks can be manufactured and processed by a traveling crane from one point to another, and handily hefted to trucks at his loading docks. Parking for customers is ample. For forty years the wholesaler has prospered at this location, in these apparently outmoded buildings, doing an annual business of several millions of dollars.

Subsequently, you appraised land and buildings here for Fair Market Value as though the property (not the business operation) was for sale on the open market. You produced Comparable Sales under Market Data to show that this type of property had been recently purchased in the same city by another firm in the same business for $250,000. You produced a Depreciated Cost Approach, using authorized manuals, to show Reproduction Value at about $255,000, the upper limit of value, in your opinion. And, using comparable warehouse, office and showroom rentals of space in the same vicinity, you produced an Income Approach supporting Fair Market Value at $245,000. You placed greatest weight on the Market Data Approach, because the property was not held as an income-producing investment, but was operated as a utility by the owner. There was no lease, and the property was not the type customarily traded as investment realty.

You did not consider *Value in Use* here; your state's eminent domain custom forestalls this approach in Condemnation procedure and leaves *Value in Use* to be determined by the Judge, Jury, Committee, or Referee before whom the case may come, if taken to Court.

The plumbing wholesaler in this case received $1,000,000 for his condemned land and buildings as *Value in Use* in a settlement determined by the Referee, who held that if the wholesaler was selling to another plumbing wholesaler, the value of the particular design and layout of his special purpose land and buildings, bins and tank yard, would be four times greater than in the open market. This was considered as Just Compensation for the plumbing wholesaler's dislocation in business. You did the job that was asked of you, but the court emphasized a different value. Not all courts agree on definitions of value where "Just Compensation" is concerned in condemnation cases.

Remuneration

Most clients will expect you to quote a firm fee in advance of their request for an appraisal. This means an appropriate estimate of the scope and complexity of the problem, the work hours involved and the personnel and travel time needed. This estimate should not be given hastily. If the property is nearby and well-known to you, it may be evaluated in a few days. With a more complex problem to resolve, it can take weeks, or months, to research and cull significant data, and can require the services of professional assistants to supplement your own staff. In the latter case, for example, the fee should cover your time spent with lawyers, realtors, contractors, engineers, accountants, architects, bankers, and building managers. It must include consultation fees the appraiser has to pay for engineering, architectural, and other specialized services.

In particular, an experienced appraiser working on urban investment properties might set his fee at the rate of $50 per hour, or $400 per day, for his own time on the job, plus $25 per hour for each assistant required. A figure over the base rate can be added to include an estimate of extra expenses such as long-distance travel, photographs, mechanical drawings, and the like.

Relations with Client—Your proposal to your prospective client should be set forth in a letter, acquainting him with the problem in this manner:

A. Identification of the property.
B. Statement of rights to be appraised.
C. Purpose of the appraisal.
D. Definition of the value to be estimated.
E. Date as of which the estimate is to be made.
F. Date on which the appraisal report will be delivered.
G. Quotation of the fee.

The client's agreement that he approves the terms can be his signature on a copy of your letter. This commitment from your client is important. It puts client and appraiser in agreement about the nature of the problem, and will avoid misunderstanding when the report finally is presented.

II

Valuation Principles Aiding in Definition of the Problem

To be accounted economically as Wealth, an object must have three qualities: *Utility,* that is, the power to satisfy wants; *Scarcity,* meaning limited in its amount; and it must be *Transferable,* capable of being possessed. Land and buildings are such objects, while stocks and bonds are symbols of objects.

Property is the right of economic use of the object, or use of the symbol of the object.

The principles of land uses are anchored in economics. Because appraising is the valuation of the rights of use of real property, these fundamentals of economics are the basic principles of valuation. A knowledge of these principles is necessary to your grip on the purposes, techniques and procedures of appraising.

The most important principles which must be understood in estimating Fair Market Value of commercial properties include:

The Principle of Supply and Demand

In economic terms, Supply means the quantity of objects that are offered for sale at various prices in a given market. Demand (desire) refers to the quantity of objects that will be purchased at various prices. The price of a property is set by the relation between the Supply of its type and the Demand for it. If the Supply is great as compared with the Demand, the price will be low. If the Supply is small, as compared with the Demand, the price will be high.

The poles of Supply and Demand oscillate and vibrate on the winds of change. Local changes in population growth, purchasing power, price and wage levels, transportation facilities, taxation and government controls are factors in addition to Scarcity which influence the ratio between Supply and Demand, in a given area.

Scarcity of labor, and high wage rates, can carry the cost of building beyond the purchasing power of the market, discouraging builders from adding to the Supply.

Government regulations such as rent control, tightening of mortgage money, and zoning regulations affect Supply and Demand by the restrictions they insist upon.

The Principle of Change

The Principle of Change is always at work on real property.

Change is relentless, its mutations falling upon individual properties, commercial districts and whole cities. Change may be slow or rapid, progressive and regressive by turns.

You must always realize that you are looking at change. You should be sensitive to the economic and social forces working on the property you are evaluating.

As an appraiser you are not expected to determine with absolute clarity all the forces that may appear in the future to change the character of a specific property, a commercial district or a city. But reasonable interpretations of probable directions, based on your best judgment, are desirable.

In all your deliberations, you can always fall back on the Market as a guide. The Market Value of a recent comparable property is seldom based on a price paid for it in the past, nor on the cost to produce it. Its price indicates what the owners believe it will do for them in the future. The Market-place will tell you much about the district's future trend. Income data in the form of rising or falling comparable rentals are sure-fire trend indicators.

Highest and Best Use

Highest and best, or most likely-profitable, use of real property is that use which prudence dictates will, over a reasonably foreseeable period of time, produce for the typical owner the highest net return or benefits, thus reflecting the highest capital asset value, and will, generally, at the same time preserve the utility of the property.

In general, when buildings constitute a substantial part of the total Fair Market Value of a property, the remaining economic life of the improvements and the preservation of the utility of the property are extremely important factors in determining that use which will produce the highest capital value and in consequence be considered as the highest and best use of the property.

Highest and best use is a most important principle and must always be given primary consideration and dealt with specifically in appraisal reports. It is a major factor of Fair Market Value as pointed out by an 1894 U.S. Supreme Court decision that—

> The value of the property results from the use to which it is put and varies with the profitableness of that use, the present and prospective, actual and anticipated. There is no pecuniary value aside from that which results from such use—the amount and profitable character of such use determines the value.

Many things must be considered in estimating highest and best use, including: supply and demand; competitive properties; use conformity; size of the land and possible economic type and size of structures or improvements which may be placed thereon; zoning; building restrictions; neighborhood or vicinity trends. The principle of highest and best use has some of its most practical applications in condemnation procedure under Eminent Domain powers where purchasing parts of ownership, or flowage, clearance and other types of easements. The value of the part left to an owner, after a partial taking, is governed largely by the highest and best use of the owner's remainder after the taking. It is, therefore, extremely important that great care be used in estimating and supporting an opinion of the highest and best use of the remainder in such cases.

The Principle of Substitution

When property is replaceable, its value tends to be set at the cost of acquisition of an equally desirable and valuable substitute property. That which may be substituted may be either a replica structure, a similar structure with equivalent functional utility, or an investment having an equal degree of increment opportunity. Thus, the fair market value of a property is to a major extent limited and controlled by the value of similar available properties having like utility and comparable locations, characteristics, and foreseeable future benefits. The principle of substitution is important to the market data approach and the cost approach in appraisals.

Increasing and Decreasing Returns

The rule of "diminishing returns" is that larger and larger investments in structures and improvements on land will produce larger and larger net income up to a certain point at which the maximum of valuation will be developed and beyond which point any additional investments will not produce a commensurate return for the additional investments. The point of "diminishing returns" is that point beyond the point of maximum value at which additional investments do not produce an increased net return.

The Principle of Balance

The law of balance, in appraising, holds that value is originated and stabilized in the equilibrium reached through essential uses of real estate. The value of a property is dominated by the balance of the four agents in production, as follows:

1. Labor (Wages).
2. Management (entrepreneur coordination).
3. Capital (investment in buildings and equipment).
4. Land.

When the agents in production are in proportionate balance to one another, the property's maximum value is achieved.

There is a theoretical point of balance in every property which will produce the greatest net return.

An imbalance obtains when a building is too small or too large for the investment in its site, and now it becomes an *underimprovement or overimprovement.*

Imbalance also occurs where the cost of services such as elevators, doormen and janitor in an apartment house are too little or too much for the building, its class of tenancy, and its rent roll. The principle of balance says that loss in value occurs when there is an excess or deficiency in the contribution of the four productive agents as they affect one another.

The principle of balance is used in estimating *highest and best use.* The proportioning of the agents in production is fundamental if maximum net return is to be produced and maximum land value developed. Because Land has last claim on the gross income produced by the careful balancing of the four agents, *the Land is residual.*

This technique applies when the value of the Land cannot be accurately estimated by the Market Data Approach. *It is used to estimate the value of the land by capitalizing the net income imputable to the land at a reasonable rate.*

The Theory of Surplus Productivity

The net income which remains after the costs of Labor, Management, and Capital have been paid is *surplus productivity.*

This surplus can be credited to the land, and it tends to establish the land's value. Surplus productivity rests upon *the principle of balance,* the law of increasing and decreasing returns, and the proportioning of the four agents in production. It is the greatest net return to the land, which when capitalized at a reasonable rate, gives value to the land. *Highest and Best Use* of the land is shown by the greatest net yield produced by trial and test of proportioning the four agents in production.

The Principle of Contribution

This is actually the law of *increasing and decreasing returns,* as it applies to some aspect of real property. It affirms that the value of an item in production is accounted for by its contribution to the net return of the enterprise. In this regard, enterprise connotes the combination of all items in production such as land, buildings, and other improvements.

The principle of contribution has practical application in many valuation problems; it must be considered before undertaking a modernization or remodeling job.

An instance in which this principle would have bearing might be this: the owners of a retail store property are told by the tenant that rental can be increased on a new lease if the owners will install a new store front and air-conditioning. The cost of these improvements amounts to $40,000. The tenant, however, is offering an increase of $8,000 per annum for only five years, which is no real contribution to net income.

The problem might be solved by negotiation extending the lease to ten years at the same rental.

The Principle of Competition

This principle affirms that profit may excite competition, and that excess profit can attract disastrous competition. Profit is that residue of net income from real property over and above the costs of Labor, Management, Capital and Land.

Merchants who first locate in, say, a new shopping center in a suburban area where merchandising services have long been needed are apt to make unusually large profits. Competing merchants are then drawn to the district, putting up their own structures or leasing new locations, and they begin to share in the total amount of business.

The volume of business originally going to the pioneer merchants declines, and so do their net incomes. This can continue to the point where none of the merchants makes a fair return.

Because the value of land rests upon the use producing the greatest return, competition, in this instance, by spoiling the net return, has reduced the net yield to the land, hence the value of the land. Profit will evaporate if competitive forces build up beyond economic demand.

The Principle of Conformity

Conformity of use can be seen in the harmonious grouping of retail stores in any primary retail district. Experience has taught the merchant that he can achieve a larger sales volume if his store is located near other stores selling the same type and quality of goods. (Gimbel's and Macy's again; or have you noticed that A&P, First National, Food Fair, Safeway, Shop-Rite and Pathmark often cluster together within a block or two?)

On the contrary, the same teacher has ruled that success rarely comes to the merchant handling an expensive line of merchandise if he locates in a district where the same types of goods are sold but of inferior quality. (You can bet that Abercrombie & Fitch will not locate across the street from a Ninth Avenue Army-Navy store, even with unlimited customer parking and a bus terminal built into the picture.) There are numerous other principles besides conformity which are applied to the selection of a store site, but conformity is important.

The elements of conformity have grown out of common social experience as our cities have developed and land uses have multiplied.

The Principle of Anticipation

People buy future benefits, when purchasing real property. The principle of anticipation accounts for value created by benefits expected in the future. It is the future, not the past, which is important in estimating value. The only importance of past experience is when it points to possible future developments in real property. The investor purchasing commercial property has done so *anticipating* income he will receive from the investment, but in deciding to buy the property, he had to examine its past income. In examining income history, the buyer had to discover the magnetisms which brought the property that income. He examines the income data to review all influences, adverse or progressive, to form an opinion as to whether the income stream will decline in a few years, or is likely to level or increase in the future.

While value may be defined as *the worth of all present and future benefits deriving from ownership,* the quality, quantity, and duration of these benefits in the future must be estimated against past experience. This principle will be applied in your choice of capitalization methods, under the Income Approach, as described in Chapter V.

Trends and Cycles

Trends and cycles are daily bread to the appraiser of commercial property. He must sense the drift of a property's life cycle, and be able to articulate the phase in the life of the commercial district he is analyzing. The appraiser must know a property's age to forecast the life of its income stream. To this end, the appraiser allows for the principle of integration and disintegration which avers that the rhythms of existence are cadenced in three stages: to begin with, integration, or birth; in the intermediate form, the balance of life, or equilibrium; and finally disintegration, or death, after which a renewal of life on a new foundation is possible, which may be called renaissance, or redevelopment.

The pattern of human existence speaks of such cycles since the beginning of recorded time. Individual properties, and neighborhoods, and entire cities and towns develop by the rule of demand at the dawn, often living out the stasis of the long day, and in the dusk crumbling into decay and eclipse, figuratively speaking. And then the cycle may begin again, like the phoenix arising from the ashes, and a renaissance, as in Rome, Athens, Istanbul and Jerusalem, takes place at or near the original site.

In our time, Urban Redevelopment agencies tend to reassert the cycle of renewal in our cities and towns, which in turn tends to preserve the long day in the life of the nation.

The growth factor in a cycle also takes into account trend-making influences such as the principles of *regression* and *progression,* which are logical extensions of the principles of conformity and change. *Regression* suggests that the value of a superior property suffers by the introduction of a less valuable property as neighbor. *Progression* holds that the value of the lesser property is enhanced by adjacent association with a superior property.

There is a close and rational relationship among all the principles discussed in this chapter. They are tied to one another by the same web of social and economic dynamics listed in Chapter I. Each principle is linked and interwoven into a master pattern of cyclical cause and effect, and each must be applied in a given appraisal with care and thought, as an influence builds into a trend, and the trends become parts of the cycle, and the cycle becomes Leviathan.

III

Land at the Root of the Problem: How to Analyze and Evaluate the Site

Land is one of the twin sources of all wealth and sustenance; entrepreneur-directed labor is the other. When land is worked, or put to use, it produces value.

At the root of all appraisal problems concerned with commercial property is Land Value, so it is necessary to appraise commercial land as separate and distinct from its improvements.

In the evaluation of commercial property, the improvements must be separately evaluated in order to apply depreciation as a deduction against the property's income under Federal Income Tax regulations. For Federal Income Tax purposes, the owner of improved commercial property can apply depreciation only to the improvements —not the land, which physically remains unchanged even though it may rise or fall in value. For this purpose, the depreciable value of the improvements must be that as of the time of construction or acquisition. The owner, or his appraiser, must differentiate between the original cost of land versus improvements.

Furthermore, separation of land and building is vital in utilizing the Income Approach to value. The Building Residual Technique is an avenue of the Income Approach. A rational rate of return on the land value is taken away from the net income earned by the total property in this technique. Therefore, a separate land value is paramount.

Segregated land value may also be needed in the residual technique where you are appraising properties with long-term leases. Here one must estimate what the land will be worth at the end of the structure's economic life, or at the termination of the lease. This estimate will be assumed as present value unless there is reason to believe that the land will become more or less desirable.

In most states appraisals made for condemnation purposes require that land and buildings be separately evaluated and the appraiser testify to separated values of land and improvements.

If buildings are destroyed by fire, wind or flood, the owner and his insurers will require a segregated value of land versus improvements.

In most parts of the nation, local real estate tax ordinances call for land and buildings to be assessed as distinct entities, in the interest of uniform land use levies.

Using the cost approach, value of the land is added to the appraiser's estimate of the building's value, based on reproduction cost less depreciation. Therefore, a separate valuation for the land is required. Site valuation is important, too, in determining the degree of economic obsolescence in the improvements.

In sum, the reasons for separate site analysis and valuation are these:

1. Deductible depreciation rates for buildings only, on Federal Tax schedules.
2. Necessary applications of Income Approach techniques.
3. Use in condemnation testimony.
4. Remainder value where buildings are destroyed.
5. Local property tax assessment.
6. Estimating value of building only, based on Reproduction cost less depreciation.
7. An index to building obsolescence.

THE BASIC PRINCIPLES IN SITE VALUATION

Chief among many of the principles described in Chapters I and II are these, in site valuation:

A site's most likely-profitable *(highest and best)* use is calculated in terms of the income imputable to it *after* the other agents in production have been satisfied. This is called *surplus productivity,* attributable to the land.

The larger the surplus, the greater is the value of the land.

The *Principle of Substitution* is an acid test of value because the value of the site being appraised inclines to be ascertained by the price required for an equally desirable substitute parcel.

BASIC DATA IN THE MARKET SURVEY AND PRCPERTY ANALYSIS

Various types of data must be gathered and correlated in developing site analysis. Area data *must be* pertinent to the site's location. If the site is in a downtown retail district, the appraiser must determine whether it is accessible to suburban areas which will patronize it. If it is in the suburbs or in the countryside, he must be equally definitive about the trade area on which the site will depend.

Gauging the site's probable best use the appraiser sets out to accumulate precise data to affirm or negate his intuitions. Thus, he begins his Market Survey and Property Analysis, a study which starts with his inspection of the property, proceeds to town hall, and ends in conscientious research, comparison and calculations.

Title Information

Proper identification of the parcel must embrace the legal description and data relating to taxes, zoning, restrictions, easements, and other pertinent legal matters.

Legal Description. This must delineate the property so that it cannot be confused with any other. Metes and Bounds may be copied from the recorded deed. A civil engineer's survey or a copy of the plat map from the Municipal Assessor's Records should be cited and appended to the report.

Taxes. These are levied to pay for services which make ownership desirable. However, net benefits wither when taxes go beyond proportion to income. So the appraiser measures the tax status against that of competitive sites, comparing assesments, mill rates, and tax annually collected, or burden on the property.

The assessed value of land for taxes may relate to a percentage of market value, if a recent reassessment has been made.

But one cannot draw value conclusions from this, since the assessed value of land is subject to question as an evidence of value in the courts. It is inadmissible in condemnation proceedings.

Zoning. This is an arbitrary, legally enforced, restriction of land use. The *Highest and Best Use* of a site may not be the use permitted by local zoning ordinance. But the appraiser must evaluate a site only on the basis of permitted use.

Zoning has become a device for protecting or walling-off the upper-income, single-family suburb from the encroachments of urban growth. As such, it often coincides with *Highest and Best Use* where residential appraising is concerned, and frequently where suburban shopping centers and medical buildings are to be appraised. But in urban commercial appraising there are sometimes great anomalies, particularly where more land has been assigned to one type of use than is economically supportable.

Nevertheless, as an appraiser, you must accept the zoning code governing the district and site which you are examining, and evaluate your subject in the light of its zoned limitations.

Someday, regional or state planning and zoning may give us a more comprehensive and equitable balance of police power, as it has in England and most of Europe. Until then we will have to live with our antiquated parochial follies where one town has on its side of the border junk-yards and abattoirs, while the adjoining one has residential zoning.

The appraiser should study the latest zoning maps and zoning ordinances regulating the site he is analyzing. Citations from these should be included in his reports to document his statement of permissible uses.

Public and private restrictions. Above and beyond zoning ordinances, there are limitations by fire ordinances; building, plumbing, anti-pollution, and sanitation codes; housing acts; and other legislative regulation. Public restrictions usually are less stringent than private restrictions but both deal with legal impositions on uses.

Private restrictions are cited in deeds conveying title. They are often part of a general plan of restriction for an entire tract recorded by the developer of the land. Then, when a lot is deeded to a buyer, the deed states that title is conveyed subject to the recorded restrictions.

Easements. Inherent elements in the succession of title, such as easements and rights of way across the property can either limit or benefit the rights of owners. An easement for entry and exit on a given property can inhibit the property's flexibility and value. But an easement crossing to neighboring property may be beneficial to ownership of the subject parcel.

Party wall agreements, and other easements running with the land can either limit or benefit the land's utility and value.

When asked to value easements or rights of way independent of the fee simple title to the land, the appraiser is only evaluating one or more of the rights to use the land, but not all of the rights. Value of an easement may vary from a small percentage of the area up to the value of the entirety. The value of the easement depends upon the number of rights embraced. Also, value loss to adjacent land in the same ownership can be added to that actually taken for easement purposes. Riparian, mineral and air rights, pipelines, electric transmission lines, cable lines, railroad rights of way, and often roadways are examples of easement leases or ownerships which have substantial interests in the bundle of rights of the land which they transect.

Weighing title and record data, one is estimating their effect upon property rights, and then evaluating the property rights.

TYPE OF ESTATE TO BE APPRAISED—IN FEE SIMPLE OR OTHERWISE

Fee Simple denotes valuation of an entire property, clear, free, and unencumbered. It is the largest estate and *the most extensive interest in land* that can be enjoyed, being an entire property with all of the rights arising from ownership. The fee simple valuation of a commercial property is developed through the orderly correlation of the generally accepted approaches of the appraisal process, where possible.

If the estate being appraised is less than the fee simple, that is to say, only certain rights or easements, this should be clearly stated before further site specifications are delineated.

Linear Specifications of the Site

The site's geometrical proportions may foreclose its presupposed highest and best use, or utility. The site's frontage, width, depth, plottage, shape, area, topography, utilities and subsoil, landscaping and the uses of neighboring land, including streets and sidewalks, should be painstakingly described.

Cross-checks

Appraisers frequently cross-check both front-foot and square foot comparisons against other considerations when evaluating land for shopping center, office building, motel and apartment house development.

Frontage is the length of the street-side boundary which a lot adjoins. If the lot should be graced with frontage on two or more streets, it may then be credited with double, triple, quadruple or other multiple frontages, which in commercial evaluation will undoubtedly add to its utility and value.

Frontage is often of greater utility than width, since the spread at the street line is better for store display and customer access, and the mean width of the property may diminish as it recedes from the street line.

Width is the distance between side lines, and may vary at certain distances from the front, as in the case of a rhomboid.

Depth is important for uses such as office and apartment buildings.

A lot which is wider than another may have greater utility and value because a larger building, with parking adjunct, can be erected on it, providing sufficient depth is present. Units of land measurement referring to width or frontage alone may be misleading. The "front foot" scale conveys nothing about width or depth at points behind the front boundary. However, the "front foot" is one way of making a fast evaluation of small retail sites, if its limitations are kept in mind. The "front foot" rule of thumb is often used by brokers making hasty retail storefront or small waterfront estimates of sale price or rental value, but experienced appraisers will cross-check for width, depth and shape, applying both square foot and front-foot cross-checks in comparisons.

To some degree, utility varies directly with width, if the width is uniform throughout the depth of the lot. Value varies in a like manner. Because one lot is twice as wide as another does not mean that its value is twice as great even though the depth may be the same in each case. Some widths are better than others for particular buildings intended for special purposes, for instance, gasoline stations and dairy bars.

Plottage is the increase in value per front foot or square foot in depth resulting from improved usability when smaller plots are combined into a larger one. For example, to acquire a proper parcel for a new drive-in bank building in a suburb, several formerly residential plots have to be assembled, from different owners. This procedure entails extra costs. The lots, with expensive homes on them, have to be purchased for more than their independent value as land, for the homes will be demolished.

Now put together, the cleared assembly will have to support the acquisition costs of land in addition to the other capital costs involved. It is not the cost of assembling which is responsible for plottage value. For plottage increment to be realized, there must be an economic *higher and better use*. Size alone is no proof of plottage increment. For the whole to be worth more than the sum of its parts, *the character of use must change;* a more likely-profitable use must have been established.

Depth Tables. These are percentage graphs showing a uniform system of measuring additional value owing to added depth. A standard depth is established, usually fixed at 100 feet. The series of percentages in the depth table begins with a lot of 100 foot depth which is designated as 100%. It courses downward for less depth and upward for more depth, according to past utility experience.

For the most part used by assessors trying for uniformity in assessing practices, these tables are not always dependable. They should be used only as a check in support of square foot calculations based on recent comparables. A depth table attuned to conditions in one locale may not relate to the conditions existing in another community. Land is a local commodity. Some of its value is founded on local conditions and customs.

Depth tables vary for different types of property. Greater depth is more important in a site for an apartment building than in the site for a gasoline station. Some commercial uses require great depth for customer parking space. In many shopping centers, the stores are situated near the rear of the site, with customer parking in front. In this instance a depth table would be absurd since it could not be supposed that the land closer to the street and used for parking is worth more than the land underlying the stores. A square foot, or overall acreage, value would rule, in this case.

Shape. Irregularity of shape can be a detriment. Construction costs, due to a site's irregular shape, might be so high as to make it impractical to erect a building which might otherwise be the highest and best use.

Topography and Subsoil Conditions. Sites will have lower value if they are costly to improve because of topographical conditions. A lot higher or lower than the abutting street level could cause additional costs in filling, or cutting to road grade.

Surface and subsoil figure in the cost of preparing a site for building and could also influence the design of the structure to be erected on the site. The cost of improvements increases if it becomes necessary to blast or if quicksand is present. Extra expense would be entailed for foundation walls and the sinking of piles if a site must be filled in. A sandy or rocky soil would make it necessary to bring in topsoil for lawns and landscaping. Site analysis must treat all such possibilities.

Since plantings are most often matters of personal taste and subject to dislocation on commercial sites, buyers are apt to discount the cost of trees and plantings. While the value of perimeter planting might have plus value, as a buffer "fence," it does not usually contribute more than a nominal sum to the value of the property. In condemnation appraising, plantings must be described, and frequently are compensated as loss to the owner.

Utilities. The presence or absence of connections for sewers, water, electricity, gas, and telephone must be stated in any appraisal. Where vacant land is concerned the presence of utility lines of adequate capacity is a vital asset.

Electricity is of prime importance to raw land. It is needed for pumping water, lighting, and construction power. Three-phase current is needed for restaurants, apartment house elevators, bowling alleys, laundromats, and office buildings. Some types of retail uses, such as lighting display, or gasoline stations with hydraulic lifts, wheel alignment machines, and body shops where welding is employed, will require as much as 440 volts.

Water supply with adequate pressure is vital to the site. If the site is in a rural area, an artesian well will have to be bored, probably at a cost of several dollars per running foot. In either case, one should state the chemical analysis of the water (pH factor), and whether a softener will be needed.

Storm sewers are a must for any commercial site. If sanitary sewers are not available, septic tanks are one answer but in some soil conditions they will require exceptionally long leaching fields.

Corner Influence, Intersections and the Environs

Analysis of a site requires a final scrutiny of its relationship to its immediate environs. A study of the site's desirability in the light of adjoining streets, abutting parcels, alleys, neighboring buildings and traffic conditions, must be detailed in the appraisal.

An intersection of streets has advantages for some commercial users. A corner location provides more light and air and has more display features. These distinctions enhance value. However, a corner location often means higher assessments because of more street frontage. It is subject to more noise and greater traffic. Whether a site on a corner is advantageous or disadvantageous can only be judged in the light of its most likely-profitable use.

A corner naturally has greater influence on the value of a site in a business district than in other areas. This has led to the development of corner influence tables. These are tables of percentages which show an increase in value because corner location affords greater exposure, light and air, and is more readily accessible to pedestrian traffic, at the street crossings. The percentage applies to the first 100 feet from a corner. It is often related to frontage value on the minor street of the two involved. Or, it may be a percentage applied to the main street unit. These tables, like those on depth influence, should be used with discretion, if at all.

Corner influence tables usually apply only to business and apartment properties, but square foot evaluation is generally a less complicated, and more satisfactory method of approaching land value on such corners.

THE INFLUENCES OF CLIMATE AND TRAFFIC ON SITE VALUE

Local shopping customs may affect store location value. If, in the Deep South and Southwest, shoppers have a tendency to avoid the sunny side of the street in the long, hot afternoons, stores so located will do less business. Most people avoid crossing heavily traveled streets unnecessarily, so the shops on the long side of a rectangular block usually receive the most patronage. Sites on the short side tend to draw fewer people.

Arterial lay-out and automobile traffic must be considered in analyzing commercial districts; and easy entrance and exit are factors which play upon the site under appraisement. Wide avenues present extended view to their frontage and develop allure for gasoline station corners and other uses which can capitalize on advertising display value, such as motels and automobile agencies.

One-way streets, rotaries, stoplights and median strips, can be good or detrimental influences. These factors should be exposed in the appraisal report with an opinion as to their influence on the value of the site.

Bus stops and on-site or nearby car parking are of great importance to commercial sites; and smooth, hard-paved streets without potholes are of equal weight in influencing value. Street lights, proper grading, solid curbs and well-kept, wide sidewalks can be attractions to customers, and customer-attraction is of the essence in commercial site analysis.

The end product of site analysis is the appraiser's conviction as to highest and best use. Then he is ready to evaluate the land.

The following is a checklist of points to be remembered in analysis and evaluation of a commercial site:

A. *Title Information*
   1. Legal description.
   2. Tax assessments, rate and burden.
   3. Zoning-classification of use, setbacks, ground coverage, height limitations, etc.
   4. Public and private restrictions, fire codes, building codes, etc., and uses requiring consent of neighbors, etc.
   5. Easements, rights of way, party wall agreements, etc.
   6. Type of estate to be appraised; in Fee Simple, or otherwise.

B. *Site Specifications*
   1. Frontage, width, depth and plottage.
   2. Area in square feet, and frontage feet.
   3. Shape.
   4. Topography and subsoil conditions.
   5. Trees and plantings.
   6. Utilities, available or connected.
   7. Corner influence, intersections and the environs.

C. *Influences of Climate and Traffic on the Site*
   1. Effect of sunlight and shade and prevailing breezes, A.M. and P.M.
   2. Width of street, surfacing, curbs, walks and presence of street lighting.
   3. Traffic load, traffic direction, stop lights, arterial layout feeding the district.
   4. Bus stops and auto parking.
   5. Display value, and ease of entry and exit.

D. *Most likely-profitable, or highest and best use.*

E. *Evaluation Method*—Market Data Approach or Land Residual Technique or both.
   1. Comparable sales—adjustments.
   2. Land Residual—testing for actual planned or hypothetical highest and best income building.
   3. Market Survey, calculations and value conclusions.

How to Evaluate the Site

Primarily, there are two methods of evaluating commercial land in appraisal practice. These are:

1. *The Market Data Approach.* This method calls for comparing, weighing, and relating sales of similar vacant sites to the land under appraisement.
2. *The Land Residual Technique.* This Income Approach technique capitalizes into value the residual income imputable to the land as derived from an actual or hypothetical new building improvement. (This is fully described in Chapter V.)

Market Data Approach

Of the two methods the Market Data Approach of land valuation is the best indicator. This method requires the gathering, recording, and comparing of sales of comparable sites. The greatest weight should be placed on actual recent sales of similar nearby sites.

Price found in the market-place is strong evidence of value. Most courts do not permit the presentation of evidence regarding mere asking prices. But a contract of sale is acceptable.

Where to Find Market Data

Market data can be gathered from brokers, builders, bankers, lawyers, assessors and town clerks. Local newspapers often report real estate transactions; news reports can be verified at city hall. Real estate sales are shown in the public records by the transfer of deeds.

Unless one is personally familiar with the details which have consummated a sale, he will interview the grantor, the grantee, or the broker, or all three. Such verification will provide firsthand information about the unrecorded conditions which might have influenced either or both parties in the transfer.

Qualified local opinion is a source of data which may help. Bankers and investors who loan against or trade in real estate will provide background and circumstance bearing on questions of value. One should not overlook any source of information.

Begin the quest for market data at the public records-transfer maps or books, the index of deeds, and the deeds themselves. From the deed the following can be extracted:

1. Name of the grantor (seller).
2. Name of the grantee (purchaser).
3. Date of sale. Recorded in volume and page, land records.
4. Legal description, metes and bounds (dimensions).
5. Zoning, and restrictions of record.
6. Mortgage indebtedness.
7. Sale price (and price per square foot).

Relating Comparable Sales to the Subject

The data in the comparable sales must be spelled out and the characteristics most similar to the subject must be stressed. Where the comparable sale differs from the subject, a plus or minus adjustment in dollars should be made in the subject's estimated value.

The character and use of the comparable sites must be stressed; size, shape and locational features must be compared with the subject, point for point; both comparable and subject must be contrasted against the background of the commercial district and block in which they are situated.

The comparable sale must have taken place within a reasonable period of time, say three years. In a land sales market which has been rising steadily for the past 25 years, and shows every sign of continuing to rise, one may add an increment of 5% per annum to the subject for each full year since the comparable sale took place.

In making adjustments, work from the comparable toward the subject. It is the subject which is adjusted and ascribed a value related to the comparable's superiority, inferiority or equality.

Examples of these relationships are demonstrated in the Model Appraisals shown in Part II, in various types of land uses.

Land Residual Technique Under the Income Approach

Determining highest and best use is the initial step in the income capitalization approach to site valuation.

The building most likely-profitable to the land is suggested by present land-use in the commercial district. But the quality of size of the structure is not so easily calculated.

Say the site suggests an apartment house. How large should the building be? The question can only be answered by testing back and forth between the gross and net income yields of imaginary buildings of various sizes until the size that will show the highest net rate of return to the land has been estimated. In effect, you project a series of hypothetical buildings upon the site until you determine which will show the greatest residual return imputable to the land. This is an application of the principle of surplus productivity.

The net income hypothetically imputed to the land in the income capitalization approach is the amount remaining after payment of all operating charges, plus interest on and recapture of the building investment. The *land earnings are the last consideration* and are therefore *residual.*

The Land Residual Technique must be applied cautiously in evaluating a site. Your choice of highest and best use can result in a broad variance in the net income assigned to the land. If the rates of capitalization are slightly varied, one way or another, the final result will also change substantially.

The Land Residual Technique is useful as a check against the Market Data Approach, or as the principal means of estimating land value when adequate comparable sales are not available.

The Model Appraisal in Chapter VI demonstrates use of the Land Residual Technique in site valuation.

Market Survey

The appraiser's market survey really begins with his inspection of subject property and remains uppermost in his mind all the way through the steps of evaluation, from the Title Information research to the last calculation in value conclusion. The principal value considerations to be applied to all commercial land, and any improvements proposed or existing on such land, are these:

1. Zoning approbation.
2. The most likely-profitable, or highest and best use.
3. Location in the region and trade area (Macro-market study).
4. The commercial district's purchasing power (Micro-market study).
5. The relative availability of comparable sites, nearby.

This is the root, sum and substance of any value problem in the appraisal of commercial land. All those parts of the Market Survey which really begin in the land records section of the town hall, along with property analysis, are now brought to conclusion in a concise form, as suggested above, to influence calculations as to value estimate, stated in terms of money.

IV

Setting Up the Problem for Solution

Turning from land to buildings, the appraiser moves into the age-life part of his valuation problem, and encounters depreciation factors in questions of functional performance, and condition and quality of materials and equipment in all types of commercial structures.

In appraisal practice, the word *functional* applies only to the physical aspects of a building. *Functional inutility* refers to a loss of usefulness because of an inherent physical defect. Commercial *functional inutility* and *functional obsolescence* are synonymous for the purposes of this book, and future references to the opposite of *functional utility* will read *functional obsolescence.*

Functional utility versus functional obsolescence in a given building is revealed by closely comparing old and new buildings with the typical in modernity.

There is great variety in architectural design from era to era, but utility tends to conform for commercial buildings of the same age. The basic floor plan is of primary importance because its shape will determine degrees of usefulness. A rectangle or square lends itself to retail store adaptations more readily than L-shapes, or other configurations. But in apartment houses and office buildings an L-shape or H-shape might be advantageous. Modernization of older buildings is often economical and advisable when the location is good, and patronage is assured. Improvements can then be a contribution to net income.

Construction and Materials

Quality of construction must be measured carefully in your accrued depreciation estimates, and on the whole in the Cost Approach. It will also be measured in comparability with similar properties in the Market Data Approach.

Conversely, economy of construction must not be given bad marks, where it is properly applied. Thrifty methods might be most advisable in building a small, neighborhood store, say a delicatessen or a retail liquor outlet, which over the term of the lease may produce a good rent. This is better judgment than if such a building was of superior construction quality, say built like a branch bank, which would mean a higher tax assessment, and a larger investment against the rent.

Use your common sense in weighing quality of materials and workmanship against the property you are appraising.

Weather pattern influences the type of construction and material used in various parts of the country. Climate affects the capacity of heating equipment, and the depth of foundations. Driveways and parking areas must have a heavier base and thicker coat of macadam or concrete where the frost level reaches down. Pipes and drains must be set deeper. Roofing must be properly sloped for snow load in Alaska. In Florida this is unimportant. But common sense is important in both places, and in appraising all the time.

Availability of materials may bear as heavily as climate in methods of construction. The cost of light aggregate block may be much cheaper in Bridgeport, Connecticut (where it is made portside from lava brought from Greece in ship bottoms) than in Chillicothe, Ohio (where it would have to be transported by truck or rail). The cost of steel in Pittsburgh might be considerably less than in Connecticut, where there are no smelting furnaces.

In the South, cypress siding for storefronts and small office buildings is plentiful. The same is true of redwood on the West Coast. In evaluating materials and quality of construction, you must judge the locale as it is related to climate, availability of materials, architectural tastes and traditions, and popular purchasing power.

Equipment

As much as 40% of the total cost of a large office building may be in equipment such as heating, ventilating, air-conditioning, lighting, plumbing, water supply, waste disposal, elevators and telephone cables.

Equipment is a prime factor of depreciation in a commercial property. Compared to the structure itself, some of the equipment such as air-conditioning compressors may have a life of, say, ten years, where the life of the building may be fifty years, so the rate of depreciation on equipment is generally higher than on the structure.

Commercial properties may suffer by loss of tenant appeal when competing properties install improved equipment.

When appraising income property, remember that operating and maintenance costs relate directly to the equipment. Shoddy equipment will mean high maintenance and operating costs. Elevator trouble will run up repair bills and tenant dissatisfaction. Breakdowns in the heating or air-conditioning systems will do the same. So study the equipment carefully when making your appraisal. You may find signs of equipment shortcomings in the operating expense statement. You may be asked to assist in the selection of a plan for modernizing equipment. But in any event, make a thorough disclosure of equipment operability in your estimate of depreciation.

Estimating Building Costs

Reproduction cost is the present cost of reproducing a building with one of approximately identical construction. *Replacement cost* is the present cost of replacing a building with one having identical utility.

The two terms are frequently juxtaposed in appraisal practice, and by usage have come to mean the same thing in *regard to construction and utility.*

Both terms are synonymous for the purposes of this book, which will henceforth refer to Reproduction Cost in the technique of the Cost Approach.

Buildings must be valued separately for some of the same reasons calling for separate land valuation:

1. For property assessment purposes (when *ad valorem* tax laws decree such separation.)
2. For accounting and federal income tax purposes (when it is important to show depreciation of structures and equipment.)
3. To determine the most likely-profitable use of the land and to estimate income imputable to buildings when using the Land Residual Technique, under the Income Approach.

Methods of Estimating Reproduction Cost

Construction cost estimates are never precise. While exact prices of materials and labor can be gleaned from manuals, the cost of putting them together in a finished building cannot be assessed with exactness.

The labor and supervision factors, and the contractor's appetite for the job can inflate or deflate the cost estimate. When contractors are bidding on a job, it often occurs that cost estimates on the same set of blueprints will vary by 25% or more. The busy contractor with too many jobs will bid an indifferent high. The contractor starving for work may bid too low.

Estimating Reproduction Cost means taking an inventory of the materials and equipment in a building under appraisement and pricing these components, plus labor and overhead and architect's fees, to reproduce the property as of the date of appraisal.

Quantity Survey Method

This is the most reliable, but most expensive method of cost estimating. It provides a detailed Reproduction Cost which is unassailable from any quarter. It is, in effect, a duplication of the contractor's original pricing of the quantity and grade of each item of material used, estimate of labor involved, and applying unit costs to the material and labor quantities.

Unit-in-Place Method

Except for use on large, newly constructed buildings, the Quantity Survey Method is impractical and costly. Most appraisers are not builders, and unless they have free access to a recent quantity breakdown, they will find this costly to obtain from a qualified builder. A Quantity Survey is time-consuming and arduous to put together, and too expensive to include in the average appraisal. It should be done by a professional builder, who will of course want to be compensated for his time and thought.

A quicker, modified version of the Quantity take-off, is the Unit-in-Place Method, generally used by contractors who are asked by appraisers for supporting evidence on new construction.

This consists of using installed prices for materials, employing a convenient unit of measurement, such as cubic or square footage. It eliminates counting the exact number of board feet of lumber, yards of ready-mix cement, bales of shingles, and the like, and facilitates your computation by including labor overhead, insurance and supervision in the square or cubic foot count.

Once basic units are established, the cost of an entire building can be estimated quickly.

You need not qualify as a professional cost estimator, since this calls for specialized training and experience, but you should know builders from whom you can obtain cost estimates, the limitations of available methods when applied to your problems, and the nature of the estimate sought in each case. You should be aware that it is most practical to have the cost estimate, the inspection of the building for depreciation, and the rehabilitation cost estimate prepared as a related process under the control of one person. This person does not have to be you, but should be someone working closely with you in whose work you have confidence.

Square Foot and Cubic Foot Comparisons

The pros and cons of the square-foot versus cubic-foot methods have to be judged in the light of local custom, and individual choice. Most commercial appraisers lean to the square-foot method which is ideally applicable to warehouses, loft buildings, store buildings, and structures of commercial character. The cubic-foot method is sometimes applied to apartments and frequently to office buildings, that is, structures with a considerable degree of interior finish and partitions.

Two kinds of *indirect costs* figure in cost estimating: first, the contractor's overhead and profit; and second, the general overhead, including architect's fees and accounting and legal services, taxes, insurance, survey expenses, and interest during the period of construction. With income properties, costs are often incurred after construction while tenants are being solicited and until total occupancy is achieved.

Familiarity with the make-up of the cubic-foot or square-foot cost per unit not only produces more accurate cost estimates, but also figures in estimating depreciation. With proper maintenance, a structure might have a long life. It's equipment might require replacement sooner and can be separately depreciated at an advanced rate.

Cost Manuals and Services

You should subscribe to one or more of the accredited cost-reporting services. Illustrations and alternative adjustments to the standard index example may help you to keener insights on costs. Some manuals provide adjustment to the individual territory in which the appraiser is interested. Some demonstrate cubic-foot costs, some square-foot, and some are designed for unit-in-place information. Actual knowledge of what it costs locally to build is still the best evidence. Even so, a good cost service is excellent supporting evidence.

As foundation for the Cost Approach, and often as an indicator in the Market Data Approach, the reproduction cost estimate contributes to the estimate of final value. Its accuracy and its presentation must be given careful review. As a rule, one of two general methods is best suited to your use: (1) the modified quantity survey (or unit-in-place); (2) the cubic-foot or square-foot (comparative). The former method is preferred where builder's testimony in court is important.

Depreciation

Depreciation is loss of value from any of several causes. In general, there are three classifications of depreciation: (1) Deterioration; (2) Functional Obsolescence (Inutility); (3) Economic Obsolescence. These classifications may be broken down as follows:

1. *Deterioration* is loss in value to a building which occurs by wear and tear in use, from decay, because of structural defects, and from exposure to the elements.

There are generally two kinds of deterioration: *Curable* and *Incurable.*

a) *Curable deterioration* is that which may be controlled by an owner who may cure the decay with good, ordinary maintenance. The amount of accrued curable deterioration is expressed as the *Cost to Cure* such deterioration. The estimate of Cost to Cure, however, must be limited by the amount which a prudent owner would be justified in spending to cure the deterioration.

b) *Incurable deterioration* is actual loss in strength or in remaining life of the basic components of the structure which cannot ordinarily be reached by a prudent owner for repair and replacement. This is a loss in value occurring as a direct result of age or inferior construction that cannot economically be cured. It is the only type of depreciation which must be estimated on the basis of the age life of the portions of the structure that are not ordinarily maintained by a prudent owner.

2. *Functional Obsolescence.* This is loss in value which occurs within a structure as a result of its inability to perform adequately the function for which it should be used. It may be represented by antiquated design, appearance, overdesign, out-of-date features, such as excessively high ceilings, oversized corridors and lobbies, and other structural features out-of-date by comparison with modern design and construction.

There are again two forms of *functional obsolescence:*

a) One form of functional obsolescence is *curable,* that is to say, can be cured economically by a prudent owner. Examples of curable functional obsolescence include replacement of old style lavatories and toilets with modern fixtures, the replacement of old-style electrical fixtures with modern recessed fluorescents, the lowering of ceilings, and installation of modern wiring and plumbing, heating and air-conditioning. The measure of the amount of accrued curable functional obsolescence is the cost to cure. This estimate is of course limited to that amount which a prudent owner would spend in curing the accrued functional obsolescence.

b) There is, in addition, *incurable functional obsolescence.* This is functional obsolescence that would be so costly to cure that a prudent owner would find it unreasonable to do so. Examples of this type of functional obsolescence are excessive foundations and buildings that are far too large for a land area. In general, the amount of *accrued incurable functional obsolescence* is estimated by capitalizing the rental loss suffered because of the inability of the structure to perform adequately the functions for which it was designed. In many cases, the rental loss is measured in reverse, that is to say, by increased ownership expenses without a corresponding increase in gross income. Sometimes the measure includes the combination of the two. The total amount of loss in value due to *incurable functional obsolescence* is therefore the capitalization of either the rental loss or the increased ownership cost, or a combination of the two, for the *remaining economic life* of the structure.

3. *Economic Obsolescence.* This is a form of depreciation which contemplates a downward price level adjustment that is not concerned with the physical condition of real property improvements. It has to do not only with the value of the particular property itself but with *all unfavorable economic influences* on the value of competing properties. It occurs primarily from a reduction in adaptability to a lower use. Among other causes it may arise from changes in legislation, the encroachment of noxious enterprises or inharmonious neighbors, shifting business centers and decline in opportunities for gainful employment.

Depreciation caused by legislation is aptly illustrated by the decline in value of property adapted to the liquor industry when the manufacture and sale of that commodity was prohibited, or what would probably happen to the market value of a profitably operated race track if the pari-mutuel betting system was outlawed.

REMAINING ECONOMIC LIFE OF STRUCTURES

All estimates of future depreciation must be based upon the remaining economic life of structures. The remaining economic life is the estimated number of years that a building will produce a net income sufficient to pay a return on, and a return of, its value.

Such an estimate of remaining economic life can be made only after a careful study of a structure. This study must include not only a complete examination of the physical characteristics of the structure itself, but must also include careful consideration of the probable *future* demands to be made upon the functions which the structure was designed to perform and upon a possible change in the future in the use of the land. Thus, the estimate of remaining economic life is an estimate of *future* deterioration, *future* functional obsolescence, and *future* economic obsolescence; all reflected by the number of years in the *future* which, in the judgment of the appraiser, a building can logically be expected to pay a return on and of the value remaining in it as of the day on which an appraisal is made. Such an estimate is only made on an observed condition basis and is tempered always by experience and by a careful study of a subject property and similar properties.

"Recapture" is the preferred term to define the setting aside of annual sums to recover or recapture within a period of years the present value of a structure.

Accrued depreciation, as such, is estimated directly only in the cost approach. However, it is estimated indirectly by the market in both the Income Approach and the Market Data Approach. In the earnings approach, the loss in value or depreciation is reflected in the income that the property will produce. It results in a lowered income and a consequently lowered value indicated by the Income Approach. Thus, the Income Approach *automatically* reflects accrued depreciation.

In the Market Data Approach, by comparing the property under appraisement with comparable properties recently sold, all accrued depreciation is deducted from the value of the property as it is actually deducted by actual buyers and sellers of comparable property. Thus, the accrued depreciation is indirectly estimated by the use of comparative sales, in which all types of depreciation have been taken into consideration by buyers and sellers in establishing prices.

It is imperative always, in giving consideration to accrued depreciation, to bear in mind that this is depreciation that has already occurred. Accrued depreciation is estimated only on the basis of observed condition. There is no arbitrary fixed amount per annum which accurately represents accrued depreciation. Such estimates are made only on the basis of what the appraiser actually finds in the inspection of the subject property.

Depreciation may be further described as the difference between the value of a structure and the cost of reproducing it as of the same date.

Accrued depreciation is estimated in the appraisal process by one or more of five different methods, as follows:

1. The capitalized income method.
2. The market method.
3. The straight-line method (age-life depreciation).
4. The engineering method (observed depreciation).
5. The breakdown method (observed depreciation).

Of these, the capitalized income method and the market method are actually indirect systems of estimating depreciation through the Market Data and Income Approaches to value.

The remaining three, the straight-line method, the engineering method, and the breakdown method, are direct systems of estimating depreciation, employed in the Cost Approach.

The straight-line method puts a percentage of depreciation, such as 2% or 2-1/2% or 3% for each year of a building's life. Thus, a building 10 years old, depreciated at the rate of 2-1/2%, will have suffered a reduction in value of 25%.

Observed depreciation is the term used for both the engineering and breakdown methods.

In the engineering method, percentage deductions are applied to the separate components of building cost.

In the breakdown method, deductions (either percentage or in lump sum amounts) are applied to rehabilitation cost, general deterioration, functional obsolescence curable, functional obsolescence incurable, and economic obsolescence.

The nature of the problem best determines the method and detail you should use in making depreciation estimates.

Legal Basis of Depreciation

Definite legal precedents for the treatment of depreciation have been established through much legal controversy.

The U.S. Supreme Court has repeatedly held that the observed condition method of estimating accrued depreciation should be accorded the greatest weight. The court comprehends the intangible nature of the estimate. It has taken the position that the opinion of a qualified witness, based upon personal inspection of the property, together with his skill in estimating depreciation, must take precedence over more mathematical computations.

In cases contested by the Internal Revenue Service, you may be called on to set up the foundational figures and premises both as to depreciation and life expectancies. Qualified appraisal opinion is steadily gaining more recognition in income tax procedure.

Generally, in law and by regulation of the various government agencies, the observed depreciation methods are preferred.

Application

Using the observed depreciation methods, the property is compared with a new property or an index example of the typical in modernity. The methods are based upon direct inspection, detailed estimates of accrued deterioration and studies of functional deficiencies, affecting the property and its desirability. Close comparison of the property against a 100 percent perfect property as a model lends more weight to your judgment of value. Your estimate will stand scrutiny if you report in enough detail so that your reasons are coherent and logical, as well as arithmetically correct.

At this point, the typical appraisal problem has been set up for solution.

The laws of supply and demand, the principles of appraising, the analysis and evaluation of land have been set forth. Analysis of physical and functional utility of structures, and methods of estimating depreciation heighten our researches.

We are now ready to proceed with solution of the appraisal problem, the final step in the appraisal process. This is done by working out one or more of the three approaches to value, and then correlating their indicated values into a final value estimate.

V

Solving the Problem with the Tools of the Profession

The solution to any appraisal problem is its value conclusion.

Your value conclusion is a correlation of the value indications ensuing from your investment analysis of a commercial property via three approaches — *Income,* Market Data, and Cost, when possible. In general appraising practice, the emphasis you place on any one of the approaches is a matter of your own opinion, based on your research, judgment and experience; but where *income property* is concerned, almost always (except for gasoline stations), the *Income Approach,* closely supported by Market Data, will count most heavily with the sophisticated investor and the courts.

The principles and approaches, and the techniques and methods of appraising commercial properties are tools to be used in solving your particular appraisal problem. They are recognized in the courts of the nation, and carry the authority of many years of thoughtful development by highly experienced appraisers.

The emphasis of this book is on the *Income Approach,* as bearing greatest weight in estimating value of income-producing properties, which are usually owned for investment purposes. But the Market Data and Cost Approaches will also be explored here for the roles they play in support of the Income Approach.

The Market Data Approach should be given great weight because it is the most easily comprehended, and because value estimate is taken from actual market transactions of similar properties. It is most likely to reflect accurately the "market value" of a property when applied to non-income bearing land or buildings. *It is conclusive in raw land evaluations.*

However, you should never entirely forget the benefits to be gained from using all the tools made available to you by applying all three approaches to value in cases where reliable data is at hand, so that you can develop three value indications.

Eminent domain proceedings require that all three approaches to fair market value be used insofar as possible.

The Income Approach

This approach to value is an appraisal technique in which the anticipated net income is processed to indicate the capital amount of the investment which produces the net income. Therefore, extreme care must be used in estimating the net income to arrive at the value indicated by the Income Approach.

Processing Earnings

This will be accomplished by taking the following deliberate steps:

1. In the appraisal of commercial property the first step is to estimate the gross income that the property mav logically be expected to bring in the rental market at the time the appraisal is made. From this estimate of rentals, which is tested by comparison with similar properties, you must then deduct a proper figure to compensate for normal losses in rents and normal collection losses. This is called a vacancy allowance, and is usually accorded 5 to 10% of the gross income. The remaining income may then be considered as the *effective gross income.*
2. From the effective gross income you must next deduct the normal ownership expenses of the subject property, which may include taxes, insurance, normal replacements, maintenance, and management. When these ownership expenses are deducted from the effective gross income, the remaining income is known as the *net income* to the property before depreciation, including the land and building.
3. Here your selection of the rate of capitalization becomes extremely important. The most effective guide to the proper rate at which the net income should be capitalized is the rate at which buyers and sellers of similar properties are capitalizing the net income to arrive at their sale prices. This can be determined *only by a study of recent sales made in the open market and net income of the properties sold.* The rate developed should include adequate coverage of the safe rate, the penalty for lack of liquidity, the penalty for the management of the money, and the penalty for risk of regularity of net money income as well as the risk for the possible future loss of the capital investment. The rate so found in the market and tested as to its components as referred to above may then be considered to be the proper capitalization rate for the subject property.
4. When the value of the land can be found in the market by the use of the Market Data Approach it is then proper to process the net income to the property by the use of the *Building Residual Technique.* (See Chapter VI.) In using this technique, the needed income required to service

the investment in the land at the value found by the Market Data Approach is charged against the net income to the property and the remainder is considered as the *net income remaining to the building.* This income is then processed to indicate the capital value of the building.

5. In the processing of the income to the building, great care must be exercised to estimate the *remaining economic life* of the building. When the remaining economic life of the building is estimated, the net income remaining to the building is then processed for the period of the remaining economic life by the proper capitalization rate to indicate the capital value of the building.

Capitalization Methods

The capitalization method to be used is determined by the *quality of the net income stream* that is anticipated from the property.

For example, if the rentals are on a month-to-month or short-term basis, if net income before depreciation is liable to decline, and if the property is generally in mid-life, the straight-line (age-life) depreciation plus the capitalization-rate method may be used. In using this method, the number of years of the remaining economic life of the building is divided into 100 to determine the percentage of future depreciation per year. Then the percentage of future depreciation is added to the capitalization rate to arrive at the overall rate which will produce a return on the invested capital for the remaining economic life of the building and the return of the invested capital over this same period.

The value of the building found by this method, plus the value of the land found by the market data approach, becomes the indicated value of the property.

Depending upon the *quality and durability* of income flowing from the property you are appraising, you can elect to follow either of the following courses of capitalization:

1. You use the straight-line depreciation plus capitalization-rate method of capitalization when you anticipate that the net income before depreciation *may decline* in the future. The rate of decline anticipated is represented by the formula —

$$\left.\begin{array}{l}\text{Annual rate of decline}\\ \quad\text{anticipated in the}\\ \quad\text{net income before}\\ \quad\text{depreciation}\end{array}\right\} = \frac{\text{Capitalization rate} \times \text{rate of depreciation}}{\text{Capitalization rate} + \text{rate of depreciation}}$$

For instance, in the evaluating of a building having a remaining economic life of 20 years, using a capitalization rate of 5 percent, the annual rate of decline anticipated in the net income before depreciation is as follows:

$$\left.\begin{array}{l}\text{Annual rate of decline}\\ \quad\text{anticipated in the}\\ \quad\text{net income before}\\ \quad\text{depreciation}\end{array}\right\} = \frac{0.05 \times 0.05}{0.05 + 0.05} = \frac{0.0025}{0.10} = 2.5 \text{ percent per year}$$

2. But if the net income before depreciation is expected to be level or better, and is *of a contract nature,* if the financial stability of the tenants is substantial and the leases extend over a period of at least twelve years, then the Inwood premise may be used. This premise is used in good, chain-store lease properties. When this method is used, it is only necessary to select the factor in the Inwood table which represents the number of years of the remaining economic life of the building and the capitalization rate selected. This factor is then multiplied by the net income remaining to the building to indicate the capital value of the building. The value of the building is then added to the value of the land as found in the Market Data Approach, and the sum of the two is the indicated value of the property, as shown here:

Building Residual—Inwood Annuity

Value of the land by Market Data	$100,000.	
Reported annual net before recapture		$32,000.
Interest imputable to land value 7%		7,000.
Annual net income imputable to building		$25,000.
Remaining economic life 20 years, interest rate 7%. Then, the present worth of 1 per annum for 20 years, discounted at 7%, is found to be 10.594 (Inwood table factor): Table II		
Building value $25,000 × 10.594		$264,850.
Add Land Value, Market Data Approach		100,000.
		$364,850.

Residual Techniques

When it is not possible to find the value of the land by the use of the Market Data Approach, it is best to find the value of the land by using the *Land Residual Technique* under a hypothetical *highest-and-best-use* building. When this technique is employed, after making a careful study of the vicinity, you estimate the type of building that will produce the highest net return to the land. You then estimate the cost of constructing the building, the income that the building will produce, and the expenses that will have to be paid to produce that income. After the estimated expenses are deducted from the estimated effective gross income, the net income to the property is then processed by first finding the amount of the net income necessary to meet the building charges. These building charges include not only a return on the money invested in the building at the proper rate of capitalization but also the return of the capital invested in the building during the remaining economic life of the building.

The income may be processed by the straight-line depreciation plus the capitalization rate method or by the Inwood method, depending upon the quality of the income stream. The total amount of the annual income necessary to service the building is next deducted from the net income to the property before depreciation, to arrive at the income remaining to the land. The land income is then capitalized at the same capitalization rate to indicate the capital value of the land.

The value of the land found in this method is used in appraisal of the subject property in connection with the *Building Residual Technique.* In other words, the income required by the land on the value found under a hypothetical highest-and-best-use building is deducted from the net income produced by the subject property before depreciation, and the remaining income is considered as the income applying to the existing building. The income applying to the existing building is then processed by the proper capitalization method to indicate the capital value of the building. The capital value of the building found in this way is now added to the value of the land found under the hypothetical highest-and-best-use building, and the sum of the two is the value indicated.

The term "residual" means that which remains after all deductions.

Using the *Property Residual Technique,* land and building are not valued separately, but as a whole. In this process, most applicable to properties leased long-term, you capitalize the present worth of the anticipated net income before depreciation for the estimated economic life of the building, or the term of the lease. At the anticipated end of the income, land and building are assumed to revert to the owner. This reversion is valued by discounting its then anticipated value against its present-day worth. The total value is the sum of the capitalized value of the income plus the present worth of the reversionary interest. Another application of this technique applies an overall rate for the entire net before depreciation with no reversion. It is, in effect, the same as direct capitalization with an overall rate.

Residual techniques are mathematical avenues by which you take certain known factors and then find the unknowns. To recapitulate:

1. In the *Land Residual Technique,* the known factors are net income before recapture, building value, interest rate, and the useful life of the building. The unknown or residual factor is land value.
2. In the *Building Residual Technique* the known factors are net income before recapture, land value, interest rate, and the remaining economic life of the building. The unknown factor is the building value.
3. In the *Property Residual Technique* the known factors are the net income before recapture, the capitalization rate, the useful life of the building, and land value. The unknown is the property value.

These techniques are tied in with the processes of straight capitalization with straight-line recapture, sinking fund, and Inwood or Hoskold. Regardless of the capitalization process used, each of the residual techniques has a function.

Selection of Rates

In commercial properties which are primarily bought and sold on the basis of the capitalization of their anticipated net income, the Income Approach becomes the favored indication of fair market value. In such properties, the value indicated by the Market Data Approach and the value indicated by the Income Approach should emerge close together.

Experienced appraisers often use the device of constructing a rate based upon the primary elements involved which first considers the generally accepted nonrisk or safe rate applicable to government bonds or good municipal bonds. An illustration of this device follows:

	Percent
The safe rate (nonrisk)	5
Rate for management	1
Rate for nonliquidity	1
Rate for risk	1
Total	8

Selection of Method

You can now assume a soundly estimated stream of income and the skillful selection of an interest rate reflecting all risks involved in a capital investment in the property. But your task is not complete. You are now confronted with selecting the method with which you will treat the income and interest rate to produce the most logical answer which these important tools can assist you in developing.

There are four methods of treatment to this vital last step in the Income Approach each of which can produce a substantially different answer subject to the basic assumptions involved in the methods indicated below:

Method	*Result Produced*
1. Straight-line depreciation plus interest	Lowest
2. Inwood premise (compound interest)	Highest
*3. Hoskold premise (sinking fund depreciation, plus interest)	Intermediate
4. Declining annuity premise (applies to variable income stream only)	Degree of decline.

Selection of the method for use in any specific case is dependent upon the type of property as an investment, the skill and depth of experience of the appraiser in dealing with investment properties, and the degree of conformity in the pattern of the data upon which his judgment has dictated his estimate of the income stream and his choice of interest rate. You must have a complete understanding of the basic assumptions inherent in each to the end that you may best reflect the viewpoint of the typical investor in real estate.

The Market Data Approach

This approach is the most convincing *support* in estimating fair market value of a commercial property. In evaluating land and gasoline stations it is *conclusive.* Simply, it means estimating the market value of a given property by comparing it with similar properties in the same vicinity which have been sold recently in the open market. The Market Data Approach is concerned with the *principle of substitution* in that typical investors will not purchase a property at a price greater than the prices of similar properties having comparable locations, characteristics and future earning or use capabilities.

*Sometimes called "straight capitalization with sinking fund recapture."

This is the only approach to value that reflects the *balance of supply and demand* in actual trading in the open market, and it develops clinching evidence, in support of the Income Approach, in condemnation proceedings. Where active *income-producing* properties are under scrutiny, except for gasoline stations, the Income Approach must edge the Market Data Approach as chief indicator of value. Occasionally, the Income Approach and the Market Data Approach coincide almost exactly in value conclusion. When this happens, value estimate is overwhelmingly confirmed, providing that all the factors and calculations have been soundly developed.

The first step in the use of the Market Data Approach, after a thorough inspection of the property to be appraised, is to obtain accurate and completely detailed information on the sales of comparable properties in the neighborhood or in the general vicinity. This is the most important step because without actual sales of comparable properties or actual offerings of comparable properties, the market test is not complete. The complete appraisal is much more convincing if it has well chosen comparable vicinity property sales which have been thoroughly tested and investigated than if it were overburdened with reference to property sales which may be questionable as to prices, dates, conditions of sales, or degree of comparability.

Selection of Comparables

In selecting the comparables to be used in valuing a given property, it is fundamental that those chosen for close comparison should be similar in size, construction, use and location to the property you are appraising. Each appraisal should contain a sufficient description of the comparables used so that it is possible for the reader to understand the conclusions drawn by the appraiser from the comparable sales used. Photographs of the comparable sales are valuable visual aids in proving the comparability of the property recently sold against the property under appraisement.

Depreciated Reproduction Cost Approach

In this approach the fair market value of the land raw is added to the depreciated replacement cost new of the improvements to arrive at an indication of the value of the property. The value of the raw land is always estimated, separately, by a study of comparable sales. The estimate of reproduction cost new of the improvements is based on current cost of labor and materials for construction of improvements of like utility. From this cost new estimate is then deducted the depreciation that can actually be observed in the buildings. The resulting value is known as the value indicated by the Cost Approach.

In a sense, this approach is another type of comparative or Market Data Approach in that the land value is estimated by comparison with similar tracts of land recently sold, and the cost estimate of the structures is developed by comparison with the cost of comparable structures.

The Cost Approach develops the upper or maximum limit of fair market value. This is because the value indication is found by adding together the land and the buildings, and further because it is extremely difficult to estimate accurately accrued depreciation. Thus, this approach is most generally used as a check on the estimate of value indicated by the Market Data or Income Approach because it definitely indicates the upper limit of market value, which is the cost of the property.

The Cost Approach requires the use of unit cost prices in the estimation of building replacement cost new. While it is true that the most accurate estimates of cost are generally made by an actual material and labor estimate, or by a unit cost in place estimate, the use of cubic-foot or square-foot cost estimates is considered to be reasonably accurate providing the actual unit cost figures used are taken from similar buildings that have recently been constructed. The standard construction cost reports are of help in estimating unit cost of construction but are not to be considered as accurate or dependable as is actual cost experience in the building of similar structures.

All three types of accrued depreciation which include deterioration, functional obsolescence, and economic obsolescence must be accurately reflected and deducted from the replacement cost new before the land and the buildings are added together to find the value indicated by the use of the Cost Approach.

The Cost Approach does have a peculiar and controlling application in the case of certain special-purpose types of structures which may be normally nonmarketable in character. These structures include schools, churches, fire stations, hospitals, municipal buildings, town halls, courthouses, and other institutional uses. The courts have held that while such properties have no ready market value in that they are not freely bought and sold, they do have a use value to the owner which must be compensated for when expropriated. Probably the best estimate of the *use value* to the owner is the value indicated by the Cost Approach.

Correlation of the Approaches

Use of the Income Approach is particularly applicable when appraising properties with improvements which were designed primarily for income purposes, properties involving severance damages, and easements, and properties involved in condemnation actions.

In relying on the Income Approach as the principal indicator of value, you should also, as support bring in the Market Data Approach. Even when it is difficult to find comparable sales, it is possible by enlarging your geographical vicinity and by using other comparable properties that are similar in their income capacities to find Market Data that will be of assistance in estimating the market value of the property under appraisement.

A minimum of two approaches is recommended, and all three should be considered to the fullest extent possible when appraising improved commercial properties involved in condemnation actions.

The Cost Approach is often used as a check against both the Market Data Approach and the Income Approach to insure that the market value estimate does not exceed cost, which is generally conceded to be the upper or miximum limit of market value.

Severance Damage

This is any loss in value of property remaining to an owner after the condemnation of part of his real estate. Severance damage is not a part of the value of the land to be taken. It is a measure of reduction in value as a result of a partial taking of real property. Severance damages are recognized only when there exists identity of ownership and unity of use with respect to parts taken and parts remaining. These damages result when a partial taking lowers the highest and best use or otherwise limits the use of the remainder. Severance damage should never be assumed merely because of partial taking. It always must be fully supported by the facts in each case.

Estimates of severance damages are developed by use of what is known as the "before" and "after" appraisal methods. For example, the "before" (before a taking) fair market value of a neighborhood shopping center on 7 acres is, say, $750,000. The part to be acquired by your state highway department, in fee, say, is 2 acres of parking area with a fair market value of $40,000 @ $20,000 per acre. Simple arithmetic would indicate the value of the part left to the owner to be $710,000. Such, however, is not necessarily the case. The "after" appraisal (appraisal of the remainder left to the owner) may indicate a fair market value in fee, of say, $675,000, thus reflecting a severance damage of $35,000. This damage may have occurred from one or more of several causes. The owner may have been left with an imbalance in shoppers' parking-to-buildings ratio, thus leaving him with decidedly "overimproved" land. The damage could be occasioned by the fact that so much of his land was taken that the remainder was appreciably limited as an economic commercial unit due to reduced road frontage and irregular boundary. This example may be illustrated in a more brief form as follows:

"Before" appraisal, fair market value of shopping center on 7 acres	$750,000.
"After" appraisal, fair market value of shopping center left to owner (the remainder) with 5 acres	675,000.
	$ 75,000.
Fair market value, appraisal of part to be taken, 2 acres @ $20,000. per acre	40,000.
The difference, severance damages	$ 35,000.

As shown in the preceding example three distinct appraisals are required:

1. The entire property before the taking.
2. The part to be taken.
3. The remainder.

Some courts have held that only two steps are essential, viz. the value before and the value after the taking. However, all three evaluations are required in appraisals for most government agencies where partial takings are involved.

Partial-taking appraisals serve to emphasize the use of all of the three approaches to value in the appraisal process as the "remainder" is often rendered entirely dissimilar from lands used as comparable sales. In many cases, you may find the final answer to your problem in your skillful use of the Income Approach. Reasonably accurate maps showing all physical conditions pertinent to the entire property, and to the separate parts, are considered vital.

Here are some typical causes of severance damages:

1. Reduction in highest and best use of the remainder.
2. Resulting insufficiency of the remainder to support normal typical operation.
3. Loss of access to transportation facilities, roads, streets, rails, and water.
4. Distortion in plottage or shape which handicaps use or marketability.
5. Bulwarking the remainder with wall or fence along the taking line.

Offsetting Benefits in Condemnation

The Act of July 18, 1918 (H. R. 10069), (Public No. 200), vol. 40, p. 904 (ch.55), sec. 6, reads as follows:

> That in all cases where private property shall be taken by the United States for the public use in connection with any improvement of rivers, harbors, canals, or waterways of the United States, and in all condemnation proceedings by the United States to acquire land or easements for such improvements, where a part only of any such parcel, lot, or tract of land shall be taken, the jury or other tribunal awarding the just compensation or assessing the damages to the owner, whether for the value of the part taken or for any injury to the part not taken, shall take into consideration by way of reducing the amount of compensation or damages any special and direct benefits to the remainder arising from the improvement, and shall render their award or verdict accordingly.

This language can be applied to offsetting benefits in partial-takings by eminent domain condemnors other than the federal government, such as the states, municipalities and utility companies. Some states, however, still maintain a legal tradition of ignoring offsetting benefits.

As described in the partial-taking process outlined above, if special and direct benefits arising from an improvement increase the value of the remainder, then that increase in value will be offset against the value of the remainder and of the part taken, if necessary.

A special and direct benefit value to a remainder should be reflected into the "after" appraisal of the remainder. Therefore, it is crucial that you become familiar with the developed benefit, its operation and its effects.

An illustration of net results of an appraisal of a partial-taking involving special and direct benefits, is as follows:

"Before" appraisal, fair market value, entire property	$ 60,000.
"After" appraisal, fair market value remainder	18,000.
	$ 42,000.

Part taken, fair market value	45,000.
Enhancement in value of remainder arising from special and direct benefits; to be offset against value of part taken	$ 3,000.

Another way to express the same results is this:

"Before" appraisal, fair market value, whole property	$ 60,000.
"After" appraisal, fair market value, including special and direct benefits	18,000.
Value of the part taken, offset by benefits	$ 42,000.

Benefits must be special and direct, real and imminent. They cannot be speculative or conjectural or for an indeterminate future time.

Easements

An easement denotes ownership of limited real property rights, thus falling short of full fee simple estate ownership. The "before" and "after" method of appraising, described in preceding paragraphs, should ordinarily be employed in their evaluation. The difference between the value of a tract of land and its value with an easement imposed thereon, is the value of the easement.

Air Rights

All real estate has three distinct physical elements: sub-surface, surface and air space. The right to mine ore, or take out gravel (mineral rights) is an example of the first, while the right to traverse the surface (via rail, road, pipe and cable) illustrates the second.

The third element, air space, is aptly described in the following excerpt from the June 8, 1970 issue of *The Mortgage and Real Estate Executives Report,*[1] edited by Alvin L. Arnold, LL.B., Adj. Asst. Professor of Real Estate, New York University:

> Beginning about twenty years ago, developers realized that prime in-city locations were available in quantity above railroad rights of way, highways, schools, post offices and other low-rise developments. Since then, the treatment of air space (or air rights) as an independent interest in real estate has steadily gathered momentum.

[1]Copyright 1970 by Hanover Lamont Corporation, a research affiliate of *The Bankers Magazine* and *The Banking Law Journal,* 89 Beach Street, Boston, Mass. 02111. Volume 3, No. 7.

New York City Selling Air Rights

New York has been a leader in creating a market for air rights. Several years ago, it set up the New York City Educational Construction Fund which issues bonds to finance school construction. The Fund simultaneously sells or leases the air space above a school to private developers who annually pay it a sum in lieu of real estate taxes. The payments are used to pay off bonds.

Observation: Two goals are thus achieved: Real estate is kept on the tax rolls and badly needed housing space is made available.

Now, New York has gone one step further by leasing air space over a public building (the Appellate Division Courthouse) to the developer of adjoining property. In this way, the developer can increase the floor area of the new building since the acquired air space is considered part of the plot for purposes of complying with the zoning ordinance.

Negotiating the Transfer of Air Space

One of four approaches is used, depending upon the particular circumstances:

1. *Sale of Fee Interest:* Air space can be sold just as can real estate in its entirety. However, the buyer must be sure he isn't left up in the air; he must have "support easements" so that he can base a building on columns resting on the surface. Negotiating the terms and conditions of the easement often is the most difficult part of the transaction. Such problems must be resolved as placement of the columns to minimize interference on the ground, and the duty of each party to repair and maintain the columns.

Observation: If real estate taxes are imposed on the entire parcel, an allocation must be agreed upon.

2. *Lease of Air Space:* Here, the physical interest (air space) is divided into two legal interests, a fee and leasehold. Sometimes, a lease must be used because the owner of the parcel (e.g., a railroad) is not permitted by law to sell any part of the property.

3. *Air Space Easement:* While in theory an easement in air space may be created, the more common method is for the owner of the parcel to sell the entire physical interest and reserve an easement of the surface. For example, a railroad or highway requires only a right of way at ground level.

4. *Air Space Condominium:* Here the air space is divided up into "space lots" with all of the lot owners sharing title to the common areas, including the surface. Condominium apartment buildings illustrate this approach.

Examples of Air Space Development

At one time or another, all of the following have been adopted or proposed:

*Office building over post office;
*Commercial building over railroad tracks;
*Apartment over street;
*Office building over garage;
*Building over reservoir;
*Building over school;
*Railroad tracks over surface use (e.g., connecting links between buildings; here the railroad is using the air space).

Beware the "Navigation Servitude"

One approach that is not feasible is the use of air space over navigable waters. The United States Constitution gives the federal government the absolute right to control navigable waters for purposes of commerce. Thus, any construction over such waters may be taken by the federal government in condemnation proceedings without any compensation. Proposals have been made to limit this "navigation servitude" but so far none of them has met with success.

INTEREST TABLES AND HOW TO USE THEM

Because investment value depends upon anticipated future income, or other benefits, the Income Approach calls for the calculation of the *present worth* of such estimated future benefits. In appraisal technique this is termed the annuity process, and its applications are set forth here as described in *McMichael's Appraising Manual,* 4th Edition, pages 78-113 (Prentice-Hall, Inc., Copyright 1951, Englewood Cliffs, N.J.):

An annuity represents a stream of payments, made usually at annual or semiannual periods, of amounts usually, although not necessarily, equal. It is necessary for the appraiser to translate such payments into value by computing their *present worth.* The sum of $1, in hand today, is worth exactly that sum. As the time until collection increases, the *present-day value* of the amount to be collected diminishes. This discount in value is due to the loss of interest in the interim.

For illustration, assume that you hold a well-secured note for $4,000, payable $1,000 at the end of each year, *without interest.* Would anyone be justified in paying $4,000 for that note *today*? Certainly not! How, then, is its *present* value to be computed? This is done by means of tables to be found later in this chapter. When so calculated, it will be found that the present-day value of the stated $4,000 note is just $3,312.12. It is in this manner that future rentals of properties under appraisement are processed.

In any system of appraising in which value is based upon the expected future earnings of property, it becomes necessary to use compound interest tables, or to be able to compute the proper percentages of present values. There are a number of tables used for this purpose that meet most requirements. They are:

Table I (pages 74–75): Present value of $1 per annum used in computing the present worth of the rentals to a lessor and the present value of a lessee's profit in a lease, if any.

Table II (pages 76–77): Present value of a single payment, used in computing present worth of a reversion.

Table III (page 78): For computing sinking funds or amortization requirements.

Table IV (page 79): The future of $1, at compound interest, at the end of a given time.

Table V (page 79): The future value of $1 per annum, at compound interest at the end of a given time.

Table VI A (page 80): The present value of an annuity of 1, Hoskold premises, with sinking fund interest at 3 per cent.

Table VI B (page 80): Same as Table VI A, except that sinking fund interest rate is 4 per cent.

Table VI C (page 81): Same as VI A and VI B, except that the interest rate is 5 per cent.

Table VII A (page 81): Present value of increasing and decreasing annuities, compound interest valuation premise, 6 per cent interest rate.

Tables VII B, VII C, and VII D (pages 82, 83 and 84) are also increasing and decreasing annuities, with interest rates at 7 per cent, 8 per cent, and 10 per cent, respectively.

Annuity Theories

An annuity is a series of periodical payments, usually although not necessarily equal in amount, and usually made at equal intervals of time, such as annually or semiannually. These periodical payments, although portions of an income stream, are not wealth or value. But they are the reflection of value.

In valuation technique, it becomes necessary to translate these periodical amounts —the annuity—into value. This is accomplished by means of a discounting process wherein the future amounts receivable are discounted for interest. Stated differently, the future amounts have a present worth that is less than their face value in an amount equal to the loss of interest during the time until collection.

Present money commands a premium over future money. That money remote in time when subjected to a present money statement suffers in the perspective of desire very much as things distant in space suffer in the visual perspective. One is disposed to pay less for that which is to be enjoyed in the future than for that which is to be enjoyed at present.

This discounting of future amounts receivable, because of the loss of interest, is an interest computation of the compounding order. And the present worth of a series of future annual payments, such as the present worth of a series of future annual payments, such as the present worth of the income stream from a ground lease, will depend upon several factors, such as the rate or rates of interest employed, the time duration between conversions, that is, between compounding periods, and last, but not least, the premises assumed in providing for the return of the capital invested.

An investor can afford to pay \$3,312.12 in cash today for the privilege of collecting an annuity of \$1,000 each year for a term of four years; and he can also afford to pay \$3,134.50 for this same series of future payments. The difference in present worth is occasioned by a difference in assumptions regarding provisions for the return of capital.

Of the several different valuation premises dedicated to the mathematical process of assigning a present-day worth to a definite income stream, perhaps the best-known are the *Hoskold sinking fund valuation premise* and the *compound interest valuation premise* (by Inwood's Coefficient). Each reflects a present worth consonant with the premises upon which it is predicated.

Before discussing either method, it may be well to remark, for the sake of clarity later, that when a sum of money is lent, the lender is entitled to two things: (1) rental for the hire of his money, that is, interest; and (2) the return of his money, somehow, sometime.

Both of the above-mentioned premises contemplate that a portion of each periodical (for example, annual) payment is (1) *interest* and (2) a partial return of the *capital,* by which is meant that lump sum paid for the privilege of collecting the periodical payments, the annuity.

But, one method (Inwood's) assumes that the annual principal return is credited to the capital account; that is, applied toward the reduction of the outstanding investment. The other method (Hoskold's) assumes that the annual principal return is immediately reinvested in a sinking fund, and thus is not credited to the capital account; that is, not applied toward the reduction of the outstanding investment.

Therefore, by the Inwood process, a portion of the investment is returned each year and the outstanding investment becomes less after the collection of each payment, as in an amortizing mortgage.

The Hoskold process, however, assumes that a portion of the investment is returned each year, in the annual payment as in Inwood's method, but differs in that this principal return is immediately reinvested in a sinking fund. Therefore, it does not reduce the outstanding capital investment, which remains constant at its original figure until the end of the term, at which time the original investment is returned in one lump sum from the sinking fund.

The Hoskold theory is similar to a straight (nonamortizing) mortgage note in which the principal is returned in the full original amount at the maturity of the loan, in one lump sum, rather than piecemeal annually.

The Compound Interest Valuation (By Inwood's Coefficient)

By this process, the present worth of an annuity of $1,000 each year, payable at the end of the year, for a term of four years, discounted for 8 per cent interest, is found to be $3,312.12. By this is meant that, if an investor were to pay $3,312.12 in cash today for the privilege of collecting $1,000 at the end of each year for a term of four successive years, he would be receiving 8 per cent interest on his investment, and would have his investment returned to him, a portion of it each year.

The premise upon which this present worth is predicated is that out of the first $1,000 payment, which is collected at the end of one year from today, a portion of it—$264.97—is interest, being 8 per cent on $3,312.12 for one year; and the balance—$735.03—is a partial return of the capital invested, and upon which no more interest is to be paid. Therefore, at the commencement of the second year, the outstanding capital investment has been reduced to $2,577.09.

At the end of the second year, when the second $1,000 payment has been made, likewise a portion of it is interest, being $206.17, which is 8 per cent on $2,577.09 for one year; and the balance—$793.83—is another partial return of the capital invested, and upon which no more interest is to be paid. Therefore, at the commencement of the third year the outstanding capital investment has been reduced to $1,783.26.

Similarly, omitting the third year for the sake of brevity, at the commencement of the fourth and last year, there is found to be an outstanding capital balance of $925.92. Then, at the end of the fourth year, when the last payment of $1,000 has been made, a portion of it—$74.08—is interest, being 8 per cent on the balance of $925.92 for one year; and the balance of the payment—$925.92—is the return of the last dollar of the original investment of $3,312.12.

The operation is now complete. Interest has been received annually on the outstanding annual balances, and the full amount of the original investment has been returned, a part of it each year, increasing from $735.03 out of the first $1,000 payment, to $925.92 out of the last. This operation is shown in the following tabulation:

COMPOUND INTEREST VALUATION PREMISE 8%

	The Annual Apportionment			
Time of Payment	*The Annual Payment*	*Interest on Outstanding Capital*	*Annual Partial Return of Principal*	*Outstanding Capital Investment*
Beginning of 1st yr.	.....	......	......	$3,312.12
End of 1st yr.	$1,000	$264.97	$ 735.03	— 735.03
				2,577.09
End of 2nd yr.	1,000	206.17	793.83	— 793.83
				1,783.26
End of 3rd yr.	1,000	142.66	857.34	— 857.34
				925.92
End of 4th yr.	1,000	74.08	925.92	— 925.92
		$687.88	$3,312.12	$ 00

On the face of these operations, only one interest rate is involved—a simple interest on the investment. No reinvestment in a sinking fund is contemplated. But the same problem computed by the Hoskold sinking fund valuation premise, using an 8 per cent speculative interest rate and an 8 per cent interest rate for the sinking fund, wherein interest is compounded annually, will show the same present worth—$3,312.12.

As before stated, the present worth of an annual payment of $1,000 each year, for four years, payable at the end of the year, when discounted at 8 per cent, by the Inwood process is found to be $3,312.12. Now let it be assumed that this sum of $3,312.12 is invested in a sinking fund wherein 8 per cent interest is added to the annual balance at the end of each year; and that at the end of each year the sum of $1,000 is withdrawn from the sinking fund and paid to the depositor. The tabulation on page 79 shows that at the end of the fourth year, when the last $1,000 withdrawal has been made, that is, when the investor has received his last $1,000 payment out of the sinking fund, the sinking fund will be evenly exhausted.

This is a further evidence of the fact that the present worth of an annuity found by use of the Inwood premise hereinbefore stated is exactly the same figure as that found by the use of the Hoskold premise in which two identical rates are employed; or that the Inwood value is the same as it would be if a sinking fund provision were assumed in which the sinking fund interest rate is the same as the speculative rate, in this case 8 per cent.

The original investment	$ 3,312.12
Interest for 1st yr.—8% in sinking fund	+ 264.97
End of 1st yr.—in sinking fund before withdrawal	3,577.09
Annual withdrawal—at end of 1st yr.	—1,000.00
Beginning 2nd yr.—in sinking fund	2,577.09
Interest for 2nd yr.—8% in sinking fund	+ 206.17
End of 2nd yr.—in sinking fund before withdrawal	2,783.26
Annual withdrawal—at end of 2nd yr.	—1,000.00
Beginning of 3rd yr.—in sinking fund	1,783.26
Interest for 3rd yr.—in sinking fund	+ 142.66
End of 3rd yr.—in sinking fund before withdrawal	1,925.92
Annual withdrawal—at end of 3rd yr.	—1,000.00
Beginning of 4th yr.—in sinking fund	925.92
Interest for 4th yr.—in sinking fund	+ 74.08
End of 4th yr.—in sinking fund before withdrawal	1,000.00
Annual withdrawal—at end of 4th yr.	—1,000.00
Sinking fund evenly exhausted	$ 00

The Hoskold Sinking Fund Valuation Premise

By this method, the present worth of the same annuity of $1,000 each year, payable at the end of the year for a term of four years, assuming that an investor demands 8 per cent for the use of his money (as before) but further assuming that money can be safely invested in a sinking fund at 8 per cent interest, compounded annually, would be exactly the same—$3,312.12.

Here we assume a different method of returning the original capital investment. Instead of returning a portion of the annual payment to the investor as a partial return of capital each year, that portion representative of capital is reinvested in a sinking fund; and at the end of the term (four years) the full amount of the original investment is withdrawn from the sinking fund, which has then fulfilled its purpose, and the entire amount is returned to the investor.

By the Inwood method, it is assumed that the original investment is returned piecemeal—a portion each year; by the Hoskold method, it is assumed that none of it is returned to the investor until the end of the term, and then all is returned in one payment. Thus, the Hoskold premise employs a reinvestment feature that the Inwood does not, although identical answers are found if the rates are the same.

This particular problem, by the Hoskold premise, assumes that $3,312.12 was paid for the annuity, as before stated. It further assumes that at the end of the first year the first payment of $1,000 is apportioned as before—$264.97 as interest, being 8 per cent on the investment, and $735.03 as capital. But this capital amount is not returned, in theory, to reduce the outstanding investment. It is assumed to be reinvested in a sinking fund in which 8 per cent interest is paid on annual balances.

Therefore, inasmuch as the original investment is not annually reduced and remains the same for the full term, it follows that the apportionment of each payment, as between principal and interest, will be the same. In this example it will be $735.03 and $264.97, respectively, and thus the annual reinvestment in the sinking fund will be $735.03.

At the end of the fourth year there will have been invested in the sinking fund the following amounts: $735.03 at 8 per cent for three years; $735.03 at 8 per cent for two years; $735.03 at 8 per cent for one year; and $735.03 for, say, one day. These four equal sinking fund investments, in addition to the interest accrued thereon in the sinking fund, will amount to $3,312.12 at the end of the fourth year. Then this full amount is returned to the investor in a single payment, and the transaction is complete. This is shown in the following tabulation.

HOSKOLD SINKING FUND VALUATION PREMISE—
8% SPECULATIVE, 8% SAFE RATES

	THE ANNUAL APPORTIONMENT				
Time of Payment	*The Annual Payment*	*Interest on Outstanding Capital*	*Annual Partial Return of Capital for Reinvestment*	*Interest Earned in Sinking Fund*	*Sinking Fund Balance*
Beginning 1st yr.					00
End of 1st yr...	$1,000	$ 264.97	$ 735.03		$ 735.03
During 2nd yr.				$ 58.80	+ 58.80
End of 2nd yr.					793.83
End of 2nd yr.	1,000	264.97	735.03		+ 735.03
					1,528.86
During 3rd yr...				122.31	+ 122.31
End of 3rd yr...					1,651.17
End of 3rd yr...	1,000	264.97	735.03		+ 735.03
					2,386.20
During 4th yr...				190.89	+ 190.89
End of 4th yr...					2,577.09
End of 4th yr...	1,000	264.97	735.03		+ 735.03
Totals	$4,000	$1,059.88	$2,940.12	$372.00	$3,312.12

The use of an 8 per cent interest rate in the sinking fund, the safe rate, in the above tabulation, wherein interest is compounded annually, unquestionably trespasses the bounds of reason. Financial history has adequately shown that the maximum rate at which money can be compounded, over reasonably long periods of time, is about 5 per cent, the savings bank interest rate.

But the use of the 8 per cent sinking fund rate in this problem was for the sole purpose of showing that the present worth of the annuity stated, when computed by the Inwood process, is exactly the same as that found when an 8 per cent sinking fund provision is employed.

Similarly, the present worth of an annuity by Inwood, using 6 per cent, is the same as that found by Hoskold, using 6 per cent and 6 per cent; 7 per cent by Inwood is the same as 7 per cent and 7 per cent by Hoskold; and so forth.

These tables will be briefly discussed under their individual headings.

Table I (pages 74–75). The uses to which this annuity table may be put are quite fully outlined in the preceding pages. It calculates the value of $1 at compound interest at the end of a given time.

Table II (pages 76–77). This table shows the present value, or *today's cash value,* of a single sum of money that will be paid *at some future date, without interest.* This table differs from Table I (annuity table) in that Table I shows the present worth of a *series* of annual payments, while Table II shows the present worth of a *single* future payment.

Example.—Today's value of $1, which will be paid 50 years hence, without interest, is today 5.4288 cents, when discounted for 6 per cent interest, which is to say that an investor could afford to pay 5.4288 cents ($0.054288) today for each $1 he will receive in a lump sum 50 years hence without interest. In this case, he will have his money returned to him, and, in addition, he will receive 6 per cent interest on his invested capital. This, in effect, is discounting a future payment for interest. The most common usage of Table II is in calculating the present worth, or *today's value,* of a reversion.

Assume that a parcel of land valued at $100,000 and under lease for 50 years will revert to the lessor at the expiration of that term. The present value of this reversion may be computed as follows:

In Table II (pages 76–77), opposite 50 years and in the column under 6 per cent, may be found the factor 0.054288, which means that $1 payable 50 years hence, when discounted for 6 per cent interest, is today worth only $0.054288 (5.4288 cents). Therefore, $100,000 payable 50 years hence is today worth

$$\$100{,}000 \times .054288, \text{ or } \$5{,}428.80.$$

Table III (page 78). This table shows the amound of money that must be set aside annually and invested in a compound interest account so that, at the end of a predetermined period, such equal annual investments, in addition to the interest thereon, will amount to the sum desired.

Example.—The sum of money that must be set aside each year for a period of 50 years in a 6 per cent compound interest account, necessary to produce $1 at the end of 50 years, is today $0.00344. (See Table III, page 78, opposite 50 years and in the 6 per cent column.) The sum that must be annually invested in a 6 per cent interest-bearing account, compounded annually, necessary to provide $100,000 at the end of 50 years is

$$\$100{,}000 \times 0.00344, \text{ or } \$344.00.$$

This table is most commonly used in computing the annual requirements for sinking fund or other amortization purposes.

Table IV (page 79). This is a table showing the amount of 1, with interest at the end of various periods of years, by which the future value of $1, at compound interest, at the end of a given time may be ascertained. Following are several problems and answers that indicate the manner in which this table is used.

Problem.—What will be the amount of a today's deposit of $1, a single investment in a sinking fund, at the end of 10 years, assuming interest to be computed annually at 3 per cent?

COMPARATIVE FEATURES OF THE COMPOUND INTEREST AND THE HOSKOLD SINKING FUND VALUATION PREMISES FOR EQUAL ANNUAL INCOMES*

		Compound Interest (Inwood) Premise	*Hoskold Premise*
Initial Capital Investment		Decreases with each payment of income.	Remains unchanged during the entire period of the investment.
Allocation of the Annual Income	to interest	1st, simple interest at the speculative rate upon capital outstanding at the beginning of any year is paid to the investor for the use of his funds;	1st, simple interest at the speculative rate, upon the entire initial capital investment, is paid to the investor. This figure remains the same throughout the term.
	to capital	then, the remainder of the annual income, which is a partial return of capital, is returned to the investor, and deducted from the amount of capital outstanding at the end of the year.	The remainder, which is a partial return of capital, is reinvested in a sinking fund at a safe interest rate, to accumulate, with interest, to the amount of the original investment at the end of the loan term.
Return of Capital		Partially annually, from the annual income, in increasing amounts.	None annually; it is returned in the full initial amount, at the end of the investment term, from the sinking fund.
Miscellaneous Features		Requires reinvestment of capital (the annual capital returns) in smaller amounts than were originally lent, hence in smaller enterprises requiring a greater number of transactions to invest the same amount.	Permits the reinvestment of capital in the full amount originally lent, hence in similar enterprises of similar magnitude.
		Is desirable for valuations where the financial policy requires an annual diminution of outstanding capital.	Is desirable for valuations where the financial policy requires a constant outstanding capital.
		If the annual capital returns are reinvested in a sinking fund to accumulate, with interest, to the amount of the initial investment at the end of the term (as in the Hoskold premise), then the sinking fund interest rate must be the same as the speculative rate to accomplish this result.	Is widely used for the commercial valuation of speculative incomes, especially from mines and real estate.

* To the appraiser interested in further explanations of this subject, the book by Geo. L. Schmutz, 4725 Ledge Ave., North Hollywood

Answer.—In Table IV, in the 3 per cent column, opposite 10 years, is found the factor 1.3439, or $1.3439, the answer.

Problem.—What amount of money must be invested in one lump sum today, with interest compounding annually at 3 per cent, to amount to $10,000 at the end of 30 years?

Answer.—In Table IV, in the 3 per cent column, opposite 30 years, is found the factor 2.4273. Then, $10,000 ÷ 2.4273 = $4,119.80, the answer.

Problem.—What would be the quantity of monetary gold held by the central banks and governments at the end of the year 1933 if at the end of the year 1925 it was $8,974 millions, assuming that it increased at the uniform rate of 3½ per cent per annum, compounded annually?

Answer.—In Table IV, in the 3½ per cent column, opposite eight years, is found the factor 1.3168. Then, $8,974 × 1.3168 = $11,816 + millions, the answer.

Table V (page 79). A table for estimating the future worth of $1 per annum, at compound interest, being the amount of 1 per annum, with interest, at the end of a given term. Two problems follow that indicate the manner in which this table is utilized:

Problem.—If $210.20 is invested in a 3 per cent sinking fund at the beginning of each year for 30 years, how much will have accumulated in the sinking fund at the end of the 30th year?

Answer.—In Table V, in the 3 per cent column, opposite 30 years, is found the factor 49.0027. Then, $210.20 × 49.0027 = $10,300.37, the answer.

Problem.—In the foregoing problem, if the $210.20 was invested at the end of the year, instead of at the beginning, all other conditions remaining the same, how much will accumulate in the sinking fund?

Answer.—In Table V, in the 3 per cent column, opposite 29 years (30 years less 1) is found the factor 46.5754. To this must be added the factor 1 for the one deposit upon which no interest will be earned, making 47.5754. Then, $210.20 × 47.5754 = $10,000.35, the answer.

Tables VI A, B, and C (pages 80–81). Present worth of an annuity of 1, Hoskold evaluation premises.

Problem.—What is the present worth of a net income of $1,000 per year, for 20 years, with interest on the investment at 8 per cent, assuming that that portion of the annual return ($1,000) which represents the return of the capital invested can be safely invested in a compound interest-bearing account (for example, savings bank) in which 3 per cent interest will be paid on annual balances, so that at the end of 20 years the full amount of the original investment can be withdrawn from the compound interest savings account, thus returning the investment in one lump sum at the end of the term?

Answer.—In Table VI A, under 8 per cent and opposite 20 years, we find the factor 8.5313, meaning that $1 per year for 20 years under the above assumptions has a present worth of $8.5313. Then, $1,000 × 8.5313 = $8,531.30, the answer.

Tables VII A, B, C and D. Present worth of increasing and decreasing annuities.

Problem.—What is the present value of an annual income for five years, the initial payment of which is $1,000, succeeding payments decreasing at the rate of 4 per cent each year, that is, $40 per year, being $960, $920, $880, and $840, respectively, discounting for interest at 7 per cent?

Answer.—In Table VII B, in the −4 per cent column, opposite five years, is the factor 3.79. Then, 3.79 × $1,000 = $3,790, the answer.

The use of tables and mathematical data is interesting, particularly to those who have a turn of mind for figures, but care should be taken to see that one does not become a slave to processes that involve the use of interest tables.* They should be used skillfully but only when needed to prove a point or present a situation which cannot be covered otherwise. If one is prone to the excessive use of such data, good judgment may not have a chance to exercise itself; and good judgment is the most important element to be found in the solution of any appraisal problem.

**Author's Note:* It is possible that, in an uptrend commercial district, a business property in a given instance might be accorded an 8% rate with a straight-line Building Residual Technique, but a few years later be re-capitalized with a 7% rate and an Inwood Building Residual. This can happen when the property's income has, in the course of time, developed the quality and durability of an annuity. The physical property remains the same, but the risk has been mitigated, and the income guaranteed. The appraiser can chart the change by reasonable use of these tables.

TABLE 1. PRESENT VALUE OF $1 PER ANNUM

(For Computing Lessor's Interest in Rentals or Lessee's Profit in a Lease)

This table will be found invaluable in determining today's worth of any saving or increase of income which extends through future years. It shows the present worth of an annually recurring saving or rental or income of $1 per year for any number of years at a given rate of interest. For example, what is the value of an annuity in the form of a leasehold estate to lessor calling for $6,000 annually for 25 years, money being worth 6%? See factor 25 periods, 6%, equals $12.783, which equals the value of $1, multiplied by $6,000 equals $76,698.00. If the rental is payable semiannually, multiply the periods, viz., 25, by 2 and divide the rate by 2, making 50 periods at 3%, which factor is 25.730 multiplied by $3,000 equals $77,199.00. If the rental is payable quarterly, multiply the periods, viz., 25, by 4 and divide the rate by 4, making 100 periods at 1½%, which factor is 51.6247 multiplied by the quarterly payment of $1,500 equals $77,437.05. It will be observed that the difference between a semiannual and an annual calculation is approximately $492 or ⅝ of 1% in the aggregate amount, while the difference between a quarterly and an annual calculation is about $640, or about ⅝ of 1%. Note that these calculations are for full years commencing on the first day of the year. The present worth of such worth as of a particular day should be taken, plus the intervening interest and payment.

Yrs.	1¼%	1½%	1¾%	2%	2¼%	2½%	2¾%	*Yrs.*
1	.988	.986	.983	.980	.978	.976	.973	1
2	1.963	1.956	1.949	1.942	1.934	1.997	1.920	2
3	2.927	2.912	2.898	2.884	2.870	2.856	2.842	3
4	3.878	3.854	3.831	3.808	3.785	3.762	3.739	4
5	4.818	4.783	4.748	4.713	4.679	4.646	4.613	5
6	5.756	5.697	5.649	5.601	5.554	5.508	5.462	6
7	6.663	6.598	6.535	6.472	6.410	6.349	6.289	7
8	7.568	7.486	7.405	7.325	7.247	7.170	7.094	8
9	8.462	8.360	8.260	8.162	8.066	7.971	7.878	9
10	9.346	9.222	9.191	8.983	8.866	8.752	8.640	10
11	10.218	10.071	9.927	9.787	9.649	9.514	9.382	11
12	11.079	10.907	10.740	10.578	10.415	10.258	10.104	12
13	11.930	11.731	11.538	11.348	11.164	10.983	10.807	13
14	12.771	12.543	12.322	12.106	11.896	11.691	11.491	14
15	13.601	13.343	13.093	12.849	12.612	12.381	12.157	15
16	14.420	14.131	13.850	13.578	13.313	13.055	12.805	16
17	15.230	14.908	14.596	14.292	13.998	13.712	13.436	17
18	16.030	15.673	15.327	14.992	14.668	14.353	14.049	18
19	16.819	16.426	16.046	15.678	15.323	14.979	14.646	19
20	17.599	17.169	16.753	16.351	15.964	15.589	15.227	20
21	18.370	17.900	17.448	17.011	16.590	16.185	15.793	21
22	19.131	18.621	18.130	17.658	17.203	16.765	16.343	22
23	19.882	19 331	18.801	18.292	17.803	17.332	16.879	23
24	20.624	20.030	19.461	18.914	18.399	17.885	17.401	24
25	21.357	20.720	20.109	19.523	18.962	18.424	17.908	25
26	22.081	21.399	20.746	20.121	19.523	18.951	18.402	26
27	22.796	22.068	21.372	20.707	20.071	19.464	18.883	27
28	23.502	22.727	21.987	21 281	20.608	19.965	19.351	28
29	24.200	23.376	22.592	21.844	21.132	20.454	19.806	29
30	24.889	24 016	23.186	22.396	21.645	20.930	20.249	30
31	25.569	24.646	23.770	22.938	22.147	21.395	20.681	31
32	26.241	25.267	24.344	23.468	22.638	21.849	21.100	32
33	26 905	25.879	24.908	23.989	23.117	22.292	21.509	33
34	27.560	26.482	25.462	24.499	23.587	22.724	21.906	34
35	28.208	27.076	26.007	24.999	24 046	23.145	22.293	35
36	28.847	27.661	26.543	25.489	24.495	23.556	22.670	36
37	29.479	28.237	27.069	25 969	24.934	23 957	23.036	37
38	30.102	28.805	27.586	26.441	25.363	24.349	23.393	38
39	30.718	29.365	28.095	26 903	25 783	24.730	23.740	39
40	31 327	29.916	28.594	27.355	26.193	25.103	24.078	40
41	31 928	30.459	29 085	27 799	26.595	25.466	24.407	41
42	32.521	30 994	29 568	28.235	26.988	25.821	24.727	42
43	33.107	31 521	30.042	28.662	27.372	26.168	25.038	43
44	33 686	32 041	30 508	29 080	27.748	26.504	25.341	44
45	34.258	32 552	30 966	29.490	28.115	26.833	25 636	45
46	34 823	33.056	31.416	29.892	28.474	27 154	25.924	46
47	35.381	33 553	31.859	30.287	28.822	27.467	26.203	47
48	35.931	34 043	32.294	30 673	29.170	27.773	26.475	48
49	36 475	34 525	32.721	31.052	29.506	28.071	26.740	49
50	37.013	35.000	33.141	31.424	29.834	28.362	26.998	50

Yrs.	3%	3½%	4%	4½%	5%	5½%	6%	7%	8%	*Yrs.*
1	.971	.966	.962	.957	.952	.948	.943	.935	.926	1
2	1.913	1.900	1.886	1.873	1.859	1.846	1.833	1.808	1.783	2
3	2.829	2.802	2.775	2.749	2.723	2.698	2.673	2.624	2.577	3
4	3.717	3.673	3.630	3.588	3.546	3.505	3.465	3.387	3.312	4
5	4.580	4.515	4.452	4.390	4.329	4.270	4.212	4.100	3.993	5
6	5.417	5.329	5.242	5.158	5.076	4.996	4.917	4.767	4.623	6
7	6.230	6.115	6.002	5.893	5.786	5.683	5.582	5.389	5.206	7
8	7.020	6.874	6.733	6.596	6.463	6.335	6.210	5.971	5.747	8
9	7.786	7.608	7.435	7.269	7.108	6.952	6.802	6.515	6.247	9
10	8.530	8.317	8.111	7.913	7.722	7.538	7.360	7.024	6.710	10
11	9.253	9.002	8 760	8.529	8.306	8.093	7.887	7.499	7.139	11
12	9.954	9.663	9.385	9.119	8.863	8.619	8.384	7.943	7.536	12
13	10.635	10.303	9.986	9.683	9.394	9.117	8.853	8.358	7.904	13
14	11.296	10.921	10.563	10.223	9.899	9.590	9.295	8.745	8.244	14
15	11.938	11.517	11.118	10.740	10.380	10.038	9.712	9.108	8.559	15
16	12.561	12.094	11.652	11.234	10.838	10.462	10.106	9.447	8 851	16
17	13.166	12.651	12.166	11.707	11.274	10.865	10.477	9.763	9.122	17
18	13.754	13.190	12.659	12.160	11.690	11.246	10.828	10.059	9.372	18
19	14.324	13.710	13.134	12.593	12.085	11.608	11.158	10.336	9.604	19
20	14.877	14.212	13.590	13.008	12.462	11.950	11.470	10.594	9.818	20
21	15.415	14.698	14.029	13.405	12.821	12.275	11.764	10.836	10.017	21
22	15.937	15.167	14.451	13.784	13.163	12.583	12.042	11.061	10.201	22
23	16.444	15.620	14.857	14.148	13.489	12.875	12.303	11.272	10.371	23
24	16.936	16.058	15.247	14.495	13.799	13.152	12.550	11.469	10.529	24
25	17.413	16.482	15.622	14.828	14.094	13.414	12.783	11.654	10.675	25
26	17.877	16.890	15.983	15.147	14.375	13.663	13.003	11.826	10.810	26
27	18.327	17.285	16.330	15.451	14.643	13.898	13.211	11.987	10.935	27
28	18.764	17.667	16.663	15.743	14.898	14.121	13.406	12.137	11.051	28
29	19.188	18.036	16.984	16.022	15.141	14.333	13.591	12.278	11.158	29
30	19.600	18.392	17.292	16.289	15.372	14.534	13.765	12.409	11.258	30
31	20.000	18.736	17.588	16.544	15.593	14.724	13.929	12.532	11.350	31
32	20.389	19.069	17.874	16.789	15.803	14.904	14.084	12.647	11.435	32
33	20.766	19.390	18.148	17.023	16.003	15.075	14.230	12.754	11.514	33
34	21.132	19.701	18.411	17.247	16.193	15.237	14.368	12.854	11.587	34
35	21.487	20.001	18.665	17.461	16.374	15.391	14.498	12.948	11.655	35
36	21.832	20.290	18.908	17.666	16.547	15.536	14.621	13.035	11.717	36
37	22.167	20.571	19.143	17.862	16.711	15.674	14.737	13.117	11.775	37
38	22.492	20.841	19.368	18.050	16.868	15.805	14.846	13.193	11.829	38
39	22.808	21.103	19.584	18.230	17.017	15.929	14.949	13.265	11.879	39
40	23.115	21.355	19.793	18.402	17.159	16.046	15.046	13.332	11.925	40
41	23.412	21.599	19.993	18.566	17.294	16.157	15.138	13.394	11.967	41
42	23.701	21.835	20.186	18.724	17.423	16.263	15.225	13.452	12.007	42
43	23.982	22.063	20.371	18.874	17.546	16.363	15.306	13.507	12.043	43
44	24.254	22.283	20.549	19.018	17.663	16.458	15.383	13.558	12.077	44
45	24.519	22.495	20.720	19.156	17.774	16.548	15.456	13.606	12.108	45
46	24.775	22.701	20.885	19.288	17.880	16.633	15.524	13.650	12.137	46
47	25.025	22.899	21.043	19.415	17.981	16.714	15.589	13.692	12.164	47
48	25.267	23.091	21.195	19.536	18.077	16.790	15.650	13.730	12.189	48
49	25.502	23.277	21.341	19.651	18.169	16.863	15.708	13.677	12.212	49
50	25.730	23.456	21.482	19.762	18.256	16.932	15.762	13.801	12.233	50

TABLE I (*Continued*)

Yrs.	1¼%	1½%	1¾%	2%	2¼%	2½%	2¾%	Yrs
51	37.544	35.468	33.554	31.788	30.156	28.646	27.248	51
52	38.068	35.929	33.960	32.145	30.470	28.923	27.492	52
53	38.585	36.383	34.358	32.495	30.778	29.193	27.729	53
54	39.097	36.830	34.750	32.838	31.078	29.457	27.960	54
55	39.602	37.271	35.135	33.175	31.373	29.714	28.185	55
56	40.100	37.706	35.514	33.505	31.660	29.965	28.404	56
57	40.593	38.134	35.886	33.828	31.942	30.210	28.617	57
58	41.079	38.555	36.252	34.145	32.217	30.448	28.824	58
59	41.560	38.971	36.611	34.456	32.486	30.681	29.026	59
60	42.035	39.380	36.964	34.761	32.749	30.909	29.223	60
61	42.503	39.783	37.311	35.060	33.006	31.130	29.414	61
62	42.966	40.181	37.652	35.353	33.258	31.347	29.600	62
63	43.423	40.572	37.987	35.640	33.504	31.558	29.781	63
64	43.875	40.958	38.317	35.921	33.745	31.764	29.957	64
65	44.321	41.338	38.641	36.197	33.980	31.965	30.128	65
66	44.761	41.712	38.959	36.468	34.211	32.161	30.295	66
67	45.196	42.081	39.272	36.733	34.436	32.352	30.458	67
68	45.626	42.444	39.579	36.994	34.656	32.538	30.616	68
69	46.051	42.802	39.881	37.249	34.871	32.720	30.770	69
70	46.470	43.155	40.178	37.499	35.082	32.898	30.919	70
71	46.884	43.502	40.470	37.744	35.288	33.071	31.065	71
72	47.292	43.845	40.756	37.984	35.490	33.240	31.207	72
73	47.696	44.182	41.038	38.220	35.687	33.405	31.345	73
74	48.095	44.514	41.315	38.451	35.879	33.566	31.479	74
75	48.489	44.842	41.587	38.677	36.068	33.723	31.610	75
76	48.878	45.164	41.855	38.899	36.252	33.876	31.737	76
77	49.262	45.482	42.118	39.117	36.432	34.025	31.861	77
78	49.642	45.795	42.376	39.330	36.609	34.171	31.981	78
79	50.016	46.103	42.630	39.539	36.781	34.313	32.099	79
80	50.387	46.407	42.880	39.744	36.950	34.452	32.213	80
81	50.752	46.707	43.125	39.946	37.115	34.587	32.324	81
82	51.113	47.002	43.366	40.143	37.276	34.719	32.432	82
83	51.470	47.292	43.603	40.336	37.434	34.848	32.537	83
84	51.822	47.579	43.836	40.525	37.588	34.974	32.640	84
85	52.170	47.861	44.065	40.711	37.739	35.096	32.740	85
86	52.514	48.139	44.290	40.893	37.886	35.216	32.836	86
87	52.853	48.412	44.511	41.072	38.031	35.332	32.931	87
88	53.188	48.682	44.728	41.247	38.172	35.446	33.023	88
89	53.519	48.948	44.942	41.419	38.310	35.557	33.112	89
90	53.846	49.210	45.152	41.587	38.445	35.666	33.199	90
91	54.169	40.468	45.358	41.752	38.577	35.771	33.284	91
92	54.488	49.722	45.560	41.914	38.706	35.875	33.366	92
93	54.803	49.972	45.760	42.072	38.832	35.975	33.345	93
94	55.114	50.219	45.955	42.228	38.956	36.073	33.525	94
95	55.421	50.462	46.148	42.380	39.077	36.169	33.601	95
96	55.725	50.702	46.337	42.529	39.195	36.263	33.674	96
97	56.024	50.938	46.523	42.676	39.310	36.354	33.756	97
98	56.320	51.170	46.705	42.819	39.423	36.443	33.816	98
99	56.613	51.399	46.885	42.960	39.534	36.529	33.885	99
100	56.901	51.625	47.061	43.098	39.642	36.614	33.951	100

Yrs.	3%	3½%	4%	4½%	5%	5½%	6%	7%	8%	Yrs.
51	25.951	23.629	21.617	19.868	18.339	16.997	15.813	13.832	12.253	51
52	26.166	23.796	21.748	19.969	18.418	17.058	15.861	13.862	12.272	52
53	26.375	23.957	21.873	20.066	18.493	17.117	15.907	13.890	12.288	53
54	26.578	24.113	21.993	20.159	18.565	17.173	15.950	13.916	12.304	54
55	26.774	24.264	22.109	20.248	18.633	17.225	15.991	13.940	12.319	55
56	26.965	24.410	22.220	20.333	18.699	17.275	16.029	13.963	12.332	56
57	27.151	24.550	22.327	20.414	18.761	17.332	16.065	13.984	12.344	57
58	27.331	24.686	22.430	20.492	18.820	17.367	16.099	14.003	12.356	58
59	27.506	24.818	22.528	20.567	18.876	17.410	16.131	14.022	12.367	59
60	27.676	24.945	22.623	20.638	18.929	17.450	16.161	14.039	12.377	60
61	27.840	25.067	22.715	20.706	18.980	17.488	16.190	14.055	12.386	61
62	28.000	25.186	22.803	20.772	19.029	17.524	16.217	14.070	12.394	62
63	28.156	25.300	22.887	20.834	19.075	17.558	16.242	14.084	12.402	63
64	28.306	25.411	22.969	20.894	19.119	17.591	16.266	14.098	12.409	64
65	28.453	25.518	23.047	20.951	19.161	17.622	16.289	14.110	12.416	65
66	28.595	25.621	23.122	21.006	19.201	17.651	16.310	14.121	12.422	66
67	28.733	25.721	23.194	21.058	19.239	17.679	16.331	14.132	12.428	67
68	28.867	25.817	23.264	21.108	19.275	17.705	16.350	14.142	12.433	68
69	28.997	25.910	23.330	21.156	19.310	17.730	16.368	14.152	12.438	69
70	29.123	26.000	23.395	21.202	19.343	17.753	16.385	14.160	12.443	70
71	29.246	26.087	23.456	21.246	19.374	17.776	16.401	14.169	12.447	71
72	29.365	26.171	23.516	21.288	19.404	17.797	16.416	14.176	12.451	72
73	29.481	26.253	23.573	21.328	19.432	17.817	16.430	14.183	12.455	73
74	29.592	26.331	23.628	21.367	19.459	17.836	16.443	14.190	12.458	74
75	29.702	26.407	23.680	21.404	19.485	17.854	16.456	14.196	12.461	75
76	29.807	26.480	23.731	21.439	19.509	17.871	16.468	14.202	12.464	76
77	29.910	26.551	23.780	21.473	19.533	17.887	16.479	14.208	12.467	77
78	30.010	26.619	23.827	21.505	19.555	17.903	16.490	14.213	12.469	78
79	30.107	26.685	23.872	21.536	19.576	17.917	16.500	14.218	12.471	79
80	30.201	26.749	23.915	21.565	19.596	17.931	16.509	14.222	12.474	80
81	30.292	26.810	23.957	21.593	19.615	17.944	16.518	14.224	12.476	81
82	30.381	26.870	23.997	21.620	19.634	17.956	16.526	14.228	12.477	82
83	30.466	26.927	24.035	21.646	19.651	17.968	16.534	14.232	12.478	83
84	30.550	26.983	24.072	21.671	19.667	17.979	16.542	14.235	12.480	84
85	30.631	27.037	24.109	21.695	19.684	17.990	16.549	14.238	12.482	85
86	30.710	27.089	24.142	21.717	19.698	18.001	16.555	14.241	12.483	86
87	30.786	27.139	24.175	21.739	19.713	18.010	16.562	14.244	12.484	87
88	30.861	27.187	24.207	21.760	19.726	18.019	16.568	14.247	12.485	88
89	30.933	27.234	24.237	21.780	19.739	18.027	16.573	14.250	12.486	89
90	31.002	27.279	24.267	21.799	19.752	18.035	16.579	14.253	12.488	90
91	31.070	27.323	24.295	21.817	19.764	18.043	16.584	14.255	12.488	91
92	31.136	27.365	24.322	21.834	19.775	18.051	16.588	14.257	12.489	92
93	31.200	27.406	24.348	21.852	19.786	18.058	16.593	14.259	12.490	93
94	31.263	27.445	24.373	21.867	19.796	18.064	16.597	14.261	12.491	94
95	31.323	27.484	24.398	21.883	19.806	18.069	16.601	14.263	12.492	95
96	31.381	27.520	24.420	21.897	19.815	18.075	16.605	14.264	12.492	96
97	31.438	27.556	24.443	21.911	19.823	18.081	16.608	14.265	12.493	97
98	31.494	27.590	24.464	21.924	19.832	18.086	16.611	14.266	12.493	98
99	31.547	27.623	24.485	21.937	19.840	18.091	16.614	14.267	12.493	99
100	31.599	27.655	24.505	21.950	19.848	18.096	16.618	14.269	12.494	100

TABLE II. PRESENT VALUE OF A SINGLE PAYMENT OF $1 AT A FUTURE DATE

(For Computing the Present Value of a Reversion)

This compound interest table showing the present worth of a dollar payable hereafter will be found useful in determining the worth of annuities or interests, arising under long term leases. For example, what is the value of $5,000 rent payable ten years hereafter, money being worth 6% payable annually? The factor at 6% for 10 years of 1 dollar is $0.558395, which, multiplied by $5,000, equals $2,791.97. This table may also be used when interest is compounded semiannually by doubling the period and dividing the rate by two. Thus, to find the factor for 20 years at 6% compounded semiannually, use factor $0.306557 (factor for 40 years at 3%).

PRESENT WORTH OF $1 FOR ANY TIME FROM 1 TO 100 YEARS AT

Yrs.	1%	1¼%	1½%	2%	2½%	3%
1	.990099	.987654	.985222	.980392	.975610	.970874
2	.980296	.975461	.970662	.961169	.951814	.942596
3	.970590	.963418	.956317	.942322	.928599	.915142
4	.960980	.951524	.942184	.923845	.905951	.888487
5	.951466	.939777	.928260	.905731	.883854	.862609
6	.942045	.928175	.914542	.887971	.862297	.837484
7	.932718	.916716	.901027	.870560	.841265	.813092
8	.923483	.905398	.887711	.853490	.820747	.789409
9	.914340	.894221	.874592	.836755	.800728	.766417
10	.905287	.883181	.861667	.820348	.781198	.744094
11	.896324	.872277	.848933	.804263	.762145	.722421
12	.887449	.861509	.836387	.788493	.743556	.701380
13	.878663	.850873	.824027	.773033	.725420	.680951
14	.869963	.840368	.811849	.757875	.707727	.661118
15	.861349	.829993	.799852	.743015	.690466	.641862
16	.852821	.819746	.788031	.728446	.673625	.623167
17	.844377	.809626	.776385	.714163	.657195	.605016
18	.836017	.799631	.764912	.700159	.641166	.587395
19	.827740	.789759	.753607	.686431	.625528	.570286
20	.819544	.780009	.742470	.672971	.610271	.553676
21	.811430	.770379	.731498	.659776	.595386	.537549
22	.803396	.760868	.720688	.646839	.580865	.521893
23	.795442	.751475	.710037	.644156	.566697	.506692
24	.787566	.742197	.699544	.621721	.552875	.491934
25	.779768	.733034	.689206	.609531	.539391	.477606
26	.772048	.723984	.679021	.597579	.526235	.463695
27	.764404	.715046	.668986	.585862	.513400	.450189
28	.756836	.706219	.659099	.574375	.500878	.437077
29	.749342	.697500	.649359	.563112	.488661	.424346
30	.741923	.688889	.639762	.552071	.476743	.411987
31	.734577	.680384	.630308	.541246	.465115	.399987
32	.727304	.671984	.620993	.530633	.453771	.388337
33	.720103	.663688	.611816	.520229	.442703	.377026
34	.712973	.665494	.602774	.510028	.431905	.366045
35	.705914	.647402	.593866	.500028	.421371	.355383
36	.698925	.639409	.585090	.490223	.411094	.345032
37	.692005	.631515	.576443	.480611	.401067	.334983
38	.685153	.623719	.567924	.471187	.391285	.325226
39	.678370	.616019	.559531	.461948	.381741	.315754
40	.671653	.608413	.551262	.452890	.372431	.306557
41	.665003	.600902	.543116	.444010	.363347	.297628
42	.658419	.593484	.535089	.435304	.354485	.288959
43	.651900	.586157	.527182	.426769	.345839	.280543
44	.645445	.578920	.519391	.418401	.337404	.272372
45	.639055	.571773	.511715	.410197	.329174	.264439
46	.632728	.564714	.504153	.402154	.321146	.256737
47	.626463	.557742	.496702	.394268	.313313	.249259
48	.620260	.550856	.489362	.386538	.305671	.241999
49	.614119	.544056	.482130	.378958	.298216	.234950
50	.608039	.537339	.475005	.371518	.290942	.228107
51	.602019	.530705	.467985	.364243	.283846	.221463
52	.596058	.524153	.461069	.357101	.276923	.215013
53	.590156	.517682	.454255	.350099	.270169	.208750
54	.584313	.511291	.447542	.343234	.263579	.202670
55	.578528	.504979	.440928	.336504	.257151	.196767
56	.572800	.498745	.434412	.329906	.250879	.191036
57	.567189	.492587	.427992	.323437	.244760	.185472
58	.561514	.486506	.421667	.317095	.238790	.180069
59	.555954	.480500	.415435	.310878	.232966	.174825
60	.550450	.474568	.409296	.304782	.227284	.169733
61	.545000	.468709	.403247	.298806	.221740	.164789
62	.539604	.462922	.397288	.292947	.216332	.159990
63	.534261	.457207	.391417	.287203	.211055	.153330
64	.528971	.451563	.385632	.281572	.205908	.150806
65	.523734	.445988	.379933	.276051	.200886	.146413
66	.518548	.440482	.374318	.270638	.195986	.142149
67	.513414	.435044	.368787	.265331	.191206	.138009
68	.508331	.429673	.363337	.260129	.186542	.133989
69	.503298	.424368	.357967	.255028	.181992	.130086
70	.498315	.419129	.352677	.250028	.177554	.126290
71	.493381	.413955	.347465	.245125	.173223	.122619
72	.488496	.408844	.342330	.240319	.168998	.119047
73	.483659	.403797	.337271	.235607	.164876	.115580
74	.478871	.398811	.332287	.230987	.160855	.112214
75	.474129	.393888	.327376	.226458	.156931	.108945
76	.469435	.389025	.322538	.222017	.153104	.105772
77	.464787	.384222	.317771	.217664	.149370	.102691
78	.460185	.379479	.313075	.213396	.145726	.099700
79	.455629	.374794	.308449	.209212	.142172	.096796
80	.451118	.370167	.303890	.205110	.138705	.093977
81	.446651	.365597	.299399	.201088	.135322	.091240
82	.442229	.361083	.294975	.197145	.132021	.088582
83	.437851	.356625	.290615	.193879	.128801	.086002
84	.433515	.352223	.286321	.189490	.125659	.083497
85	.429223	.347874	.282089	185774	.122595	.081065
86	.424974	.343580	.277920	.182132	.119605	.078704
87	.420766	.339338	.273813	.178560	.116687	.076412
88	.416600	.335148	.269767	.175059	.113841	.074186
89	.412475	.331011	.265780	.171627	.111065	.072026
90	.408391	.326924	.261852	.168261	.108356	.069928
91	.404348	.322888	.257982	.164962	.105713	.067891
92	.400344	.318902	.254170	.161728	.103135	.065914
93	.396380	.314965	.250414	.158556	.100619	.063994
94	.392456	.311076	.246713	.155448	.098165	.062130
95	.388570	.307236	.243067	.152400	.095771	.060320
96	.384723	.303443	.239475	.149411	.093435	.058563
97	.381914	.299697	.235936	.146482	.091156	.056858
98	.377142	.295997	.232449	.143609	.088933	.055202
99	.373408	.292342	.229014	.140794	.086764	.053594
100	.369711	.288733	.225629	.138033	.084647	.052033

TABLE II (*Continued*)

Yrs.	4%	5%	6%	7%	8%
1	.961538	.952381	.943396	.934579	.925925
2	.924556	.907029	.889996	.873438	.857338
3	.888996	.863838	.839619	.816297	.793832
4	.854804	.822702	.792094	.762895	.735029
5	.821927	.783526	.747258	.712986	.680582
6	.790315	.746215	.704961	.666342	.630169
7	.759918	.710681	.665057	.622749	.583490
8	.730690	.676839	.627412	.582008	.540268
9	.702587	.644609	.591898	.543933	.500248
10	.675564	.613913	.558395	.508349	.463193
11	.649581	.584679	.526788	.475092	.428882
12	.624597	.556837	.496969	.444011	.397113
13	.600574	.530321	.468839	.414964	.367697
14	.577475	.505068	.442301	.387817	.340460
15	.555265	.481017	.417265	.362445	.315241
16	.533908	.458112	.393646	.338734	.291890
17	.513373	.436297	.371364	.316574	.270268
18	.493628	.415521	.350344	.295863	.250248
19	.474642	.395734	.330513	.276508	.231711
20	.456387	.376889	.311805	.258418	.214547
21	.438834	.358942	.294155	.241512	.198655
22	.421955	.341850	.277505	.225712	.183940
23	.405726	.325571	.261797	.210946	.170314
24	.390121	.310068	.246979	.197146	.157699
25	.375117	.295303	.232999	.184249	.146017
26	.360689	.281241	.219810	.172195	.135201
27	.346817	.267848	.207368	.160930	.125186
28	.333477	.255094	.195630	.150402	.115913
29	.320651	.242946	.184557	.140562	.107327
30	.308319	.231377	.174110	.131366	.099377
31	.296460	.220360	.164255	.122772	.092015
32	.285058	.209866	.154957	.114740	.085199
33	.274094	.199873	.146186	.107234	.078888
34	.263552	.190355	.137912	.100219	.073045
35	.253615	.181290	.130105	.093662	.067634
36	.243660	.172657	.122741	.087535	.062624
37	.234297	.164436	.115793	.081808	.057985
38	.225235	.156605	.109239	.076456	.053690
39	.216621	.149148	.103056	.071454	.049713
40	.208289	.142046	.097222	.066780	.046030
41	.200278	.135282	.091719	.062411	.042621
42	.192575	.128840	.086527	.058328	.039463
43	.185168	.122704	.081630	.054512	.036540
44	.178046	.116861	.077009	.050946	.033833
45	.171198	.111297	.072650	.047613	.031327
46	.164614	.105997	.068538	.044498	.029007
47	.158283	.100949	.064658	.041587	.026858
48	.152195	.096942	.060998	.038866	.024868
49	.146341	.091564	.057546	.036324	.023026
50	.140713	.087204	.054288	.033947	.021321
51	.135301	.083051	.051215	.031726	.019741
52	.130097	.079096	.048316	.029651	.018279
53	.125093	.075330	.045581	.027711	.016925
54	.120282	.071743	.043001	.025898	.015671
55	.115656	.068326	.040567	.024204	.014510
56	.111207	.065073	.038270	.022620	.013435
57	.106930	.061974	.036104	.021140	.012440
58	.102817	.059023	.034061	.019757	.011519
59	.098863	.056212	.032133	.018465	.010665
60	.095060	.053536	.030314	.017257	.009875
61	.091414	.050986	.028598	.016128	.009144
62	.087889	.048558	.026979	.015073	.008466
63	.084508	.046246	.025452	.014087	.007839
64	.081258	.044044	.024011	.013165	.007259
65	.078133	.041946	.022652	.012304	.006721
66	.075128	.039949	.021370	.011499	.006223
67	.072238	.038047	.020160	.010746	.005762
68	.069460	.036225	.019019	.010043	.005335
69	.066788	.034509	.017942	.009386	.004940
70	.064219	.032866	.016927	.008772	.004574
71	.061749	.031301	.015969	.008198	.004235
72	.059374	.029811	.015065	.007662	.003921
73	.057091	.028391	.014212	.007161	.003631
74	.054895	.027039	.013407	.006692	.003362
75	.052784	.025752	.012649	.006254	.003113
76	.050754	.024225	.011933	.005845	.002882
77	.048801	.023357	.011257	.005463	.002669
78	.046924	.022245	.010620	.005105	.002471
79	.045120	.021186	.010019	.004771	.002288
80	.043384	.020177	.009452	.004459	.002118
81	.041716	.019216	.008917	.004167	.001961
82	.040111	.018301	.008412	.003895	.001816
83	.038569	.017430	.007936	.003640	.001681
84	.037085	.016600	.007486	.003402	.001557
85	.035659	.015809	.007063	.003179	.001442
86	.034287	.015056	.006663	.002971	.001335
87	.032969	.014339	.006286	.002777	.001236
88	.031701	.013657	.005930	.002595	.001144
89	.030481	.013006	.005594	.002425	.001059
90	.029309	.012387	.005277	.002267	.000981
91	.028102	.011797	.004979	.002118	.000908
92	.027098	.011235	.004697	.001980	.000841
93	.026056	.010700	.004431	.001850	.000779
94	.025053	.010190	.004180	.001729	.000721
95	.024090	.009705	.003944	.001616	.000667
96	.023163	.009243	.003720	.001510	.000618
97	.022272	.008803	.003510	.001411	.000572
98	.021416	.008384	.003311	.001319	.000530
99	.020592	.007985	.003124	.001233	.000490
100	.019800	.007604	.002947	.001152	.000454

TABLE III. FOR COMPUTING SINKING FUNDS OR AMORTIZATION REQUIREMENTS

The annual amount which, deposited at the end of each year, with interest will amount to 1 at the end of a given time.

Yrs.	1½%	1¾%	2%	2½%	3%	3½%	4%	4½%	5%	5½%	6%	7%	Yrs.
1	1.00000	1.00000	1.00000	1.00000	1.00000	1.00000	1.00000	1.00000	1.00000	1.00000	1.00000	1.00000	1
2	.49628	.49566	.49505	.49383	.49261	.49140	.49020	.48900	.48780	.48662	.48544	.48309	2
3	.32838	.32757	.32675	.32514	.32353	.32193	.32035	.31877	.31721	.31565	.31411	.31105	3
4	.24444	.24353	.24262	.24082	.23903	.23725	.23549	.23374	.23201	.23029	.22859	.22523	4
5	.19409	.19312	.19216	.19025	.18835	.18648	.18463	.18279	.18097	.17918	.17740	.17389	5
6	.16053	.15952	.15853	.15655	.15460	.15267	.15076	.14888	.14702	.14518	.14336	.13980	6
7	.13656	.13553	.13451	.13250	.13051	.12854	.12661	.12470	.12282	.12096	.11913	.11555	7
8	.11858	.11754	.11651	.11447	.11246	.11048	.10853	.10661	.10472	.10286	.10104	.09747	8
9	.10461	.10356	.10252	.10046	.09843	.09645	.09449	.09257	.09069	.08884	.08702	08349	9
10	.09343	.09238	.09133	.08926	.08723	.08524	.08329	.08138	.07950	.07767	.07587	.07238	10
11	.08429	.08323	.08218	.08011	.07808	.07609	.07415	.07225	.07039	.06857	.06679	.06336	11
12	.07668	.07561	.07456	.07249	.07046	.06848	.06655	.06467	.06283	.06103	.05928	.05590	12
13	.07024	.06917	.06812	.06605	.06403	.06206	06014	.05828	.05646	.05468	.05296	.04965	13
14	.06472	.06366	.06260	.06054	.05853	.05657	.05467	.05282	.05102	.04928	.04758	.04434	14
15	.05994	.05888	.05783	.05577	.05377	.05183	.04994	.04811	.04634	.04463	.04296	.03979	15
16	.05577	.05470	.05365	.05160	.04961	.04768	.04582	.04402	.04227	.04058	.03895	.03586	16
17	.05208	.05102	.04997	.04793	.04595	.04404	.04220	.04042	.03870	.03704	.03544	.03243	17
18	.04881	.04774	.04670	.04467	.04271	.04082	.03899	.03724	.03555	.03392	.03236	.02941	18
19	.04588	.04482	.04378	.04176	.03981	.03794	.03614	.03441	.03275	.03115	.02962	.02675	19
20	.04325	.04219	.04116	.03915	.03722	.03536	.03358	.03188	.03024	.02868	.02718	.02439	20
21	.04087	.03981	.03878	.03679	.03487	.03304	.03128	.02960	.02800	.02646	.02500	.02229	21
22	.03870	.03766	.03663	.03465	.03275	.03093	.02920	.02755	.02597	.02447	.02305	.02041	22
23	.03673	.03569	.03467	.03270	.03081	.02902	.02731	.02568	.02414	.02267	.02128	.01871	23
24	.03492	.03389	.03287	.03091	.02905	.02727	.02559	.02399	.02247	.02104	.01968	.01719	24
25	.03326	.03223	.03122	.02928	.02743	.02567	.02401	.02244	.02095	.01955	.01823	.01581	25
26	.03173	.03070	.02970	.02777	.02594	.02421	.02257	.02102	.01956	.01819	.01690	.01456	26
27	.03032	.02929	.02829	.02638	.02456	.02285	.02124	.01972	.01829	.01695	.01570	.01343	27
28	.02900	.02798	.02699	.02509	.02329	.02160	.02001	.01852	.01712	.01581	.01459	.01239	28
29	.02778	.02676	.02578	.02389	.02211	.02045	.01888	.01741	.01605	.01477	.01358	.01145	29
30	.02664	.02563	.02465	.02278	.02102	.01937	.01783	.01639	.01505	.01381	.01265	.01059	30
31	.02557	.02457	.02360	.02174	.02000	.01837	.01686	.01544	.01413	.01292	.01179	.00980	31
32	.02458	.02358	.02261	.02077	.01905	.01744	.01595	.01456	.01328	.01210	.01100	.00907	32
33	.02364	.02265	.02169	.01986	.01816	.01657	.01510	.01374	.01249	.01133	.01027	.00841	33
34	.02276	.02177	.02082	.01901	.01732	.01576	.01431	.01298	.01176	.01063	.00960	.00789	34
35	.02193	.02095	.02000	.01821	.01654	.01500	.01358	.01227	.01107	.00997	.00897	.00723	35
36	.02115	.02017	.01923	.01745	.01580	.01428	.01289	.01161	.01043	.00937	.00839	.00672	36
37	.02041	.01944	.01851	.01674	.01511	.01361	.01224	.01098	.00984	.00880	.00786	.00624	37
38	.01972	.01875	.01782	.01607	.01446	.01298	.01163	.01040	.00928	.00827	.00736	.00580	38
39	.01905	.01809	.01717	.01544	.01384	.01239	.01106	.00986	.00876	.00778	.00689	.00539	39
40	.01843	.01747	.01656	.01484	.01326	.01183	.01052	.00934	.00828	.00732	.00646	.00501	40
41	.01783	.01688	.01597	.01427	.01271	.01130	.01002	.00886	.00782	.00689	.00606	.00466	41
42	.01726	.01632	.01542	.01373	.01219	.01080	.00954	.00841	.00739	.00649	.00568	.00434	42
43	.01672	.01579	.01489	.01322	.01170	.01033	.00909	.00798	.00699	.00611	.00533	.00404	43
44	.01621	.01528	.01439	.01273	.01123	.00988	.00866	.00758	.00662	.00576	.00501	.00376	44
45	.01572	.01479	.01391	.01227	.01079	.00945	.00826	.00720	.00626	.00543	.00470	.00350	45
46	.01525	.01433	.01345	.01183	.01036	.00905	.00788	00684	.00593	.00512	.00441	.00326	46
47	.01480	.01389	.01302	.01141	.00996	.00867	.00752	.00651	.00561	.00483	.00415	.00304	47
48	.01437	.01347	.01260	.01101	.00958	.00831	.00718	.00619	.00532	.00456	.00390	.00283	48
49	.01396	.01306	.01220	.01062	.00921	.00796	.00686	.00589	.00504	.00430	.00366	.00264	49
50	.01357	.01267	.01182	.01026	.00887	.00763	.00655	.00560	.00478	.00406	.00344	.00246	50
55	.01183	.01096	.01014	.00865	.00735	.00621	.00523	.00439	.00367	.00305	.00254	.00174	55
60	.01039	.00955	.00877	00735	.00613	.00509	.00420	.00345	.00283	.00231	.00188	.00123	60
65	.00919	.00838	.00763	.00628	.00515	.00419	.00339	.00273	.00219	.00175	.00139	.00087	65
70	.00817	.00739	.00667	.00540	.00434	.00346	.00275	.00217	.00179	.00133	.00103	.00062	70
75	.00730	.00655	.00586	.00465	.00367	.00287	.00223	.00172	.00132	.00101	.00077	.00044	75
80	.00655	.00582	.00516	.00403	.00311	.00238	.00181	.00137	.00103	.00077	.00057	.00031	80
85	.00589	.00519	.00456	.00349	.00265	.00199	.00148	.00109	.00080	.00059	.00043	.00022	85
90	.00532	.00465	.00405	.00304	.00226	.00166	.00121	.00087	.00063	.00045	.00032	.00016	90
95	.00482	.00417	.00360	.00265	.00193	.00139	.00099	.00070	.00049	.00034	.00024	.00011	95
99	.00446	.00383	.00328	.00238	.00170	.00120	.00084	.00058	.00040	.00028	.00019	.00009	99
100	.00437	.00375	.00320	.00231	.00165	.00116	.00081	.00056	.00038	.00026	.00018	.00008	100

TABLE IV. FUTURE VALUE OF ONE DOLLAR

At Compound Interest

The Amount of 1, with Interest, at the End of a Given Time

Yrs.	2½%	3%	3½%	4%	4½%	5%	6%
1	1.0250	1.0300	1.0350	1.0400	1.0450	1.0500	1.0600
2	1.0506	1.0609	1.0712	1.0816	1.0920	1.1025	1.1236
3	1.0769	1.0927	1.1087	1.1249	1.1412	1.1576	1.1910
4	1.1038	1.1255	1.1475	1.1699	1.1925	1.2155	1.2625
5	1.1314	1.1593	1.1877	1.2167	1.2462	1.2763	1.3382
6	1.1597	1.1941	1.2293	1.2653	1.3023	1.3401	1.4185
7	1.1887	1.2299	1.2723	1.3159	1.3609	1.4071	1.5036
8	1.2184	1.2668	1.3168	1.3686	1.4221	1.4775	1.5938
9	1.2489	1.3048	1.3629	1.4233	1.4861	1.5513	1.6895
10	1.2801	1.3439	1.4106	1.4802	1.5530	1.6289	1.7908
11	1.3121	1.3842	1.4600	1.5395	1.6229	1.7103	1.8983
12	1.3449	1.4258	1.5111	1.6010	1.6959	1.7959	2.0122
13	1.3785	1.4685	1.5640	1.6651	1.7722	1.8856	2.1329
14	1.4130	1.5126	1.6187	1.7317	1.8519	1.9799	2.2609
15	1.4483	1.5580	1.6753	1.8009	1.9353	2.0789	2.3966
16	1.4845	1.6047	1.7340	1.8730	2.0224	2.1829	2.5404
17	1.5216	1.6528	1.7947	1.9479	2.1134	2.2920	2.6928
18	1.5597	1.7024	1.8575	2.0258	2.2085	2.4066	2.8543
19	1.5986	1.7535	1.9225	2.1068	2.3079	2.5269	3.0256
20	1.6386	1.8061	1.9898	2.1911	2.4117	2.6533	3.2071
21	1.6796	1.8603	2.0594	2.2788	2.5202	2.7860	3.3996
22	1.7216	1.9161	2.1315	2.3699	2.6337	2.9253	3.6035
23	1.7646	1.9736	2.2061	2.4647	2.7522	3.0715	3.8197
24	1.8087	2.0328	2.2833	2.5633	2.8760	3.2251	4.0489
25	1.8539	2.0938	2.3632	2.6658	3.0054	3.3864	4.2919
26	1.9003	2.1566	2.4460	2.7725	3.1407	3.5557	4.5494
27	1.9478	2.2213	2.5316	2.8834	3.2820	3.7335	4.8223
28	1.9965	2.2879	2.6202	2.9987	3.4297	3.9201	5.1117
29	2.0464	2.3566	2.7119	3.1187	3.5840	4.1161	5.4184
30	2.0976	2.4273	2.8068	3.2434	3.7453	4.3219	5.7435
31	2.1500	2.5001	2.9050	3.3731	3.9139	4.5380	6.0881
32	2.2038	2.5751	3.0067	3.5081	4.0900	4.7649	6.4534
33	2.2589	2.6523	3.1119	3.6484	4.2740	5.0032	6.8406
34	2.3153	2.7319	3.2209	3.7943	4.4664	5.2533	7.2510
35	2.3732	2.8139	3.3336	3.9461	4.6673	5.5160	7.6861
36	2.4325	2.8983	3.4503	4.1039	4.8774	5.7918	8.1473
37	2.4933	2.9852	3.5710	4.2681	5.0969	6.0814	8.6361
38	2.5557	3.0748	3.6960	4.4388	5.3262	6.3855	9.1543
39	2.6196	3.1670	3.8251	4.6161	5.5650	6.7048	9.7035
40	2.6851	3.2620	3.9593	4.8010	5.8164	7.0400	10.2857
41	2.7522	3.3500	4.0078	4.9931	6.0781	7.3920	10.9029
42	2.8210	3.4607	4.2413	5.1928	6.3516	7.7616	11.5570
43	2.8915	3.5645	4.3897	5.4005	6.6374	8.1497	12.2505
44	2.9638	3.6715	4.5433	5.6165	6.9361	8.5571	12.9855
45	3.0379	3.7816	4.7024	5.8412	7.2482	8.9850	13.7646
46	3.1139	3.8950	4.8669	6.0748	7.5744	9.4343	14.5905
47	3.1917	4.0119	5.0373	6.3178	7.9153	9.9060	15.4659
48	3.2715	4.1323	5.2136	6.5705	8.2715	10.4013	16.3939
49	3.3533	4.2562	5.3961	6.8333	8.6437	10.9213	17.3775
50	3.4371	4.3839	5.5849	7.1067	9.0326	11.4674	18.4202

Factors shown are for deposits made at **beginning of year**; interest compounded annually. The factor for twice any period is the square of the factor for that period. See Problems on page 90.

TABLE V. FUTURE VALUE OF ONE DOLLAR PER ANNUM

At Compound Interest

The Amount of 1 Per Annum, with Interest, at the End of a Given Time

2½%	3%	3½%	4%	4½%	6%	Yrs.
1.0250	1.0300	1.0350	1.0400	1.0450	1.0600	1
2.0756	2.0909	2.1062	2.1216	2.1370	2.1836	2
3.1525	3.1836	3.2149	3.2465	3.2782	3.3746	3
4.2563	4.3091	4.3625	4.4163	4.4707	4.6371	4
5.3877	5.4684	5.5502	5.6330	5.7169	5.9753	5
6.5474	6.6625	6.7794	6.8983	7.0192	7.3938	6
7.7361	7.8923	8.0517	8.2142	8.3800	8.8975	7
8.9545	9.1591	9.3685	9.5828	9.8021	10.4913	8
10.2034	10.4639	10.7314	11.0061	11.2882	12.1808	9
11.4835	11.8078	12.1420	12.4864	12.8412	13.9716	10
12.7956	13.1920	13.6020	14.0258	14.4640	15.8699	11
14.1404	14.6178	15.1130	15.6268	16.1599	17.8821	12
15.5190	16.0863	16.6770	17.2919	17.9321	20.0151	13
16.9319	17.5989	18.2957	19.0236	19.7841	22.2760	14
18.3802	19.1569	19.9710	20.8245	21.7193	24.6725	15
19.8647	20.7616	21.7050	22.6975	23.7417	27.2129	16
21.3863	22.4144	23.4997	24.6454	25.8551	29.9057	17
22.9460	24.1169	25.3572	26.6712	28.0636	32.7600	18
24.5446	25.8704	27.2797	28.7781	30.3714	35.7856	19
26.1833	27.6765	29.2695	30.9692	32.7831	38.9927	20
27.8629	29.5368	31.3289	33.2480	35.3034	42.3923	21
29.5844	31.4529	33.4604	35.6179	37.9370	45.9958	22
31.3490	33.4265	35.6665	38.0826	40.6892	49.8156	23
33.1578	35.4593	37.9499	40.6459	43.5652	53.8645	24
35.0117	37.5530	40.3131	43.3117	46.5706	58.1564	25
36.9120	39.7096	42.7591	46.0842	49.7113	62.7058	26
38.8598	41.9309	45.2906	48.9676	52.9933	67.5281	27
40.8563	44.2189	47.9108	51.9663	56.4230	72.6398	28
42.9027	46.5754	50.6227	55.0849	60.0071	78.0582	29
45.0003	49.0027	53.4295	58.3283	63.7524	83.8017	30
47.1503	51,5028	56.3345	61.7015	67.6662	89.8898	31
49.3540	54.0778	59.3412	65.2095	71.7562	96.3432	32
51.6129	56.7302	62.4531	68.8579	76.0303	103.1838	33
53.9282	59.4621	65.6740	72.6522	80.4966	110.4348	34
56.3014	62.2759	69.0076	76.5983	85.1640	118.1209	35
58,7339	65.1742	72.4579	80.7022	90.0413	126.2681	36
61.2278	68.1594	76.0289	84.9703	95.1382	134.9042	37
63.7830	71.2342	79.7249	89.4091	100.4644	144.0585	38
66.4026	74.4013	83.5503	94.0255	106.0303	153.7620	39
69.0876	77.6633	87.5095	98.8265	111.8467	164.0477	40
71.8398	81.0232	91.6074	103.8196	117.9248	174.9505	41
74.6608	84.4839	95.8486	109.0124	124.2764	186.5076	42
77.5523	88.0484	100.2383	114.4129	130.9138	198.7580	43
80.5161	91.7199	104.7817	120.0294	137.8500	211.7435	44
83.5540	95.5015	109.4840	125.8706	145.0982	225.5081	45
86.6679	99.3965	114.3510	131.0454	152.6726	240.0986	46
89.8596	103.4084	119.3882	138.2632	160.5879	255.5645	47
93.1311	107.5406	124.6018	144.8337	168.8594	271.9584	48
96.4843	111.7969	129.9979	151.6671	177.5030	289.3359	49
99.9215	116.1808	135.5828	158.7738	186.5357	307.7561	50

Factors shown are for deposits made at **beginning of year**; interest compounded annually. If deposits are made at end of year, add 1 to factor for previous year. See Problems on pages 90 and 91.

TABLE VI A. PRESENT WORTH OF AN ANNUITY OF 1

Hoskold Valuation Premises

Sinking Fund Interest Rate 3%; Speculative Interest Rate as Shown

Yrs.	5%	6%	7%	8%	9%	10%	12%	15%	Yrs.
1	.9524	.9434	.9346	.9259	.9174	.9091	.8929	.8696	
2	1.8429	1.8096	1.7774	1.7464	1.7164	1.6874	1.6324	1.5562	
3	2.6772	2.6074	2.5411	2.4781	2.4182	2.3611	2.2546	2.1118	
4	3.4599	3.3442	3.2360	3.1345	3.0393	2.9496	2.7853	2.5705	
5	4.1954	4.0265	3.8706	3.7264	3.5925	3.4680	3.2430	2.9555	5
6	4.8876	4.6599	4.4524	4.2626	4.0883	3.9278	3.6417	3.2830	
7	5.5400	5.2492	4.9874	4.7504	4.5350	4.3383	3.9919	3.5650	
8	6.1555	5.7986	5.4808	5.1960	4.9393	4.7068	4.3019	3.8102	
9	6.7370	6.3118	5.9370	5.6043	5.3069	5.0395	4.5780	4.0252	
10	7.2870	6.7921	6.3601	5.9798	5.6424	5.3410	4.8255	4.2153	10
11	7.8078	7.2123	6.7532	6.3260	5.9496	5.6155	5.0485	4.3845	
12	8.3014	7.6651	7.1194	6.6462	6.2320	5.8664	5.2504	4.5359	
13	8.7697	8.0626	7.4610	6.9430	6.4923	6.0965	5.4339	4.6723	
14	9.2144	8.4369	7.7805	7.2188	6.7328	6.3081	5.6014	4.7956	
15	9.6370	8.7899	8.0797	7.4757	6.9557	6.5034	5.7548	4.9076	15
16	10.0391	9.1232	8.3604	7.7154	7.1628	6.6840	5.8958	5.0097	
17	10.4218	9.4382	8.6242	7.9395	7.3555	6.8515	6.0258	5.1033	
18	10.7865	9.7363	8.8724	8.1494	7.5353	7.0073	6.1460	5.1892	
19	11.1341	10.0186	9.1063	8.3463	7.7033	7.1524	6.2573	5.2683	
20	11.4658	10.2864	9.3270	8.5313	7.8607	7.2878	6.3607	5.3414	20
21	11.7825	10.5405	9.5355	8.7054	8.0082	7.4144	6.4570	5.4092	
22	12.0850	10.7820	9.7326	8.8694	8.1468	7.5331	6.5468	5.4720	
23	12.3741	11.0115	9.9193	9.0241	8.2772	7.6444	6.6307	5.5305	
24	12.6506	11.2300	10.0962	9.1703	8.4000	7.7491	6.7093	5.5851	
25	12.9152	11.4380	10.2640	9.3086	8.5159	7.8476	6.7830	5.6361	25
26	13.1686	11.6363	10.4234	9.4395	8.6253	7.9404	6.8522	5.6838	
27	13.4113	11.8253	10.5748	9.5635	8.7287	8.0280	6.9173	5.7286	
28	13.6438	12.0058	10.7189	9.6812	8.8267	8.1107	6.9787	5.7706	
29	13.8668	12.1781	10.8560	9.7929	8.9194	8.1890	7.0366	5.8101	
30	14.0807	12.3427	10.9867	9.8991	9.0074	8.2631	7.0912	5.8473	30
31	14.2859	12.5002	11.1112	10.0001	9.0910	8.3334	7.1429	5.8824	
32	14.4830	12.6508	11.2301	10.0963	9.1704	8.4001	7.1918	5.9155	
33	14.6722	12.7949	11.3435	10.1879	9.2459	8.4634	7.2382	5.9469	
34	14.8540	12.9329	11.4519	10.2752	9.3178	8.5236	7.2822	5.9765	
35	15.0287	13.0652	11.5554	10.3585	9.3862	8.5808	7.3239	6.0046	35
36	15.1967	13.1920	11.6545	10.4380	9.4515	8.6353	7.3636	6.0312	
37	15.3582	13.3135	11.7493	10.5140	9.5137	8.6872	7.4013	6.0565	
38	15.5137	13.4301	11.8400	10.5866	9.5731	8.7367	7.4372	6.0805	
39	15.6632	13.5421	11.9269	10.6560	9.6298	8.7840	7.4714	6.1034	
40	15.8072	13.6496	12.0102	10.7224	9.6841	8.8291	7.5040	6.1251	40
41	15.9458	13.7528	12.0901	10.7860	9.7359	8.8721	7.5351	6.1458	
42	16.0793	13.8520	12.1667	10.8470	9.7855	8.9133	7.5648	6.1655	
43	16.2080	13.9474	12.2402	10.9053	9.8330	8.9527	7.5931	6.1844	
44	16.3319	14.0391	12.3107	10.9613	9.8785	8.9904	7.6202	6.2023	
45	16.4514	14.1273	12.3785	11.0150	9.9221	9.0265	7.6461	6.2195	45
46	16.5666	14.2121	12.4436	11.0665	9.9639	9.0610	7.6709	6.2359	
47	16.6776	14.2938	12.5062	11.1160	10.0040	9.0942	7.6946	6.2515	
48	16.7848	14.3724	12.5663	11.1635	10.0424	9.1259	7.7174	6.2665	
49	16.8881	14.4481	12.6242	11.2091	10.0793	9.1584	7.7392	6.2809	
50	16.9879	14.5211	12.6798	11.2530	10.1148	9.1856	7.7600	6.2946	50

TABLE VI B. PRESENT WORTH OF AN ANNUITY OF 1

Hoskold Valuation Premises

Sinking Fund Interest Rate 4%; Speculative Interest Rate as Shown

Yrs.	5%	6%	7%	8%	9%	10%	12%	15%	Yrs.
1	.952	.943	.935	.926	.917	.909	.893	.870	
2	1.851	1.818	1.786	1.754	1.724	1.694	1.639	1.562	
3	2.700	2.629	2.562	2.498	2.437	2.379	2.271	2.126	
4	3.503	3.384	3.273	3.170	3.072	2.981	2.813	2.594	
5	4.262	4.088	3.927	3.779	3.641	3.513	3.283	2.989	5
6	4.981	4.745	4.530	4.333	4.153	3.988	3.693	3.325	
7	5.662	5.359	6.086	4.840	4.617	4.413	4.055	3.615	
8	6.308	5.934	5.601	5.304	5.037	4.796	4.376	3.868	
9	6.921	6.473	6.079	5.731	5.420	5.142	4.662	4.090	
10	7.502	6.979	6.524	6.124	5.771	5.456	4.919	4.286	10
11	8.055	7.454	6.938	6.487	6.092	5.742	5.151	4.461	
12	8.580	7.902	7.323	6.823	6.387	6.004	5.360	4.618	
13	9.079	8.323	7.684	7.136	6.660	6.244	5.551	4.759	
14	9.554	8.721	8.021	7.426	6.912	6.465	5.725	4.886	
15	10.006	9.096	8.337	7.696	7.146	6.669	5.884	5.001	15
16	10.436	9.450	8.634	7.948	7.363	6.858	6.031	5.107	
17	10.846	9.785	8.913	8.183	7.564	7.032	6.165	5.203	
18	11.237	10.102	9.175	8.404	7.752	7.195	6.290	5.291	
19	11.609	10.402	9.422	8.610	7.928	7.345	6.405	5.372	
20	11.964	10.686	9.654	8.804	8.092	7.486	6.511	5.447	20
21	12.303	10.955	9.874	8.986	8.245	7.617	6.610	5.516	
22	12.626	11.211	10.081	9.158	8.389	7.740	6.702	5.580	
23	12.935	11.454	10.277	9.319	8.524	7.855	6.788	5.640	
24	13.230	11.684	10.462	9.471	8.651	7.963	6.869	5.695	
25	13.511	11.903	10.637	9.614	8.771	8.064	6.944	5.747	25
26	13.780	12.111	10.803	9.750	8.884	8.159	7.014	5.795	
27	14.037	12.309	10.960	9.878	8.990	8.248	7.080	5.840	
28	14.283	12.498	11.109	9.999	9.090	8.332	7.142	5.882	
29	14.518	12.677	11.251	10.113	9.184	8.412	7.200	5.921	
30	14.743	12.848	11.386	10.222	9.274	8.487	7.255	5.958	30
31	14.958	13.011	11.513	10.325	9.358	8.558	7.307	5.993	
32	15.163	13.167	11.635	10.422	9.439	8.625	7.356	6.026	
33	15.360	13.315	11.750	10.515	9.514	8.688	7.402	6.057	
34	15.549	13.456	11.860	10.603	9.586	8.748	7.445	6.086	
35	15.729	13.591	11.965	10.686	9.655	8.805	7.486	6.113	35
36	15.902	13.720	12.065	10.766	9.719	8.858	7.525	6.139	
37	16.067	13.843	12.160	10.841	9.781	8.910	7.562	6.164	
38	16.225	13.960	12.250	10.913	9.839	8.958	7.587	6.187	
39	16.377	14.072	12.336	10.982	8.895	9.004	7.630	6.209	
40	16.523	14.180	12.419	11.047	9.948	9.049	7.661	6.230	40
41	16.662	14.282	12.497	11.109	9.998	9.089	7.691	6.249	
42	16.795	14.380	12.572	11.168	10.046	9.129	7.720	6.268	
43	16.923	14.474	12.644	11.225	10.092	9.167	7.747	6.286	
44	17.046	14.564	12.712	11.278	10.135	9.203	7.772	6.303	
45	17.164	14.649	12.778	11.330	10.177	9.237	7.797	6.319	45
46	17.276	14.731	12.840	11.379	10.216	9.269	7.820	6.334	
47	17.385	14.810	12.900	11.426	10.254	9.300	7.842	6.348	
48	17.488	14.885	12.957	11.470	10.288	9.330	7.863	6.362	
49	17.588	14.957	13.001	11.513	10.324	9.358	7.883	6.375	
50	17.683	15.026	13.063	11.554	10.357	9.385	7.902	6.388	50

TABLE VI C. PRESENT WORTH OF AN ANNUITY OF 1

Hoskold Valuation Premises

Sinking Fund Interest Rate 5%; Speculative Interest Rate as Shown

Yrs.	5%	6%	7%	8%	9%	10%	12%	15%	*Yrs.*
1	.952	.943	.935	.925	.917	.909	.893	.870	
2	1.859	1.825	1.793	1.761	1.731	1.701	1.645	1.568	
3	2.723	2.651	2.583	2.518	2.456	2.397	2.287	2.140	
4	3.546	3.424	3.311	3.205	3.105	3.012	2.841	2.618	
5	4.330	4.150	3.984	3.832	3.690	3.559	3.323	3.021	5
6	5.076	4.830	4.608	4.405	4.219	4.048	3.745	3.367	
7	5.786	5.470	5.186	4.930	4.699	4.488	4.118	3.665	
8	6.463	6.071	5.723	5.414	5.136	4.885	4.450	3.926	
9	7.108	6.636	6.223	5.859	5.534	5.244	4.746	4.155	
10	7.722	7.168	6.689	6.269	5.900	5.571	5.012	4.357	10
11	8.306	7.669	7.123	6.649	6.235	5.869	5.252	4.537	
12	8.863	8.142	7.529	7.002	6.543	6.142	5.470	4.699	
13	9.394	8.587	7.908	7.328	6.828	6.392	5.667	4.844	
14	9.899	9.007	8.263	7.632	7.091	6.621	5.847	4.974	
15	10.380	9.404	8.595	7.915	7.335	6.833	6.012	5.093	15
16	10.838	9.778	8.907	8.179	7.560	7.029	6.163	5.201	
17	11.274	10.132	9.200	8.425	7.770	7.210	6.301	5.299	
18	11.690	10.466	9.474	8.655	7.965	7.377	6.429	5.389	
19	12.085	10.782	9.733	8.870	8.147	7.533	6.547	5.472	
20	12.462	11.081	9.976	9.071	8.316	7.678	6.656	5.548	20
21	12.821	11.364	10.204	9.260	8.475	7.813	6.757	5.618	
22	13.163	11.632	10.420	9.436	8.623	7.938	6.851	5.683	
23	13.489	11.885	10.623	9.603	8.761	8.056	6.938	5.742	
24	13.799	12.126	10.814	9.759	8.891	8.165	7.019	5.798	
25	14.094	12.353	10.995	9.906	9.013	8.268	7.095	5.850	25
26	14.375	12.568	11.165	10.044	9.127	8.364	7.165	5.897	
27	14.643	12.773	11.326	10.174	9.234	8.454	7.231	5.942	
28	14.898	12.966	11.478	10.296	9.335	8.538	7.293	5.984	
29	15.141	13.150	11.622	10.412	9.430	8.617	7.350	6.022	
30	15.373	13.324	11.757	10.520	9.519	8.692	7.405	6.059	30
31	15.593	13.489	11.886	10.623	9.603	8.762	7.455	6.093	
32	15.803	13.646	12.007	10.720	9.682	8.828	7.503	6.124	
33	16.003	13.795	12.123	10.812	9.757	8.890	7.548	6.154	
34	16.193	13.936	12.232	10.898	9.827	8.948	7.590	6.182	
35	16.374	14.070	12.335	10.980	9.894	9.003	7.629	6.208	35
36	16.547	14.198	12.432	11.057	9.957	9.055	7.667	6.233	
37	16.711	14.319	12.525	11.131	10.016	9.104	7.702	6.256	
38	16.868	14.433	12.613	11.200	10.072	9.150	7.735	6.278	
39	17.017	14.542	12.696	11.266	10.125	9.194	7.766	6.299	
40	17.159	14.646	12.775	11.328	10.175	9.236	7.790	0.318	40
41	17.294	14.744	12.850	11.387	10.223	9.275	7.823	6.336	
42	17.423	14.838	12.921	11.442	10.267	9.311	7.850	6.353	
43	17.546	14.927	12.988	11.495	10.310	9.346	7.875	6.370	
44	17.663	15.011	13.052	11.545	10.350	9.379	7.898	6.385	
45	17.774	15.092	13.113	11.592	10.388	9.411	7.920	6.399	45
46	17.880	15.168	13.170	11.638	10.425	9.441	7.941	6.413	
47	17.981	15.241	13.225	11.680	10.459	9.469	7.961	6.426	
48	18.077	15.310	13.277	11.721	10.491	9.495	7.980	6.438	
49	18.169	15.375	13.326	11.759	10.522	9.520	7.997	6.450	
50	18.256	15.438	13.373	11.796	10.551	9.544	8.015	6.461	50

TABLE VII A. PRESENT WORTH OF INCREASING & DECREASING ANNUITIES 6%

Straight Line % Changes—Inwood Premise

Yrs.	Income Annually DECREASING at Rate Shown									*Yrs.*
	−2%	−3%	−4%	−5%	−7%	−10%	−12%	−14%	−20%	
1	0.94	0.94	0.94	0.94	0.94	0.94	0.94	0.94	0.94	1
2	1.81	1.81	1.80	1.79	1.77	1.74	1.73	1.71	1.66	2
3	2.62	2.60	2.57	2.54	2.49	2.42	2.36	2.31	2.16	3
4	3.37	3.32	3.27	3.22	3.12	2.97	2.87	2.77	2.48	4
5	4.05	3.97	3.89	3.82	3.66	3.42	3.26	3.10	2.63	5
6	4.69	4.57	4.46	4.34	4.11	3.77	3.54	3.31		6
7	5.27	5.12	4.96	4.81	4.50	4.04	3.73	3.42		7
8	5.81	5.61	5.42	5.22	4.82	4.23	3.83	3.43		8
9	6.31	6.06	5.82	5.57	5.08	4.34	3.85			9
10	6.77	6.47	6.18	5.88	5.29	4.40				10
11	7.19	6.84	6.49	6.14	5.45					11
12	7.58	7.17	6.77	6.37	5.56					12
13	7.93	7.47	7.01	6.55	5.63					13
14	8.26	7.74	7.23	6.71	5.67					14
15	8.56	7.99	7.41	6.83	5.68					15
16	8.84	8.20	7.57	6.93						16
17	9.09	8.39	7.70	7.01						17
18	9.32	8.57	7.81	7.06						18
19	9.53	8.72	7.91	7.09						19
20	9.72	8.85	7.96	7.10						20

Yrs.	Income Annually INCREASING at Rate Shown									*Yrs.*
	+2%	+3%	+4%	+5%	+7%	+10%	+12%	+14%	+20%	
1	0.94	0.94	0.94	0.94	0.94	0.94	0.94	0.94	0.94	1
2	1.85	1.86	1.87	1.88	1.90	1.92	1.94	1.96	2.01	2
3	2.72	2.75	2.78	2.80	2.85	2.93	2.98	3.03	3.19	3
4	3.56	3.61	3.66	3.71	3.81	3.96	4.06	4.16	4.45	4
5	4.37	4.45	4.53	4.61	4.77	5.01	5.16	5.32	5.80	5
6	5.15	5.26	5.38	5.49	5.72	6.06	6.29	6.52	7.21	6
7	5.89	6.05	6.20	6.35	6.66	7.13	7.44	7.74	8.67	7
8	6.61	6.80	7.00	7.20	7.60	8.19	8.59	8.99	10.18	8
9	7.29	7.54	7.78	8.03	8.52	9.26	9.75	10.24	11.72	9
10	7.95	8.25	8.54	8.84	9.43	10.32	10.91	11.50	13.28	10
11	8.58	8.93	9.28	9.63	10.33	11.37	12.07	12.77	14.86	11
12	9.19	9.59	10.00	10.40	11.21	12.42	13.22	14.03	16.45	12
13	9.77	10.23	10.69	11.15	12.07	13.45	14.37	15.29	18.04	13
14	10.33	10.85	11.36	11.88	12.91	14.46	15.50	16.53	19.64	14
15	10.86	11.44	12.01	12.59	13.74	15.47	16.62	17.77	21.22	15
16	11.37	12.01	12.64	13.28	14.55	16.45	17.72	18.99	22.80	16
17	11.86	12.56	13.25	13.95	15.33	17.42	18.80	20.19	24.35	17
18	12.33	13.09	13.84	14.59	16.10	18.36	19.87	21.37	25.89	18
19	12.78	13.60	14.41	15.22	16.85	19.29	20.91	22.54	27.42	19
20	13.21	14.09	14.96	15.83	17.58	20.19	21.94	23.68	28.91	20

Illustration: An annuity for 5 years commencing with an initial payment of $1 and decreasing 7 cents each year, discounted at 6%, is today worth $3.66.

TABLE VII B. PRESENT WORTH OF INCREASING & DECREASING ANNUITIES 7%

Straight Line % Changes—Inwood Premise

Yrs.	Income Annually DECREASING at Rate Shown									Yrs.
	−2%	−3%	−4%	−5%	−7%	−10%	−12%	−14%	−20%	
1	0.93	0.93	0.93	0.93	0.93	0.93	0.93	0.93	0.93	1
2	1.79	1.78	1.77	1.76	1.75	1.72	1.70	1.69	1.63	2
3	2.57	2.55	2.52	2.50	2.45	2.37	2.32	2.27	2.12	3
4	3.29	3.24	3.20	3.15	3.05	2.91	2.81	2.72	2.43	4
5	3.95	3.87	3.79	3.72	3.56	3.34	3.18	3.03	2.57	5
6	4.55	4.44	4.33	4.22	4.00	3.67	3.45	3.23		6
7	5.09	4.95	4.80	4.65	4.36	3.92	3.62	3.33		7
8	5.60	5.41	5.22	5.03	4.66	4.09	3.72	3.34		8
9	6.05	5.82	5.59	5.36	4.90	4.20	3.74			9
10	6.47	6.19	5.91	5.64	5.08	4.25				10
11	6.85	6.52	6.20	5.87	5.23					11
12	7.20	6.82	6.45	6.07	5.33					12
13	7.51	7.09	6.66	6.24	5.39					13
14	7.80	7.32	6.85	6.38	5.43					14
15	8.06	7.53	7.01	6.49	5.44					15
16	8.30	7.72	7.14	6.57						16
17	8.51	7.88	7.26	6.63						17
18	8.71	8.03	7.35	6.68						18
19	8.88	8.16	7.43	6.71						19
20	9.04	8.27	7.49	6.72						20

Yrs.	Income Annually INCREASING at Rate Shown									Yrs.
	+2%	+3%	+4%	+5%	+7%	+10%	+12%	+14%	+20%	
1	0.93	0.93	0.93	0.93	0.93	0.93	0.93	0.93	0.93	1
2	1.83	1.83	1.84	1.85	1.87	1.90	1.91	1.93	1.98	2
3	2.67	2.70	2.72	2.75	2.80	2.87	2.92	2.97	3.12	3
4	3.48	3.53	3.58	3.63	3.72	3.87	3.96	4.06	4.35	4
5	4.25	4.33	4.41	4.48	4.64	4.86	5.02	5.17	5.63	5
6	4.99	5.10	5.21	5.31	5.53	5.86	6.08	6.30	6.96	6
7	5.68	5.83	5.98	6.12	6.42	6.86	7.15	7.45	8.33	7
8	6.35	6.53	6.72	6.91	7.29	7.85	8.23	8.60	9.73	8
9	6.98	7.21	7.44	7.67	8.13	8.83	9.29	9.75	11.14	9
10	7.58	7.85	8.13	8.41	8.96	9.79	10.35	10.90	12.57	10
11	8.15	8.47	8.80	9.12	9.77	10.74	11.39	12.04	13.99	11
12	8.69	9.06	9.44	9.81	10.56	11.68	12.42	13.17	15.41	12
13	9.20	9.63	10.05	10.47	11.32	12.59	13.44	14.28	16.82	13
14	9.69	10.17	10.64	11.11	12.06	13.48	14.43	15.38	18.22	14
15	10.16	10.68	11.20	11.73	12.78	14.35	15.40	16.45	19.59	15
16	10.60	11.17	11.75	12.32	13.47	15.20	16.35	17.50	20.95	16
17	11.01	11.64	12.27	12.89	14.14	16.02	17.27	18.53	22.28	17
18	11.41	12.09	12.76	13.44	14.79	16.82	18.17	19.53	23.58	18
19	11.79	12.51	13.24	13.97	15.42	17.60	19.05	20.50	24.86	19
20	12.14	12.92	13.69	14.47	16.02	18.35	19.90	21.45	26.10	20

Illustration: An annuity for 5 years commencing with an initial payment of $1 and decreasing 7 cents each year, discounted at 7%, is today worth $3.56.

TABLE VII C. PRESENT WORTH OF INCREASING & DECREASING ANNUITIES 8%

Straight Line % Changes—Inwood Premise

Yrs.	Income Annually DECREASING at Rate Shown									Yrs.
	−2%	−3%	−4%	−5%	−7%	−10%	−12%	−14%	−20%	
1	0.93	0.93	0.93	0.93	0.93	0.93	0.93	0.93	0.93	1
2	1.77	1.76	1.75	1.74	1.72	1.70	1.68	1.66	1.61	2
3	2.53	2.50	2.48	2.45	2.41	2.33	2.28	2.24	2.09	3
4	3.22	3.17	3.13	3.08	2.99	2.85	2.75	2.66	2.38	4
5	3.84	3.77	3.70	3.62	3.48	3.26	3.11	2.96	2.52	5
6	4.41	4.31	4.20	4.10	3.89	3.57	3.36	3.15		6
7	4.92	4.78	4.65	4.51	4.22	3.80	3.52	3.24		7
8	5.39	5.21	5.04	4.86	4.50	3.97	3.61	3.25		8
9	5.81	5.59	5.38	5.16	4.72	4.07	3.63			9
10	6.19	5.93	5.67	5.41	4.89	4.11				10
11	6.53	6.23	5.93	5.63	5.02					11
12	6.84	6.50	6.15	5.80	5.11					12
13	7.12	6.73	6.34	5.95	5.17					13
14	7.37	6.94	6.51	6.07	5.20					14
15	7.60	7.12	6.64	6.16	5.21					15
16	7.80	7.28	6.76	6.24						16
17	7.99	7.42	6.86	6.29						17
18	8.15	7.54	6.94	6.33						18
19	8.32	7.65	7.00	6.35						19
20	8.45	7.74	7.06	6.36						20

Yrs.	Income Annually INCREASING at Rate Shown									Yrs.
	+2%	+3%	+4%	+5%	+7%	+10%	+12%	+14%	+20%	
1	0.93	0.93	0.93	0.93	0.93	0.93	0.93	0.93	0.93	1
2	1.80	1.81	1.82	1.83	1.84	1.87	1.89	1.90	1.95	2
3	2.62	2.65	2.68	2.70	2.75	2.82	2.87	2.92	3.07	3
4	3.40	3.45	3.50	3.55	3.64	3.78	3.87	3.96	4.24	4
5	4.14	4.21	4.29	4.36	4.51	4.73	4.88	5.03	5.47	5
6	4.83	4.94	5.04	5.15	5.36	5.68	5.89	6.10	6.73	6
7	5.53	5.63	5.77	5.91	6.19	6.61	6.89	7.17	8.01	7
8	6.18	6.28	6.46	6.64	6.99	7.53	7.88	8.24	9.31	8
9	6.76	6.90	7.12	7.34	7.77	8.43	8.86	9.30	10.61	9
10	7.30	7.49	7.75	8.01	8.53	9.31	9.83	10.35	11.90	10
11	7.82	8.05	8.35	8.65	9.26	10.16	10.77	11.38	13.19	11
12	8.30	8.57	8.92	9.27	9.96	11.00	11.69	12.38	14.46	12
13	8.79	9.07	9.47	9.86	10.64	11.81	12.59	13.37	15.71	13
14	9.24	9.55	9.98	10.42	11.29	12.59	13.46	14.33	16.94	14
15	9.65	9.99	10.47	10.95	11.91	13.35	14.30	15.26	18.14	15
16	10.03	10.42	10.94	11.46	12.51	14.08	15.12	16.17	19.30	16
17	10.38	10.82	11.39	11.95	13.08	14.78	15.91	17.05	20.44	17
18	10.72	11.19	11.81	12.41	13.63	15.46	16.67	17.89	21.54	18
19	11.03	11.55	12.20	12.86	14.16	16.11	17.41	18.71	22.61	19
20	11.33	11.89	12.58	13.28	14.66	16.73	18.11	19.49	23.64	20

Illustration: An annuity for 5 years commencing with an initial payment of $1 and decreasing 7 cents each year, discounted at 8%, is today worth $3.48.

Years	PER CENT						PER CENT								
	5	5¼	5½	5¾	6	6¼	6½	6¾	7	7½	8	8½	9	9½	10
15	7.29	7.20	7.10	7.01	6.92	6.83	6.75	6.66	6.58	6.42	6.27	6.12	5.98	5.84	5.71
16	7.70	7.60	7.49	7.39	7.29	7.20	7.10	7.01	6.91	6.74	6.57	6.40	6.25	6.10	5.95
17	8.11	7.99	7.88	7.76	7.65	7.55	7.44	7.34	7.24	7.04	6.86	6.68	6.51	6.34	6.19
18	8.51	8.38	8.25	8.13	8.01	7.89	7.77	7.66	7.55	7.34	7.14	6.94	6.76	6.58	6.41
19	8.90	8.75	8.61	8.48	8.35	8.22	8.09	7.97	7.85	7.62	7.40	7.20	7.00	6.81	6.62
20	9.28	9.12	8.97	8.82	8.68	8.54	8.41	8.27	8.15	7.90	7.66	7.44	7.22	7.02	6.83
21	9.65	9.48	9.32	9.16	9.01	8.86	8.71	8.57	8.43	8.16	7.91	7.67	7.44	7.22	7.02
22	10.01	9.83	9.66	9.49	9.32	9.16	9.00	8.85	8.70	8.42	8.15	7.89	7.65	7.42	7.20
23	10.37	10.17	9.99	9.80	9.63	9.45	9.29	9.12	8.96	8.66	8.37	8.10	7.85	7.60	7.37
24	10.72	10.51	10.31	10.11	9.92	9.74	9.56	9.39	9.22	8.90	8.59	8.31	8.03	7.78	7.53
25	11.05	10.83	10.62	10.41	10.21	10.01	9.82	9.64	9.46	9.12	8.80	8.50	8.21	7.94	7.69
26	11.38	11.15	10.92	10.70	10.49	10.28	10.08	9.88	9.70	9.34	9.00	8.68	8.38	8.10	7.84
27	11.70	11.45	11.21	10.98	10.75	10.54	10.32	10.12	9.92	9.55	9.19	8.86	8.55	8.25	7.97
28	12.02	11.75	11.50	11.25	11.01	10.78	10.56	10.35	10.14	9.74	9.37	9.03	8.70	8.39	8.10
29	12.32	12.04	11.77	11.51	11.26	11.02	10.79	10.56	10.35	9.93	9.55	9.18	8.84	8.53	8.23
30	12.61	12.32	12.04	11.77	11.50	11.25	11.01	10.77	10.54	10.11	9.71	9.33	8.98	8.65	8.34
31	12.90	12.59	12.30	12.01	11.74	11.47	11.22	10.97	10.74	10.29	9.87	9.48	9.11	8.77	8.45
32	13.18	12.85	12.54	12.25	11.96	11.69	11.42	11.16	10.92	10.45	10.02	9.61	9.24	8.88	8.55
33	13.45	13.11	12.79	12.47	12.18	11.89	11.61	11.35	11.09	10.61	10.16	9.74	9.35	8.99	8.65
34	13.71	13.35	13.02	12.69	12.38	12.09	11.80	11.52	11.26	10.76	10.29	9.86	9.46	9.09	8.74
35	13.96	13.59	13.24	12.91	12.58	12.27	11.98	11.69	11.42	10.90	10.42	9.98	9.57	9.18	8.83
36	14.20	13.82	13.46	13.11	12.77	12.45	12.15	11.85	11.57	11.04	10.54	10.09	9.67	9.27	8.91
37	14.44	14.04	13.66	13.30	12.96	12.63	12.31	12.01	11.71	11.17	10.66	10.19	9.76	9.36	8.98
38	14.66	14.25	13.86	13.49	13.13	12.79	12.47	12.15	11.85	11.29	10.77	10.29	9.84	9.43	9.05
39	14.88	14.46	14.06	13.67	13.30	12.95	12.62	12.29	11.98	11.41	10.87	10.38	9.93	9.51	9.12
40	15.09	14.66	14.24	13.84	13.47	13.10	12.76	12.43	12.11	11.52	10.97	10.47	10.00	9.58	9.18
41	15.30	14.85	14.42	14.01	13.62	13.25	12.89	12.55	12.23	11.62	11.06	10.55	10.08	9.64	9.24
42	15.49	15.03	14.59	14.17	13.77	13.39	13.02	12.67	12.34	11.72	11.15	10.63	10.15	9.70	9.29
43	15.68	15.21	14.75	14.32	13.91	13.52	13.15	12.79	12.45	11.81	11.23	10.70	10.21	9.76	9.34
44	15.87	15.38	14.91	14.47	14.05	13.65	13.26	12.90	12.55	11.90	11.31	10.77	10.27	9.81	9.39
45	16.04	15.54	15.06	14.61	14.18	13.77	13.38	13.00	12.65	11.99	11.38	10.83	10.33	9.86	9.43
46	16.21	15.70	15.21	14.74	14.30	13.88	13.48	13.10	12.74	12.07	11.45	10.89	10.38	9.91	9.47
47	16.37	15.85	15.35	14.87	14.42	13.99	13.58	13.20	12.83	12.14	11.52	10.95	10.43	9.95	9.51
48	16.53	15.99	15.48	14.99	14.53	14.10	13.68	13.29	12.91	12.21	11.58	11.00	10.47	9.99	9.55
49	16.68	16.13	15.61	15.11	14.64	14.20	13.77	13.37	12.99	12.28	11.64	11.05	10.52	10.03	9.58
50	16.83	16.26	15.73	15.22	14.74	14.29	13.86	13.45	13.06	12.35	11.69	11.10	10.56	10.06	9.61

TABLE VII D. PRESENT WORTH OF INCREASING & DECREASING ANNUITIES 10%

Straight Line % Changes—Inwood Premise

Yrs.	Income Annually DECREASING at Rate Shown									Yrs.
	−2%	−3%	−4%	−5%	−7%	−10%	−12%	−14%	−20%	
1	0.91	0.91	0.91	0.91	0.91	0.91	0.91	0.91	0.91	1
2	1.72	1.71	1.70	1.69	1.67	1.65	1.64	1.62	1.57	2
3	2.44	2.42	2.39	2.37	2.32	2.25	2.21	2.16	2.02	3
4	3.08	3.04	3.00	2.95	2.86	2.73	2.64	2.56	2.29	4
5	3.65	3.59	3.52	3.45	3.31	3.10	2.97	2.83	2.42	5
6	4.15	4.07	3.97	3.87	3.68	3.39	3.19	3.00		6
7	4.60	4.49	4.36	4.23	3.98	3.59	3.34	3.08		7
8	5.00	4.85	4.69	4.53	4.21	3.73	3.41	3.09		8
9	5.35	5.18	4.98	4.79	4.40	3.82	3.43			9
10	5.67	5.46	5.23	5.00	4.54	3.86				10
11	5.95	5.70	5.44	5.18	4.65					11
12	6.20	5.92	5.62	5.32	4.72					12
13	6.42	6.10	5.77	5.44	4.77					13
14	6.61	6.26	5.90	5.53	4.79					14
15	6.79	6.40	6.00	5.60	4.80					15
16	6.94	6.52	6.09	5.65						16
17	7.07	6.62	6.16	5:69						17
18	7.19	6.71	6.22	5.72						18
19	7.30	6.79	6.26	5.74						19
20	7,39	6.85	6.30	5.74						20

Yrs.	Income Annually INCREASING at Rate Shown									Yrs.
	+2%	+3%	+4%	+5%	+7%	+10%	+12%	+14%	+20%	
1	0.91	0.91	0.91	0.91	0.91	0.91	0.91	0.91	0.91	1
2	1.75	1.76	1.77	1.78	1.79	1.82	1.83	1.85	1.90	2
3	2.53	2.56	2.58	2.60	2.65	2.72	2.77	2.81	2.95	3
4	3.26	3.30	3.34	3.39	3.48	3.61	3.70	3.78	4.05	4
5	3.93	4.00	4.07	4.13	4.27	4.48	4.61	4.75	5.16	5
6	4.55	4.65	4.74	4.84	5.03	5.32	5.52	5.71	6.29	6
7	5.12	5.25	5.38	5.51	5.76	6.14	6.40	6.66	7.42	7
8	5.66	5.82	5.98	6.14	6.46	6.94	7.26	7.58	8.54	8
9	6.15	6.34	6.54	6.73	7.12	7.70	8:09	8.48	9.64	9
10	6.60	6.83	7.06	7.29	7.75	8.43	8.89	9.35	10.72	10
11	7.02	7.29	7.55	7.81	8.34	9.13	9.66	10.19	11.77	11
12	7.41	7.71	8.01	8.31	8.91	9.80	10.40	11.00	12.80	12
13	7.77	8.11	8.44	8.78	9.44	10.44	11.11	11.78	13.79	13
14	8.10	8.47	8.84	9.21	9.94	11.05	11.78	12.52	14.73	14
15	8.41	8.81	9.21	9.62	10.42	11.62	12.43	13.23	15.64	15
16	8.69	9.13	9.56	10.00	10.87	12.17	13.04	13.91	16.51	16
17	8.95	9.42	9.89	10.36	11.29	12.68	13.62	14.55	17.34	17
18	9.19	9.69	10.19	10.69	11.68	13.17	14.17	15.16	18.14	18
19	9.42	9.94	10.47	11.00	12.04	13.63	14.68	15.73	18.88	19
20	9.62	10.18	10.73	11.29	12.40	14.06	15.17	16.27	19.60	20

Illustration: An annuity for 5 years commencing with an initial payment of $1 and decreasing 7 cents each year, discounted at 10%, is today worth $3.31.

Part Two

Techniques and Procedures in Evaluating Commercial Properties

VI

Appraising Retail Store Property

Retail store properties with structures of one or more levels, housing one or more stores, with or without parking at hand, will be examined here.

Introduction

As distinct from shopping centers, these business units must attract shoppers by their own and their neighbors' pulling power. They are sometimes affected adversely in competition among themselves, by rivalry from nearby shopping centers, or by traffic congestion in downtown areas. They are sometimes gems.

The Income Approach is the chief guide to evaluation of income-bearing, investment properties, with Market Data and Cost Approaches used, when applicable, as supporting evidence of value.

Dominant aspects of value in retail property. Retail store properties are usually established by risk-taking entrepreneurs in the urban core and environs, in perimeter districts along arteries leading to suburbs, and in outlying rural places where the only mark of commercial activity may be the general store and gasoline pump at the cross-roads.

But in any case, valuation of such income-bearing property must begin with the appraiser's estimate of its highest and best use (i.e., "most likely-profitable use") in supplying desirable goods and services at retail to a demanding public convenienced to the spot by relatively easy access.

To determine highest and best and most productive use of land and building, the appraiser must first collect and absorb all economic data having any bearing on the operation of the retail store property under appraisement. The initial question uppermost in the appraiser's mind must be: *Is it the proper store in the proper place at this time?*

Without the answer to this question, the appraiser cannot begin to forecast the earnings expectancy of the subject property. He must determine the likely type and quality and permanence of tenant business (for instance, a rated, national chain store long-term lease vs. a month-to-month fly-by-night) in order to establish the basis of a capitalization rate which will produce a fair net return on the equity invested.

The dominant kind of value possessed by a retail property is *investment value.* This is its market value, and it is measured by the *investment analysis method* (i.e., the Income Approach, based on a comprehensive market survey and forecast of the earnings expectancy of the property). It is then possible to compute the present worth of a number of years of annual dollar benefits at a yield rate commensurate with the risk involved in purchasing the property at his appraised value. The likely length and strength of the lease guarantee is vital in this calculation.

The appraiser's forecast of annual net dollar returns and his selection of the yield rate are modified by comparative market data, which must be carefully collected by him during his examination of the district in which the subject property is lodged. He will have to make a comparative analysis of rentals of similar properties throughout the district to become convinced of an average yield rate. (See demonstration of Property Residual—Direct Capitalization, near the end of this chapter.)

Intricate mathematical formulae and tables can be useful tools in the Income Approach, but not unless they are based on common sense application of market data collection, and a practical feeling for the pulse of the market place. Only then can the approaches, techniques and procedures for value estimate be rationally employed.

How to collect data for retail property evaluation. There is no mystique to the orderly investment analysis of retail property. The nitty gritty of this hard work means collecting data which builds systematically into a comprehensive survey of market climate, embracing likely prospects for the future. The appraiser relates this survey to his physical analysis of the subject property, concluding with the kernel of the grain, in this manner: Strong Macro-market—adequate building—poor Micro-market location; or other. If there is presently a strong but suffering tenant in such a location, the appraiser knows the tenant will move at the end of the lease, and his capitalization rate will be increased to reflect this termination. A strong market and an adequate building will not recapture a tenant of equal stature if the location is in decline. It is the appraiser's first duty to measure the validity of such data and reflect it in his calculations.

Evidence from the Macro-market (national, regional, area and city) must be weighed against and meshed with proofs of data from the Micro-market (commercial district, neighborhood, block and site location). Conflicting data inferences must be boiled down and resolved. The net result will be concise appreciation of subject location.

Where to find the data for the market survey. Local (micro-market) data can be gathered through discreet inquiries of bankers, lawyers, newspapermen, real estate brokers and property managers. The local Board of Trade or Chamber of Commerce, the public relations departments of the utilities companies, and the postmaster are reliable sources for local and area data. The local police or your state highway department will furnish pedestrian and auto traffic count estimates.

For broader, macro-market data, the periodical entitled *Percentage Leases,* published by the National Institute of Real Estate Brokers, is important for its coast-to-coast rental rates and sales volume figures. *The Dollars and Cents of Shopping Centers,* revised in 1969 by the Urban Land Institute, is pregnant with facts concerning retail properties in downtown and outlying districts, and in neighborhood and regional centers. State and federal agencies frequently issue up-to-date statistics on highway planning and development, interstate commerce, labor and housing.

Most of the fifty states, following Connecticut's lead thirty years ago, now have well-established Economic Development Commissions capable of providing all kinds of Market Data.

Under the following heading and checklist, the appraiser begins to write his investment analysis, as follows:

Market Survey and Property Analysis

1. *Prospects.* Status and current trends of the macro-market, in which regional, trade area and city economic situations must be measured against a forecast of specific micro-market conditions for the particular trade in the immediate locale of the retail property being appraised. In measuring macro-market conditions, the following area factors must be analyzed:

a) Growth and change indications in the city, measuring density of population, decentralization trends for retail business and median family income in the trade area, with a brief history of retail business development there.

b) Permits for new commercial construction in the trade area, with notes on the types of retail trade likely to be added, particularly in the light of possible competition in the same business as subject property, together with a report on aggregate bank deposits and total gross retail sales in the trade area.

c) Total number of housing starts in the trade area for the current year, as compared to the past few years, and weighed against the number of starts in similar nearby areas. Total home ownership in the trade area should be cited, as against the number of residents renting, and with proportion of vacant dwellings.

d) Types and diversification of industry in and surrounding the area, with total employment figures and labor pool forecast. Any predisposition of local industry to be dependent on temporary government defense contracting should be noted. Space for industrial expansion, and airport, rail and/or harbor facilities cited.

e) Utility services available, with up-to-date forecasts from the telephone, electric power, gas and water companies on number of customer accounts in the trade area current and anticipated, together with local U.S. Post Office survey of distribution area, plus local newspaper circulation figures, and the total number of motor vehicle registrations in the trade area.

2. *Market analysis of the commercial district and block.* Micro-market factors influencing the vicinity should be set forth as follows: (a) Types of transportation

serving the locale; (b) Areas the customers are drawn from, and reasons why they shop in the locale; (c) The retail purchasing potential of these customers; (d) The types of retail outlets needed in the district to meet the maximum purchasing potential vs. the facilities now available; (e) Growth and change indications in the locale.

3. *Property Analysis and History.* Data defining the retail store property under appraisement must be outlined clearly: (a) Recitation of the title, including metes and bounds, assessments and tax levy; (b) Zoning and zone requirements; (c) Description of the topography and subsoil conditions, plottage and shape of the land area, together with list of utilities connected on site or available; (d) The type of construction, use and condition of the building, together with site improvements such as paved parking, fencing, etc.; (e) Summary of the development of the property, including five-to-ten year history of income and expense, and type of management and maintenance attending the property; (f) Estimation of the anticipated useful life of the property and allowances for depreciation and obsolescence.

4. *Comparable Sales and Leases.* The appraiser must list in detail verified data concerning sales and leases of retail store properties similar to the subject property in present or anticipated use, in the locale of the subject property or in similar micro-market districts. These comparables should be inspected and photographed to illustrate similarities to or differences from subject, summing up the market survey and property analysis.

After sifting through the data outlined in the foregoing Market Survey, using its information as a checklist on his judgments, the appraiser should by now have convinced himself of the rightness or wrongness of his earlier estimate of the subject property's highest and best and most productive use. If this is properly a retail store in the right location, the appraiser will at this point make that statement in his report, under the caption *Highest and Best Use.* The appraiser's next step is to consider the approaches to value estimate of the property.

THE APPROACHES TO VALUE

With market survey, property analysis and highest and best use established in the appraiser's mind, he now sets to work on the conclusive phase of evaluation via the investment analysis method: writing up the Income Approach on the basis of supportive Market Data. Unless the retail property under appraisement is new or recent, with little or no income and expense history, (see Model Appraisal on page 93 of this chapter) the Cost Approach will not add supportive evidence to the investment analysis procedure.

Retail properties are usually leased for rentals that, capitalized, prove values considerably greater than Reproduction Cost shows.

But the Income Approach alone is not proof of value, because an unusually high rental return might derive from management personality peculiar to that retail enterprise. Thus, substitution of the structure (as shown by Market Data) might be accomplished in the same block or in another district just as desirable, but at a lower figure than the Income Approach shows. If the Market Data Approach proves that a property or an income of equal value and use is available nearby, this evidence will temper an unusual value that the Income Approach alone indicates for the subject.

Most often, however, the capitalization of net income under the Income Approach proves market value to the sophisticated investor, when adequately supported by Market Data. Retail property is generally purchased by investors for its income yield, and therefore, the capitalization rate placed on the net income is of paramount importance in the application of the Income Approach.

Income approach. This important part of investment analysis is an appraisal technique in which the anticipated net income is processed to indicate the capital amount of the investment which produces the net income. The following thoughtful steps must be taken to arrive at the net income and to apply the proper rate to capitalize the net income to estimate value by the income approach:

Step 1—Gross income. In the appraisal of retail store property the first step is to estimate the gross income that the property may bring in the rental market at the time the appraisal is made. From this estimate of rentals, which is tested by comparison with similar properties, then deduct a proper figure (usually 10%) to compensate for vacancy allowance. The remaining income may then be considered as the *effective gross income.*

Step 2—Net income. From the effective gross income deduct the normal ownership expenses of the subject property. These expenses include taxes, insurance, normal replacements, maintenance, and management. When these ownership expenses are deducted from the effective gross income, the remaining income is known as the *net income* to the property, before depreciation including the land and building. If the property under appraisement has a long-term lease which is absolutely net to the owner, these two steps can, of course, be obviated.

Step 3—How to select a capitalization rate. Choosing the rate of capitalization is crucial. The simplest and truest way to find a rate at which the net income should be capitalized is to see how buyers and sellers of *similar properties* are capitalizing the net income to arrive at their sale prices. This market data can be collected in a study of recent sales made in the open market with verification of net income of the properties sold. The rate developed, thus automatically includes coverage of the safe rate, the penalty for lack of liquidity, the penalty for the management of the money, and the penalty for risk of regularity of net money income as well as the risk for the possible future loss of the capital investment. The rate so found in the market, where it was developed by sophisticated investors, may then be considered to be the proper capitalization rate for the subject property. This is sometimes called direct capitalization and will be demonstrated in an example given at the end of this chapter. (See Property Residual—Direct Capitalization.)

Capitalization Methods. Depending upon the *quality and durability* of income flowing from the property you are appraising, you can elect to follow either of the following courses of capitalization:

1. Use the straight-line depreciation plus capitalization-rate method of capitalization when you anticipate that the net income before depreciation *may decline* regularly each year in the future.

2. But if the net income before depreciation is expected to be level and is *of a contract nature,* and if the financial stability of the tenants is substantial and the leases extend over a period of at least fifteen years, then the Inwood premise may be used. This premise is used in good, chain-store lease properties, and good, long-term lease, commercial properties.

Clinching the income approach with market data. Capitalization rates on retail property will vary with circumstances. Yield percentages will differ. The owner of a prime property long-term leased to a Triple-A tenant in a downtown area may be willing to accept a 6 or 7 percent return. But the owner of a building in a congested area, subject to competition from shopping centers, may demand a yield of 10 to 12 percent.

The appraiser will select an adequate rate of capitalization by dividing the market value into the income of several comparable sales in the district, also to be demonstrated in the following pages.

Value through capitalization of net income now indicated, there remains in the investment analysis only the application of the final check on values sales of comparable retail properties. A keen knowledge of retail properties like the one under appraisement, plus intense research into the background of other similarly located retail properties, will formulate a basis of comparative values for the appraiser, to clinch his income approach computations.

The appraiser who performs best in retail property valuations is he who has specialized in it for years, keeping in constant contact with buyers and sellers, analyzing sales and rentals, and building a library on the subject in a rather well-defined area. Such experience equips him to work efficiently in other areas or cities, but only after he has learned his trade in his own downtown bazaars.

TECHNIQUES FOR ESTIMATING VALUE OF LAND AND IMPROVEMENTS IN RETAIL PROPERTY APPRAISAL

Procedure for Estimating a Separate Land Value Under the Retail Store Structure

In retail property appraising, it is usually essential to set up land value as separate and distinct from the improvements. Under our tax laws, land is non-depreciable, and therefore its value cannot be lumped together with depreciable improvements, and processed in the same manner as depreciable improvements. If possible, it is best to estimate land value first, particularly where Market Data on nearby vacant land is plentiful. But on occasion such Market Data may be scarce, and the appraiser may know from the outset the value of the building, particularly if the structure is new, without depreciation, and the builder's costs are competitive and at hand. In that case, the appraiser would set up his Cost Approach first, and find his land value using the Land Residual Technique. This is the only instance in which use of the Cost Approach is necessary in retail property appraising. The Model Appraisal following, details this technique.

Land value by Market Data. Land value may be estimated by: (1) Recent sales of nearby vacant land; (2) Recently executed land leases; (3) The Land Residual Technique.

Vacant land sales. Recent sales of nearby comparable vacant land present incontrovertible evidence of market value. If subject property and the comparables are located on the main retail street, and have approximately the same shape and depth, the front foot unit is the best unit of comparison. If the comparables are of varying shapes and depths on different streets, the square foot unit would be a more equitable unit of comparison.

Land lease rentals. A land value estimate derived from rentals of recent land leases may be comparatively applied to valuation of the subject site. The rental income is brought down to a net return, after deduction of all landlord's expenses of ownership, including management. Capitalization of the net yield, at the market interest rate, will indicate the value imputable to the land.

The Land Residual Technique. When it is not possible to find the value of the land by the use of the Market Data Approach, it is proper to find the value of the land by using the *Land Residual Technique* under a hypothetical *highest and best use* building or an actual building, recent or new. This technique will be fully demonstrated in the Model Appraisal on pages following.

Adjustment of comparables to subject. Each comparable sale is measured in every aspect against the subject property. The appraiser must contrast the comparables against the subject property and make plus or minus adjustments of differences between them. If the comparable is superior, equal to, or inferior to the subject, the appraiser states this qualification, and puts a dollar value on it.

1. *Location.* Plus adjustment must be made for corner influence; minus adjustment for one-way traffic, etc.
2. *Plottage.* Larger parcels may represent more value per unit, but plottage value does not accrue beyond maximum economic land use.
3. *Area and shape.* The geometry of economic frontages and economic depths must be evaluated. Odd or irregular shaped lots may show waste areas when compared to rectangles and squares. Lots with two or three frontages will show a considerable plus value over lots with one frontage, etc.
4. *Date of sale.* The appraiser contrasts price differential between the date of sale and current date.

Adjustment may also be required for other features, such as topography, subsoil, and drainage. These adjustments, plus or minus, may be made in terms of dollars or percent of dollar values, as compared to subject property. (Note adjustments to comparables in demonstration appraisals.)

Several sales or leases of comparable vacant land, with carefully documented and verified details of transfer spelled out, are requisite as supportive evidence of fair market value. Only arm's-length sales or leases of closely similar vacant land should be presented to produce a comparative estimate of value to the subject property.

When comparable land sales or leases are unavailable, or the comparative features are poor, the Land Residual Technique may be applied to produce an estimate of land value. The following Model Appraisal demonstrates this technique.

MODEL APPRAISAL OF RETAIL STORE PROPERTY USING LAND RESIDUAL TECHNIQUE

The following (abbreviated) appraisal is of a two-story retail building, with parking, in the interior of a downtown block of an industrial city in the Northeast. This structure will produce a net income sufficient until the land may be ripe for a taller building. Such properties generally represent highest and best use of the land with proper improvements.

Purpose and Function

Fair market value for permanent mortgage financing.

Valuation Premise

City population is 260,000, surrounded by suburbs aggregating a trade area of 425,000. Chief industries are aircraft manufacture, automotive parts, plastics and electronics. Median family income is $9,715. Residential areas are within a mile east or west of subject property, which is easily reached by auto, bus and walking. Main Street extends from I-95 on the south to the Merritt Parkway on the north, a distance of three miles. Small office buildings, banks, utility companies, retail stores and outlying shopping centers line Main Street for most of its length. The public library, two hospitals, and four churches are within one mile of the subject property.

MACRO-MARKET ASPECTS

New, well-constructed and strategically located, the subject building should have the advantage of commercial location and seniority for the foreseeable future. Trend is toward population increase in the area, and expanded industrial activity in the city. Area employment is at a high level, and likely to remain so.

Market Survey and Property Analysis (abbreviated)

Micro-market climate for subject location is strong and promising. The adjoining corner property is controlled by the same owners and they intend to build upon this corner also. They have been approached by several national chain organizations of varying types of businesses. These two properties will enjoy the use of the 25,000 square foot parking area in the rear of the corner property, when both sites have been fully improved.

Patronage from the well-to-do suburbs in the trade area is steady. Regional economy is strong and the national posture good.

Nature of tenancy. The tenant is a branch of a successful national chain store.

The fact that a chain organization has selected this location is an indication of the probable future of the venture, because they have full knowledge of trends and conditions in this and neighboring counties as well as the regional and national economic climate. They have very efficient planning staffs, which make thorough surveys of areas before entering into a lease. Their merchandising record has been outstandingly successful. The twenty-year lease will be of importance in maintaining the character of this project for years to come.

A new U.S. post office on Main Street, within 500 feet of this property, is nearing completion. There are 70,000 families resident in the city. Annual retail sales in the city total $340,000,000.

The shopping area within this neighborhood consists of stores with frontages of approximately 25′ by 70′ depth, which are gross leased at $800. average per month. The tenants of these stores are principally specialty shops. The tenant in the subject store should be in a favorable competitive position with these neighbors.

Capitalization of income. More reliance has been placed by this appraiser on the capitalization of the stabilized net income of the property than on a cost estimate, due to the fact that it is difficult to estimate the value of this raw land. The owners of this property and their business associates own a considerable amount of surrounding land. Some of this is owned on an inter-partner arrangement and does not of necessity reflect the value of the land generally or even the value to the buyer and seller. There have been no sales of comparable vacant land in the vicinity of subject in recent years.

There have been no recent sales of similar buildings in the immediate neighborhood. The value ascribed to the land in this appraisal will, we believe, materially increase within a short time. A low capitalization rate is therefore indicated.

Description of Site

The plot is rectangular in shape. The land is firm and at grade. The grade of the street is level. Paved sidewalks and curbs, street lights, all utilities. Dimensions: 150′ front × 100′ depth.

Parking Area

(Diagram of plat showing subject property, buildings and parking area is inserted here.) Parking area occupies eastern one-half of site area, paved with bituminous asphalt, 3″ thick, covering 7,500 square feet.

Description of Structure

Two story brick building with full basement, retail store building, fronting 75′ on Main Street with a depth of 100′ leased to a single tenant, with taxes, insurance and all maintenance provided by the tenant. The building occupies the western half of the site area.

Age

New, completed this week.

Construction

Poured concrete foundation: steel "I" beams and Lally columns; brick walls; built-up composition, 20-year bonded roof; galvanized leaders and gutters; metal sash. Facade of building is face brick—show windows have modern design of stainless steel frames and bases.

Interior

Basement—concrete floors, plasterboard ceilings, exterior walls of cement block.

Store—concrete floors covered with asphalt tile, and carpeting in some areas. Sheetrock ceilings and walls. Partition walls, wood studs, sheetrock finish. Two washrooms per floor, one each for men and women, tiled. Porcelain basins and bowls, chrome fixtures, well-lighted.

Heating—oil-fired, hot air, with a combination heating and air-condition unit with concealed ducts serving both floors. 220V—100 amp. electric service. Bx Cable.

Water supply—city water. Capacity 100 gallons a minute.

Layout and Tenancy

(Excerpts of important clauses of lease, terms, rental, type of business, size of store, with diagram of building should be given here.) A 20-year lease on the property has just been executed. Annual rental is $24,750., absolutely net.

Highest and Best Use

Development of presently zoned use as a retail facility.

Valuation of the Improvements via the Cost Approach

The following actual payments were made by the owner for the construction of the retail store's plans and specifications:

Concrete work, footing, foundation, basement, concrete floors, concrete block walls and front brick facade	$ 25,000.
Bathroom, plumbing, tile and fixtures ABC, Inc.	3,798.
Roof, including plasterboard ceilings and insulation for walls installed with styrofoam and fiberbutts on studs by DEF Company	17,141.
Windows, doors and sills by GHI Corp.	5,188.
Heating and air-conditioning, including all wiring and electrical outlets by JKL, Inc.	18,891.
Structural steel work by MNO Company—incl. tax	33,300.
Master Antenna—installed by PQR Services	820.
Thermostats by XYZ Incorporated	2,088.
Total Materials (including gutters, leaders and tile drains)	$107,066.
Total Labor, including contractor's overhead and profit, and taxes and insurance paid + architect's fee	$100,434.
Total Job Payment to Contractor, Materials and Labor overhead and profit	$207,500.

Site Improvements:

Cost Index Service
Section 61, Page 8, June 1967
Approximately 7,500 square feet
asphalt paving, 3″ asphalt, 2″ base
@ 27¢ per square foot = $2,497. rounded to $2,500.

The owner's contract figures will be used for building value, since the contract proves to be economically advantageous to the owner when compared against cost index service.

The Cost Index figure for *parking improvements* will be used, since the owner's contract payment of $3,300. for paving seemed to this appraiser to be excessive and an overpayment in the current market.

Therefore,

Actual cost of the building	$207,500.

Add site improvements	2,500.
Estimated Value of the Improvements via the Cost Approach	$210,000.

Explanation of Lack of Depreciation

The Cost Approach was used to estimate the cost of building improvements new. The Land Residual Technique will be used to estimate the value of the land at its highest and most profitable use, viz, as a site for a two-story retail store building. Since the building and site improvements are new, there is no depreciation to be deducted.

Actual Construction Cost (New) to the Owner . . . . $210,000.
(*Estimated* Construction Cost by Cost Index . . . . $225,000.)
Actual Cost of the building will be used in the Land Residual Technique, under the Income Approach.

Valuation of Land and Improvements via Income Approach
(Using Land Residual Technique)

Actual Cost of the Building New = $210,000.		
Effective, absolutely, net income per annum	$24,750.	
Interest imputable to improvements ($210,000 × 9%)	18,900.	
Interest to Land		$ 5,850.
Therefore, 5,850 ÷ 7% = $83,571.		
Estimate of Cost of the Improvement	$210,000.	
Estimated Value of the Land	83,571.	
Estimate of Market Value of the Property		$293,571.

Explanation of Capitalization

The summation method is used to estimate a proper interest rate. This method builds a rate by adding together component parts which are considered appropriate, to constitute a total interest rate. See the following illustration:

Safe Rate or Non-risk rate	5.00%
(Interest paid by Savings Bank or Government Bonds)	
Rate for lack of safety	1.00%
Rate for Non-Liquidity	.50%
Rate for Burden of Management	.50%
Total	7.00%

Recapture Rate

The expected economic life of the building improvement is influenced by the anticipated durability of the income stream, which in turn is anticipated from the credit of the tenant or lessee, the location of the improvements and the permanence of usage. The tenancy herein could be expected to last for a period of 50 years, therefore, the recapture rate would be 50/100ths, or 2.00%; therefore, interest and recapture on the improvements are 9%.

Market Data Approach

Net Income Multiplier. In appraising retail store property by the Market Data Approach, a gross income or net income multiplier may be used in support of value conclusion. Subject property is net leased property and the net income it will produce as compared with net income indicated by recent market sales of *similar* retail properties reflects evaluation by the typical knowledgeable investor.

Net income multiplier procedures used here maintain a high degree of accuracy. The net incomes applied are truly net to land and improvements. They are detailed as follows:

Sales of Retail Properties Net-Leased
to Chains in Nearby Cities

Sale No. 1:
422 Congress Street, Hope City, sold for $420,000, 2-12-68; net income: $33,600 per annum. $429,000÷33,000=13.0.

Sale No. 2:
311 Boulevard, Terminal City, sold for $350,000, 5-15-68; net income=$24,500 per annum. $350,000÷24,500=13.2

Sale No. 3:
517 Asylum Street, Capitol City, sold for $325,000, 10-10-68; net income=$24,375 per annum. $320,000÷24,300=13.3.

The above cities are all of approximately the same population and trading area as subject City, and all are within 75 miles of subject. The range of the multipliers is 13.0 to 13.3. Applying these multipliers to subject income as:

$22,500×13.0=$292,500.
$22,500×13.2=$297,000.
$22,500×13.3=$299,250.

—Value Indicated by Market Data Approach is between $292,500. and $299,000., rounded.

Correlation and Conclusion

Value Indicated by Income and Cost Approaches .... $294,000.

Value Indicated by Market Data Approach
is between .... $292,500 and $299,000.

In the absence of any sales of closely similar improved properties in the downtown area, a net income multiplier was derived from sales of net leased retail properties in neighboring cities, producing the Market Data value estimate in this report. Because properties such as subject are customarily purchased by investors for income purposes, it is the judgment of this appraiser that the Income Approach is, in this instance, the most accurate guide to value.

Therefore, in my opinion, Fair Market Value of the whole of subject property is:

Two Hundred Ninety-four Thousand Dollars
($294,000.)

Procedure for Estimating Value of the Improvements by Means Other Than the Cost Approach in Retail Store Property Appraisal

Residual techniques under the Income Approach. When a retail store building is old, and its type of construction not the sort that would be reproduced today to house a modern store, it is scarcely appropriate to use the Depreciated Cost Approach to attempt to measure its value.

If such a store nevertheless is leased long-term net to a nationally rated chain tenant, and then the tenant has constantly refurbished the premises to create the appearance of modernity, it is pure guesswork to attempt to reflect accurately rates of depreciation to include deterioration, functional obsolescence and economic obsolescence, and then to deduct this burden of time, wear and tear and patchwork refurbishment from the theoretical cost new.

This property will probably be net-leased for a rental that, capitalized, proves investment or market value much greater than Depreciated Reproduction Cost could show. So the Cost Approach is out.

Therefore, we will examine other means of finding the value of retail property improvements, when the value of the land is already known through Market Data. These means are provided by the building and Property Residual techniques. In review, these two means, under the Income Approach relying on Market Data, are as follows:

The Building Residual Technique. Here the known factors are: (1) Net income before recapture; (2) Land Value (via Market Data); (3) Interest rate (taken from current requirements of local investors and lenders); (4) The *remaining economic life* of the building. The *unknown* factor is the value of the building.

In this technique, the income required to service the investment in the land, found by the Market Data Approach, is charged against the net income to the property, and the remainder is the *net income imputable to the building.*

This income is then capitalized to reflect the investment value of the building.

Remaining economic life. In processing the income imputable to the building, care must be taken to estimate the remaining economic life of the building. The net income remaining to the building is then processed for *the period of the remaining economic life* by the appropriate capitalization rate, or Inwood factor if the lease is long-term and certain, to indicate the capital value or market value of the building. For instance:

Building Residual—Inwood Annuity

Value of the land by Market Data	$125,000.	
Verified annual net income before recapture		$ 31,500.
Interest imputable to land value 7%		8,750.
Annual net income imputable to building		$ 22,750.

Remaining economic life 25 years,
interest rate 7%. Then the present worth of
1 per annum for 25 years, discounted at 7%,
is found to be 11.654 (Inwood factor, Table II)

Building value=$22,750×11.654	$269,179.
Add Land Value via Market Data Approach.	125,000.
Estimated value of land and improvements	$394,179.
Rounded to	$394,000.

The Property Residual Technique. Here the known factors are: (1) Net income before recapture; (2) The capitalization rate; (3) The useful life of the building; (4) Land value by Market Data. The *unknown* factor is the value of *the property as a whole.*

Using this technique, land and building are not valued separately, but as a whole. (If you already know the value of the land by Market Data, simply subtract the value of the land from the value of the property as a whole, and it leaves you with building value.)

In this process, most applicable to properties leased long-term, you capitalize the present worth of the net income expectancy before depreciation for the estimated economic life of the building or the term of the lease.

At the anticipated end of the income, say 25 years, land and building are assumed to revert to the owner. This reversion is valued by discounting its then anticipated value against its present-day worth. The total value is the sum of the capitalized value of the income plus the present worth of the reversionary interest.

Another application of this technique, which will be demonstrated here, applies an overall rate for the entire net before depreciation and with no reversion. It is, in effect, the same as direct capitalization with an overall rate. For example, consider this case:

A synopsis of the lease is as follows: terms, 25 years, from July 1, 1948 to December 31, 1973, with annual rental absolutely net at $31,500, payable in quarterly instalments of $7,875. each, in advance, on the first day of July, October, January and April. The tenant is a national chain clothing store, rated Triple-A.

Utilities, repairs, maintenance, fire, boiler, plate glass and liability insurance premiums, and all claims, to be assumed and paid by the tenant; in other words, lease is net, net, net.

Option to purchase: Until the expiration of the lease on December 31, 1973, on 30 days notice to the owner, the tenant has an option to purchase the property for $450,000.

The tenant has asked the appraiser to estimate present-day market value of the property so that he can decide whether or not to exercise his option. This is the purpose and function of the following appraisal, which demonstrates the techniques:

Property Residual—Direct Capitalization

This appraiser has made a close analysis of comparable rentals in the neighborhood and city. There has been a sharply depreciating influence operating in this vicinity for the past few years. The recent completion of a large regional shopping center with two major department stores in the downtown core about five blocks south of subject property has caused vacancies immediately north and south of the subject on both sides of Main Street, where there is a consequent reduction in demand for retail space among the older buildings. To meet this trend, rentals will have to be reduced to attract less desirable tenants.

As evidence that this trend has taken effect in the neighborhood, I submit the following closeby and recent comparable rentals:

1. Location: 555 Main Street. Commencement date: 2-20-68
   First Floor: 5,500 sq. ft. Use: Men's clothing, chain.
   Second and third floors: 10,500 sq. ft., same tenant and use.
   Rent: $16,000, annually, or $1.00 per square foot, absolutely net, for ten years, no parking.
2. Location: 626 Main Street. Commencement Date: 10-1-68
   Basement: 4,000 sq. ft. Use: Branch bank drive-in
   1st Floor 4,000 sq. ft. Limited parking (10 cars).
   Rent: $16,000, or $2.00 per square foot, absolutely net for 15 years.
3. Location: 750 Main Street. Commencement Date: 2-1-69
   Basement, Ground, and two upper floors: 44,000 sq. ft.
   Use: Novelty store, chain. No parking.
   Rent: $55,000 annually, or $1.25 per square foot, absolutely net for 12 years.

There is a wide range in these comparable rents. Comparable #2 has parking for about 10 cars, while the subject and Comparables #1 and #3 have no parking. Comparable #3 is most similar to subject property in terms of area and building condition (functional utility).

Due to the movement of the prime business neighborhood toward the new regional downtown shopping center, where there is adequate public parking as against none in subject neighborhood, I have selected Comparable #3 as equal to the estimated stabilized economic rental for the subject property, or $1.25 per square foot per annum.

The net rentable area of the subject building is 42,000 square feet. Therefore, the annual rental value, net, of the subject property is estimated to be:

42,000 sq. ft. @ 1.25 p.s.f. = $52,500 per annum.

Explanation of Capitalization Rate

The owner has refused to furnish this appraiser with a record of his property expenses, because the appraiser has been retained by the Tenant. Such a record would be necessary for the purpose of processing a value estimate by the Building Residual technique.

I have, therefore, elected to use a Direct Capitalization Rate, and the Property Residual Technique to estimate value.

I have considered the risk and uncertainity reflected on the subject property by the extensive development of new retail facilities with parking just five blocks to the south.

The following sales are submitted to support the Direct Capitalization Rate:

1. Location: 642 Main Street Use: Retail
   Grantor: ABC Corp. Grantee: DEF Trust
   Date of Sale: 3-10-68 Sale Price: $132,000
   Annual Net Rental: $16,000 / $16,000 ÷ $132,000 = 12%

2. Location: 811 Main Street Use: Retail
   Grantor: GHI Co. Grantee: John Doe, Inc.
   Date of Sale: 4-15-68 Sale Price: $50,000
   Annual Net Rental: $7,800 / $7,800 ÷ $50,000 = 16%

3. Location: 823 Main Street Use: Banking
   Grantor: MNO, Inc. Grantee: XYZ Trust
   Date of Sale: 2-17-69 Sale Price: $100,000
   Annual Net Rental: $8,400 / $8,400 ÷ $100,000 = 8.4%

In the opinion of this appraiser, Comparable #1 is closest to subject in location and type of use, and I have selected a Direct Capitalization Rate of 12% as a reasonable and sound rate to be applied to subject in processing the Property Residual method.

Estimated annual net rental value of subject property as stabilized in the economic processing of selected comparable sales is $52,500, which considerably exceeds the original annual contract rent of $31,500. However, $52,500 divided by the Direct Capitalization Rate of 12% = $437,500, *a figure less than the option price to the Tenant.*

Since the subject property has been held for many years as an investment, it is the opinion of this appraiser that the Income Approach is the most reliable method to estimate value. Therefore, I have employed the Property Residual technique, under the Income Approach, for my value conclusion, in the amount of $437,500. (Land value here was estimated via Market Data at $125,000; thus, if a separate building value was required for tax purposes, the building value would be $437,500 less $125,000 = $312,500.)

Appraising vacant retail store property. The techniques and procedures recited in this chapter apply as fully to the vacant property as to the one that is tenanted. Resorting to the Depreciated Cost Approach because there is no income stream (perhaps temporarily) from a vacant store is like immediately defining an unemployed person as permanently disabled. First, go back to highest and best and most productive use. Find out why the store is vacant. Even if the business community has shifted to another locale, the vacant store may have remaining use as a delicatessen, liquor shop or neighborhood grocery, even a "flea market" junk shop. Then set up a hypothetical likely tenant on a stabilized rental based on similar comparable properties, and process the projected income by the technique indicated by your market survey and property analysis, both macro-market and micro-market.

A vacancy might be found in a highly prized location, in a store surrounded by long-term net-leased properties, where a poorly financed retailer had gone out of business due his own poor management, through no fault of the property, the business district, or regional contribution to the trade. Such a property, temporarily vacant at worst, must be appraised for its long-term lease expectancy on the basis of the investment analysis method, embracing the Income Approach as buttressed by a qualified market survey and forecast.

VII

How to Capitalize Income into Value— The Shopping Center

Stores follow people. In our mobile society, people are on the move from farms to cities, from cities to suburbs, and from the older suburbs to new ones and quasi-rural exurban green belts. They are also on the move toward second homes in summer and winter resorts, and toward retirement homes in sunny climes. Shopping centers, large and small, will be erected or expanded to serve people wherever they congregate in large numbers. But the shopping center developer will have to be more careful about his land and building costs and his mortgage interest rates in the new decade than he has been in the past quarter century, or he will not own the property long enough to see its percentage leases bear fruit.

Inflation, tight money, high interest rates and spiraling construction costs have made shopping center development a high-risk business. Department stores are going to have to shoulder more of the rent burden if big centers are to survive.

Introduction

Today's shopping center is an integrated store group with parking, planned, developed, owned and managed as a unit, a fact which most often shows itself through an attractive architectural unity tying the stores together. Off-street parking with an area at least three times that occupied by the stores must be provided on the property.

Each store tenant in the shopping center should have been selected by the developer to fit into a pre-ordained pattern of merchandizing. Together this group of tenants will supply all of a shopper's daily needs; larger centers will include the shopper's once-a-year needs, too.

The typical customer coming to the shopping center will arrive by automobile and will require 300 square feet in which to conveniently park the car. If parking is not adequate, the customer may be lost to a competing center.

In sum, for the average shopper, the modern, planned shopping center has three outstanding advantages. First, the cumulative pull of a carefully selected group of stores. Second (a corollary of the first), all of a day's needs can be met at one place. Third, parking and picking up purchases in the car is convenient.

The foregoing introduction refers to all three kinds of shopping center: the convenience or neighborhood center, the medium-sized community center and the large regional shopping center, as described in Chapter II, and reiterated here.

The convenience neighborhood center will usually consist of local or chain supermarket, pharmacy, dry cleaner, hardward store, variety or discount house, and sometimes a beauty salon, barber shop, bakery, delicatessen, branch bank and gasoline service station, ranging in size from ten to twenty stores. This center will depend on the trade of at least 3,000 families, and generally contains 25,000 to 100,000 square feet of gross leasable area.

The community center is most often built around a junior department store, with as many as twenty to forty stores arrayed around it. It is most often found in flourishing suburbs, or at city perimeters. At least 15,000 families must patronize it regularly, and it will contain between 100,000 and 200,000 square feet of gross leasable area.

The regional center will have as many as 100 stores or more totalling over 500,000 square feet of gross leasable area. It will be built around one or more large major department stores, each with not less than 100,000 square feet of gross leasable area. It is designed to accommodate the daily and annual needs of more than 50,000 families. The regional center is the equivalent of the downtown shopping district, and offers varieties of apparel and home furnishings, as well as novelties, luxuries, recreational facilities and often professional services.

UNIQUE FEATURES OF SHOPPING CENTER EVALUATION

If the shopping center is already established, or is not yet built but has achieved executed agreements to lease, valuation of the land must be based on capitalization of annual residual net income produced by the yield of the lease rentals; if the shopping center is merely projected and has no lease agreements, valuation of the land can only be based on Market Data showing comparable sales of similar land in similar situations.

The property must be valued as a whole, and not as separate individual stores or buildings.

The need for the shopping center must be proven by a macro- and micro-market survey early built into the appraisal. An estimate of rent achievement based on percentage of gross sales must be made, in addition to the minimum guaranteed yield of the leases.

Sales of improved commercial properties in the area cannot be used as comparable in evaluating the subject, because no two shopping centers are ever precisely alike in terms of land area, parking ratio to store areas, store mix, goods offered, hours open, lease particulars, gross expenses and net income produced per square foot of store occupancy.

In these respects, every shopping center is a unique entity, and can only be evaluated by capitalization of its guaranteed net income.

The first step in appraising a shopping center, already established or merely projected, is to make a thorough analysis of those land requirements unique to successful shopping center development. The appraiser may begin as follows:

Site Analysis: (Micro-market).

1. *Location.* Traffic flow for any kind of shopping center is of prime importance. The neighborhood or community center should be close to public facilities such as churches, libraries, and schools, on or near an intersection of important town roads, and close to state highways.

Proximity to cloverleaf exchanges on express highways is requisite for a regional shopping center, since it embraces a much broader market trade area. Local roads in and out of the center, and public transportation, are also important.

Pedestrians should be afforded protected, easy access to all three types of center, where they may be carried by bus, train or subway. Ample automobile parking is essential to any center. Does the location meet all these tests?

2. *Land area.* A regional shopping center, with double-decked interior mall and attached multi-level parking, can be built on a 10-acre downtown parcel. But in a suburban locale, where land is cheaper, a regional mammoth can be built on one level, with surface parking, using ten times that area. Community and neighborhood centers require much less. A vacant tract of the required size usually offers the best opportunity; land improved with buildings is too high-priced.

3. *Cost of Site.* Shopping center planners can build on only 25% of their site. The bulk of the land is assigned to parking, ingress and egress, and delivery areaways for servicing the stores. So they must acquire the site at a cost commensurate with the net income that 25% of the site can produce.

As a rule of thumb for suburban areas, most developers feel that $1.50 per square foot for land is the maximum that can be paid for a shopping center site. In downtown core urban renewal areas, developers figure on $2.50 per square foot as maximum price, and this only when a high-rise office building can be superimposed over the shopping mall. Is the price paid for subject land in line with these requirements?

4. *Zoning.* Commercial zoning for the entire tract is necessary to full development of the center. There can be no compromise in this regard with municipal authorities, without seriously inhibiting the anticipated value of the property. Does the zoning of subject site allow full development?

5. *Utilities.* Electric, sewer and water conduits are necessary attachments to the site. If they are not present, the cost of bringing them in must be in reasonable proportion to budgeted site costs. A gas line is beneficial, but bottled propane can substitute for tenants requiring it.

6. *Topography and subsoil.* Stores can be arranged in a variety of patterns on more than one level, and an experienced architect can often provide both customer convenience and great charm to an irregular site with an uneven surface. However, the costs of site preparation must be compared to acquisition costs of a level site, near road grade, if such is available. Poor subsoil conditions can be the cause of flooding, sinking and cracking of buildings and paved areas, and limitations on expansion of the center. Is subject site free of these flaws? If not, the value of the center is threatened. Test borings are advisable before planning advances.

7. *Competition.* A new regional shopping center should be seven miles or more from a regional center of the same type, in the same trade area. Community shopping centers should be at least five miles apart and neighborhood centers three miles apart, where they overlap trade areas; otherwise, the value of the center is threatened.

8. *Real Estate Taxes.* Geographically, tax rates vary. Local real estate assessments and fluctuating mill rates may make the difference between profit and loss in any shopping center. If the site is over-assessed to begin with, it is likely that buildings will also be over-taxed. Tax escalation clauses commencing upon completion should be included in every lease, in each kind of center, so that the tenant bears his share of tax increases after the first year of occupancy. Without tax escalation clauses, the value of the center can be washed out.

The second step in preparing an appraisal report of a shopping center is taken by researching, synthesizing and writing a comprehensive market survey and forecast of earnings.

Market Survey and Forecast

Its key importance. A market survey and forecast must come on the heels of site deliberation in shopping center planning and appraising, because this reconnaissance will take the measure of market strength present and future, and determine the number and size and mix of stores to be leased and built on the site. It will also become a prime tool in calculating the changed value of the land, after agreements to lease on the site have been made.

The survey must include macro-market study of the prospects and trends in the national, regional and trade area economic pictures. Further, it must see into the future far enough to predict growth or decline in the customer area, and to assess customer purchasing power over a period of years. It takes about four years for a large center to reach full-tilt operation, so the forecast must cover that period and beyond it, if the appraisal is being made at the beginning of the center's life. At that time, the architect will need your survey and forecast to give the center ultimate size and shape, and the banker will need this information to formulate the basis of financing.

The survey and forecast is in itself the major part of a preliminary appraisal of a proposed shopping center on a site under consideration. For the completed shopping center, with leases, it means confirmation of existing percentage rents, and a forecast of favorable or unfavorable elements affecting the center's earnings in the future.

The appraiser must have a feel for the developer's sense of timing. Meeting the needs of the market-place at a given location with specific facilities is an art as well as a science in market research. The developer who owns the right spot at the proper time in the growth pattern of a community is apt to command both the feasibility and success of a shopping center. The right combination of stores in the right place at the right time is the combination for success.

Reach of market survey and forecast. The macro-market survey and forecast must embrace a map of the trade area on which the shopping center under appraisement will depend, showing: (1) Number of families in the trade area; and (2) The spendable annual income of total families in the trade area, and its secondary and tertiary areas in the various sections of the trade area. (See Figure 2.)

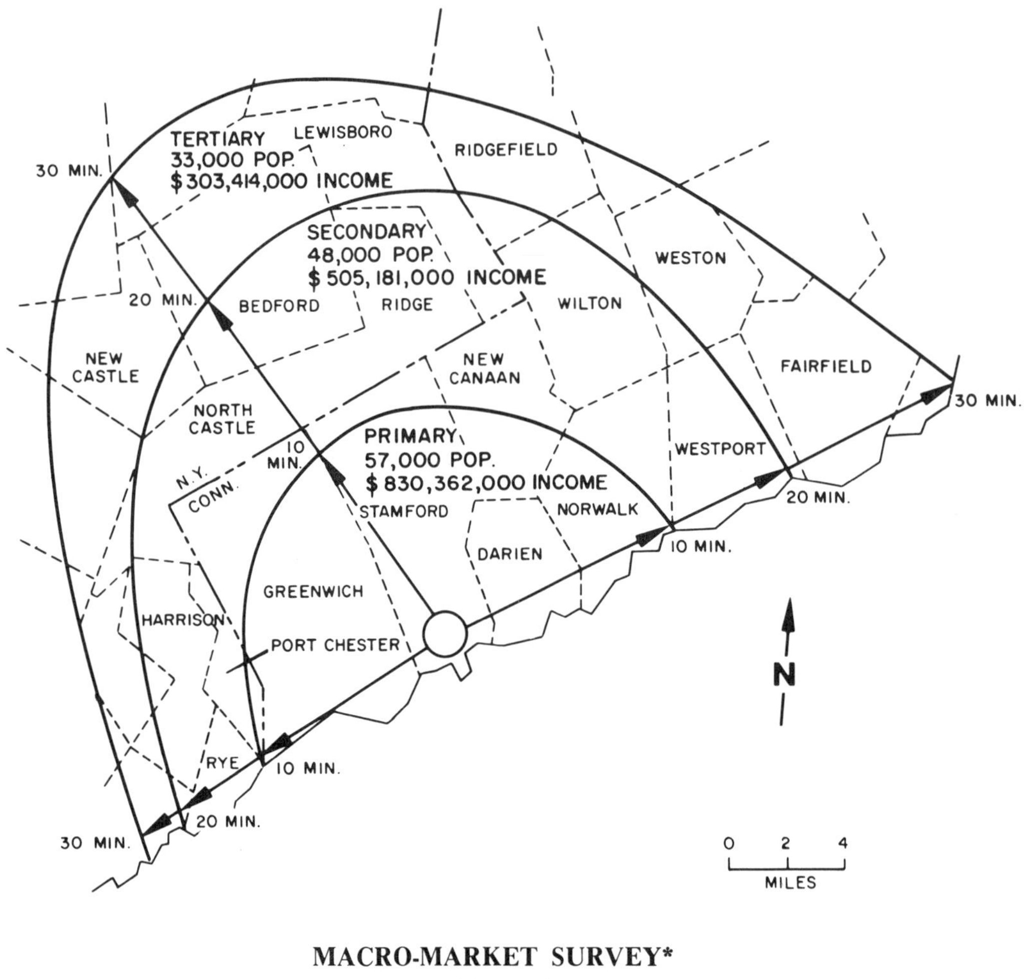

MACRO-MARKET SURVEY*
Retail Trade Areas
FIGURE 2.

A statement of the apportionment of income spent by families in the trade area in each kind of store should be appended to the map.

*Connecticut Redevelopment Commission, 1970.

The micro-market focus of the survey and forecast is on a fixed location in a definite area, so that all data appended to the trade area map, such as traveling time by automobile from the tertiary and secondary areas, should relate directly to the site.

Appraisals of shopping centers may be required at different phases of their development, from mere conception on a hypothetical site, to intermediate up-date for temporary financing, or for completed project long-term financing or sale. Whichever the phase, the survey and forecast is of paramount importance. Without it, there is no road to valuation of a center.

In the case of shopping centers, the investment analysis method of evaluation is comprised of the site analysis and the Market Survey and Forecast as interwoven in the earnings process, or Income Approach. Except when the site is virgin, comparative Market Data is of no consequence, which is where the method varies from the emphasis placed on it in Chapter VI.

MACRO-MARKET SURVEY*

Macro-Market Survey

City

Effective Buying Income

Aggregate $327,000,000
Per Household Average $10,900
Number of Households 30,000

Distribution of Household by effective buying income

Over $10,000 ....35% $2500–$3999 .... 10%
$7000–$9999 .... 15% Under $2500 .... 11%
$4000–$6999.......... 29%

Greater Metropolitan Area
Includes contiguous suburbs

Effective Buying Income

Aggregate $830,362,000
Per Household Average $14,500
Number of Households 57,000

Distribution of Households by effective buying income

Over $10,000 ....53% $2500–$3999 ....8%
$7000–$9999 .... 11% Under $2500 ....8%
$4000–$6999 .... 20%

Source: Sales Management *Survey of Buying Power* (1970)
(Secondary and Tertiary Sources through
State Development Commission.)

*Connecticut Development Commission, 1970.

Appendix to Map
Apportionment of Family Income Spent in Each Kind of Store in the Trade Area

	1969	*Percent of Total*
Total Retail Trade	$830,362,000	100.0
Food Stores	207,590,500	25.0
Eating, drinking places	58,125,340	7.0
General Merchandise	91,339,820	11.0
Apparel, Accessories	53,972,530	6.5
Furniture, home furnishings, appliances	39,027,014	4.7
Automotive	142,822,264	17.2
Gasoline service stations	52,312,806	6.3
Lumber, building materials, hardware, farm equipment	41,187,738	4.9
Drug and Proprietary	28,232,308	3.4
Liquor stores	25,741,222	3.1
Jewelry, novelties, gifts	66,098,598	7.9
Recreational and amusements (travel, books, sporting goods)	24,910,860	3.0

Source: State Development Commission.

The third step in appraising any shopping center, established or proposed, lies in the element of evaluation: The center can only be valued as a whole, or single entity, not as separate individual stores or buildings. The center is an aggregate income producer and cannot be evaluated in any other way, since each store has a direct income-producing influence on all the others and is in turn dependent upon the others and mutual parking for its own production. Your appraisal report should thus state its aim—evaluation of the whole.

Appraising the Shopping Center as a Single Entity

Factors in aggregate property analysis. Not only because of the income-producing interdependencies of all the stores within it must the center be appraised as a single entity, or aggregate; it must also be done because of its common parking area and because of the senior position of the "hinge" or "key" store or stores around which the specialty stores in the center are arranged. In the larger centers, the "hinge" will be a junior or senior department store or two; in the smaller centers, perhaps a supermarket. In any event, these "hinges" are the chief draw of the center, without which the surrounding specialty stores would flounder, and probably would not sign for leases in the first place.

Micro-market Interdependencies

Parking. A common parking area is used by the customers of all the tenants in the modern shopping center. The convenience attributes of the parking area are of great value to each merchant, whose sales volume is reflected accordingly, and who pays a percentage rent on that volume. Thus, the parking lot is a production agent of income for all. You could not separately appraise any one on the stores in the cum ulative pull of the center, nor could you separately value the general parking rights underwriting each merchant's success.

Department stores as hinges. In large shopping centers, it is common practice that the key department stores first signing up get benefits at a rental below the market, and sometimes even a gift of the land.

Example: The developer of Lafayette Plaza, in Bridgeport, Connecticut, made a gift of two acres of downtown land to Gimbel's Department Store there, and consequently raised his rents on some eighty specialty stores, spread between Gimbel's and Sears, from $6 per square foot to $12 per square foot.

Here, the increased yield could not have been attained without the magnet of Gimbel's attracting shoppers from a wide trade area.

However, it is important that the major department store not be permitted to become out-size or to occupy more than one-third of the total shopping center area. The mix of merchants and variety of goods is vital to the specialty store that will be carrying the greater burden of aggregate rents.

THE APPROACHES TO VALUE

Since shopping centers large and small are investment properties, primarily built, bought or sold on the basis of their income production, the fourth step in the appraisal of a shopping center leads us to the Income Approach, which is the emphasis of this chapter, with particular attention focussed on capitalizing income into value. The Cost Approach is employed only in conjunction with Residual Techniques under the Income Approach. The Market Data Approach is inapplicable, except in the selection of the virgin site, before agreements to lease have been signed.

TECHNIQUES FOR ESTIMATING VALUE OF LAND AND IMPROVEMENTS IN SHOPPING CENTER APPRAISAL

Procedure for Estimating Land Value by Capitalizing Percentage Rents

The market survey and forecast sets the mold for determining percentage overrides on minimum guaranteed leases to rated national retailers. Now these percentage rents will help the appraiser to estimate the land value of the center.

Once agreements to lease have been secured, the character of the virgin land changes, because it has become productive in its own peculiar way and is no longer comparable to other sites. Its value can only be deducted as follows:

1. The owner's mortgage commitment, necessary to go ahead with construction, will be based on sufficient minimum guaranteed rentals to pay debt service on his loan, after subtracting charges for property taxes, insurance, maintenance and management.
2. The amount of the percentage rents over the minimum guarantees is the *surplus income.*
3. The *surplus income* is now capitalized to create land value.

If the developer and his appraiser have done their homework carefully, comparing notes on Site Analysis and Market Survey and Forecast and the making of the percentage leases, the newly created land value will exceed considerably what the developer paid for the land. Now the *new land value* will be the developer's *equity* in the shopping center.

In sum, when the character of the raw land has been made unique by the nature of the particular percentage leases affecting it, the peculiarity of the subject site makes it nonpareil, or incomparable. *Then the land must be evaluated by capitalization of the residual net income imputable to the land.* A front foot, square foot or acreage valuation can be made to satisfy the appraiser's curiosity as to how far his new valuation may be from Market Data comparables in the vicinity, but land value conclusion must rest on the Land Residual Technique. This is the *fifth step* in shopping center evaluation.

The buildings will be evaluated by the Depreciated Cost Approach, if buildings have been completed; or by hypothetical estimate, if incomplete. This will be the *sixth and final step* in the appraisal of subject property.

Appraisal of a completed shopping center. When the shopping center is complete, with a history of say four years, it has a track record of minimum guaranteed rents plus percentage rents based on sales volumes achieved. There are also receipted payments for actual construction costs, fixed interest and amortization on permanent mortgages, and a record of operating expenses. An updated appraisal can now be made using a capitalization rate based on experience rather than anticipation. The residual net income, capitalized at a relatively low rate because of good prospects or at a high rate for poor prospects, for the center, will give you Market Value for purposes of sale, refinancing, or condemnation proceedings. (See Model Approval at the end of this chapter.)

So-called comparable sales of land or buildings are useless, since the center has established its own track record which has no relationship to sales of other commercial properties in the neighborhood. The Market Data, or comparative method, is inapplicable to shopping centers in operation.

Capitalization Rates. The rate you choose for capitalizing the residual net (surplus) income to find land value must be based on the prospects of the center. An excellent site in a good location in a growing area would call for the lower rate, say 7%; a good site in a competitive location with middling to fair area prospects, might be capitalized at 10%; a center with very poor prospects for the future of the site, location or area, might be penalized with an extreme rate of 13%.

Located on an unimpeded site in a good business section, a center in a dynamic area like Boston, Baltimore, Hartford, Atlanta, Miami, Chicago, Dallas, Los Angeles or San Francisco, where the urban region has a strong and expanding economic base, would call for the lowest capitalization rate.

In a deteriorating or static area, where dying industries, such as anthracite mining, show a pattern of erratic employment, a shopping center would be nailed with a very high capitalization rate, no matter how impressive its site might be.

Fluctuating interest rates on bonds and mortgages, as in 1969 when interest rates jumped from 7% to 9%, also cause capitalization rates to vary. A high interest rate is reflected in a capitalization rate higher than the norm.

The appraiser's common sense and nose for the market must, in the final analysis, be his guide to a precise capitalization rate in a given shopping center situation. But his thought processes must be documented, because 1% in the rate can mean a difference of many thousands of dollars in valuation.

Applications of the Land Residual Technique and the Cost Approach to Building Value

Land value by capitalization of residual net income. You reach the residual net (surplus) income attributable to the land by simple arithmetic. Add, subtract, and divide as follows:

1. Add the total of gross annual rents.
2. Subtract from the gross annual rents a vacancy allowance of 10%. This will leave you "rents collected."
3. Then total "operating expenses," including building maintenance and repairs, advertising and public relations, insurance, property taxes and management. Subtract this total from "rents collected." The balance is the sum *available* for debt service.
4. Now subtract the *actual* amount of debt service from the amount *available* for debt service. The balance is the net residual (surplus) income imputable to the land.
5. Divide the net annual income imputable to land (by percentage leases) by your chosen capitalization rate, between 7% and 13%, depending upon your interpretation of the facts revealed in the Site Analysis and Market Survey and Forecast in your appraisal.

Building value—cost minus depreciation. Steep changes upward in building costs during the past few years require that up-to-date reproduction figures be used in any appraisal as of a current date. These figures can be obtained from various reliable manuals, such as Marshall & Stevens, Dow Services and Boechk's Cost Indices. Realistic depreciation rates can then be applied to deduce current value of improvements.

A shopping center built in 1948 might have been put together for as little as $8. per square foot. Today, the same center might cost $25. per square foot.

Occasionally, all store utilities including fixtures are installed at owner expense, but this occurs only when the developer is having difficulty promoting national "big-name" tenants, in an area where competition is keen. The average tenant will receive only the "shell" of a store from the developer; that is to say, the bare floor, four walls and ceiling. The tenant will then install utilities, fixtures and decorations at his own expense, as leasehold improvements.

Large regional centers must include non-rentable areas for heating and air-conditioning plants serving the mall or plaza covered spaces, with public services such as elevators, escalators and rest rooms. Usually the merchants are asked to share the maintenance of such areas along with the owner. If an escalator or elevator is inside the department store, it is usually built and maintained at the owner's cost. Truck delivery tunnels servicing the merchants are also normally built and maintained at the owner's cost. Police security forces are usually hired and directed by the merchant's association.

National chain tenants usually require that parking areas at least three times their store area be provided. The parking areas must be readily accessible to highway entrance and exit, macadam paved, and flood-lighted at night.

As an appraiser computing all the developer's costs on the basis of each square foot of building area, you would also include architect's and engineer's fees, the contractor's profit, and interest on the interim mortgage financing during construction.

MODEL APPRAISAL OF REGIONAL SHOPPING CENTER IN THROES OF PARTIAL CONDEMNATION OF ITS LAND BY HIGHWAY DEPARTMENT: THE LAND RESIDUAL TECHNIQUE

The purpose and function of this appraisal are set forth in the following letter of transmittal from the appraiser to the owner's legal counsel. The completed report accompanies the letter.

Letter of Transmittal:

Attorney John Doe
29 Blank Street
City

July 10, 1969

Re: Appraisal of "Damages" to
Real Estate located at
West Wagonwheel and I-94
Intersection, City

Owned by: XYZ Plaza, Inc.

Dear Sir:

Upon your request, I have estimated the "Damages" to the real estate above-captioned, caused by a "Partial Take" of land by the State Highway Department for the relocation of I-94.

The "Taking and/or Easement" areas acquired by the State are as shown on the State Project Map attached.

For the purpose of this estimate of "Damages," your appraiser has calculated the State's "Taking" in this acquisition as 65,630 square feet of useable *land.*

Subject land is improved by a Regional Shopping Center, *which has a total useable land area of:*

"Before the Taking"	*1,413,248 square feet*
"After the Taking," land area remaining	*1,347,618 square feet*
Useable land taken by the State	*65,630 square feet*

As a result of this taking, the Furniture Mart, one of the major tenants, was deprived of approximately an acre and a half of customer parking, which constituted severe damage to his Lease, and would have resulted in its cancellation, had not the owner of the center purchased abutting land to replace it.

Therefore, "damages" to Land and Lease are estimated as follows:

Land Damages		
Land value "Before the Taking"=	$2,616,476.00	
Land value "After the Taking"=	2,493,000.00	
Difference and Estimated Land Damages		$123,500.00
Lease Damages		68,000.00
Total Damages		$191,500.00

After a thorough study of the facts and data obtained during this appraisal, and close inspection of the property in May and June of this year, it is my opinion that the "damages" caused by the "Partial Take" of useable land from subject property, as of the date July 1, 1969, is the sum of:

One Hundred Ninety-one Thousand Five Hundred Dollars

($191,500.00)

Respectfully submitted,

____

Appraiser

APPRAISAL REPORT

Land Valuation Before the Taking

The Center is hinged on one major department store and one junior department store, with 60 other stores strung out between them on two levels, all under cover. All percentage leases have paid anticipated returns, as of the fourth year, June 1, 1969. Calculations on land value will, therefore, include income from percentage rentals, reflecting a considerable increase over the 65¢ per square foot that was paid for the land by the owner.

The Reproduction Cost new, less depreciation, of the four-year-old improvements has been estimated by this appraiser, as of July 1, 1969, to be $5,447,053.

Unit land value will be established in this report by use of the Land Residual Technique, employing actual income figures as of July 1, 1969, deducting expenses and that income attributable to the buildings, leaving the income attributable to the land. This residual income will then be capitalized to show land value.

The Land Residual Technique indicates what the land is worth, based upon its actual earnings; in this instance, it is based upon what subject land is producing by its use, as of the date July 1, 1969:

Gross rents	$838,003.88	
Less Vacancy allowance, expenses and reserves	218,015.80	
Effective net income	$619,988.08	
Less Income Attributable to Improvements: $5,447,053 @ 8½%	462,999.50	
[6% interest plus (40-yr. life) 2½% depreciation or recapture]		
Remainder: Income Attributable to Land		$156,988.58
Indicated Land Value:		
$156,988.58 capitalized @ 6%=		$2,616,476.00
	Rounded to:	$2,616,500.00

Value per square foot, *After the Taking,* is derived as follows:

$2,616,500 divided by 1,347,618 sq. ft.=$1.94 p.s.f.

Land Area *Before the Taking* was: 1,413,248 sq. ft.
1,413,248×$1.94= $2,741,700.00
Land Value, *Before the Taking* .... Say, $2,742,000.00

Land Valuation After the Taking

Subject land has been reduced in area as follows:

$$\frac{\text{Area—Taking of useable Land}=65{,}630 \text{ sq. ft.}}{\text{Area—Total Land, Before Taking}=1{,}413{,}248 \text{ sq. ft.}} = 4.64\%$$

It is your appraiser's opinion that the *Taking* caused a *plottage* loss to subject property of 4.64%, and that value *After the Taking,* is consequently diminished by 4.64%, or 9¢ per square foot, to $1.85.

Land Value, *After the Taking,* therefore must be computed as follows:

1,347,618 sq. ft.×$1.85=$2,492,823.30
Rounded to: $2,493,000.00

Land Damages

Land Valuation "Before the Taking"	=$2,616,500.00
Land Valuation "After the Taking"	= 2,493,000.00
Difference and Estimated Land Damages	=$ 123,500.00

Lease Damages

In the Furniture Mart lease modification, the tenant *required,* as a result of the Taking, that the owner of the Center purchase an abutting parcel at the northwest corner of the Center to replace parking space taken from him. That parcel, fronting on the main road, was accordingly acquired by the owner, in substitution for his tenant's loss, at a cost of $3.00 per square foot.

The area of the substitute parcel was 160′ (front)×400′ (depth), or 64,000 square feet in all.

It is your appraiser's opinion that subject owner was damaged to the extent of being forced by the condemnation to substitute land valued at $3.00 p.s.f., for land your appraiser has valued at $1.94 p.s.f. Therefore:

$3.00 minus $1.94=$1.06
64,000 sq. ft.×$1.06=$67,840.00
Lease Damages = Say, $68,000.00

Summary and Total Damages

Land Damages	$123,500.00
Lease Damages	68,000.00
Estimated Total Damages	$191,500.00

VIII

How to Evaluate Office Buildings

In this decade and next, a proliferation of campus-style, suburban office buildings will be constructed for major corporations escaping the congestion of the inner core cities. Some of these corporate headquarters office complexes will have their own airfields or heliports, and many will have acres of parking and their own restaurants and recreational facilities. For the most part, such office complexes will be designed for a single corporate entity and owned by the occupant. Therefore, this chapter will be confined to the multi-tenanted, downtown, high-rise office-building which can be described as income, or investment property.

Introduction

Unlike retail properties, office building locations are not tested by regional or national market surveys. Location is of prime importance to the value of an office building, but chiefly in the micro-market sense as it relates to the immediate environment in which it stands. Data emphasis in the appraisal of an office building is therefore placed on the commercial block and district, on the municipality and to a limited degree, the suburban macro-market area immediately surrounding the city and the site.

A properly located and successfully rented office building, will generally be found nested in an established commercial district, where public transportation is at hand, where banks and other financial services flourish, and where stores, restaurants and parking are on the premises or nearby. No two office buildings are ever quite alike in tenant mix and income flow. Each tends to develop its own flavor or character as a "lawyers" or "doctors" building, or as headquarters for prominent companies.

The appraisal of an office building may be based on plans for a proposed structure on a given site as a feasibility study to test highest and best use of the land; or it may be a report on a finished building, brand new, recent, middle-aged, or old, with or without a long-term financial history. In any case, rents can be "stabilized" for the subject property by comparison and adjustment with other office rentals in the city. A neighborhood Tenant-profile should be developed early in the appraisal, based on comparative office occupancies. The profile should describe the typical area tenant, office sizes in demand, and general tenant requirements for maintenance and services.

Dominant aspects of value in office buildings. In any office building, large or small, it is essential that the floor plan produce out of its gross area the greatest possible number of square feet of useable, rentable space. Architectural expertise in the arrangement of the lobby on the ground floor, and placement of stairs, elevators, lavatories, corridors and utility rooms on the upper floors, is of vital significance. Column spacing should be designed to allow partition rearrangement for tenants expanding or diminishing their offices. The mechanical equipment of the building—heating, lighting, air-conditioning, elevator-capacity, plumbing, wiring, fire-equipment and sound-proofing—bears heavily on rental return as well as on comfort and safety. Tenants pay for comfort and safety and quiet enjoyment of the premises, and if they are not provided with these services, the income from the deficient office building will be poor. The aspects which make up the personality or character of the property dominate the quality of tenant the building attracts, hence the quantity and quality and durability of the building's income.

The appraiser's *initial step* in evaluating an existing or proposed office building is to process its actual or hypothetical income, gross to effective gross to net. He decides upon capitalization method, rate and valuation technique only after examining all the circumstances surrounding his subject's profitability or lackluster performance, basing his conclusions on the dominant aspects of value that created the situation.

Market Survey and Property Analysis

The *second step* the appraiser takes in evaluating a proposed or existing office-building is to gather and correlate data which exposes the likelihood of success or failure in renting up an office building at a given location within the city. He relates this information to his analysis of the subject property in this manner:

1. *Prospects.* Macro-market influence of area economic situation, measured against the micro-market demand for office space in the city. In measuring area vs. local economic conditions, the following factors must be scrutinized:

a) Type of city government and its effectiveness politically and economically, together with a synopsis of the city's reason for being (i.e. importance as a railhead, communications center, harbor and/or airport facility). Indications of growth or decline in such facilities.

b) Population of the city itself and population of suburbs within a 15-mile radius. Forms of transportation within the city and to and from the suburbs and other cities. Chief forms of employment within the city and within a 15-mile radius.

c) Principal industries within the city, their growth patterns, and public utilities that serve them. The amount and substance of industry in the area and its contribution, if any, to the commerce of the city. The city's atmosphere as an industrial, commercial or cultural (university) center, with all three described if necessary.

d) The planning and zoning practices, the tax policies, and local ordinances affecting the property and its district must be stated clearly.

e) Where is the demand for office space coming from? Is the pressure for office space from the micro-market within the city, i.e. growth of banks, law and accounting firms, medical services? or is it from the macro-market outside the city, i.e. branch offices of national corporations, insurance companies, manufacturers' representatives? or both? State the scope and intensity of this demand, or lack of it.

2. *Market Analysis of the Commercial District and block.* Micro-market data concerning the immediate vicinity of the proposed or existing office building should be set forth as follows:

a) Assuming that highest and best use of the site is an office building, with public transportation and automobile parking at hand, surrounded by banks, stock-brokerages, high grade shops, restaurants and other conveniences, where will the tenants for the proposed or existing office building come from? State the rent per square foot in competing office buildings nearby. Note number of vacancies.

b) Describe trends in the district and block. Is the district growing or decaying? Is redevelopment underway? Is the block the best one in the district? How far away is city hall, the public library, hospitals, medical clinics, the newspaper plant, public utility offices? Is the district served by main highways, and a sensible traffic pattern? Is it readily accessible to other important districts within the city?

3. *Property Analysis and History.* Specific details of the property under appraisement must be clearly delineated: (a) Recitation of the title, including metes and bounds, assessments and tax levy; (b) Zone requirements; (c) Description of the site topography and subsoil conditions, plottage and shape of the land area, together with list of utilities on site or available; (d) The type of construction, use and condition of the proposed or existing building and its machinery, together with site improvements, planned or existing, such as paved parking, fencing, outdoor floodlighting; (e) Each floor of the building must be measured and described; (f) A summary of the development of the property, if existing, with a five-to-ten year history of income and expense, and type of management and maintenance attending the property; (g) The anticipated useful life of the property must be estimated and allowances made for depreciation and obsolescence.

If the building is proposed or in the planning stage, the appraiser must project income and expenses for five years from his knowledge and experience in new office building construction, and recommend management and maintenance procedures for the proposed building that are both practical and economic.

4. *Comparable Land Sales and Office Leases.* The appraiser must list in detail verified data concerning land sales and leases of office space for buildings similar to the subject property, in the locale of the subject property. These comparables should be inspected and similarities or differences described, as compared to subject land or office space, summing up the property analysis.

THE APPROACHES TO VALUE

The appraiser's *third step* in office building appraisal lies in his choice of Approaches.

Usually an office building is somewhat different from any other, in terms of location, tenant mix and income flow, not to mention age, style and services. Thus its character tends to make it distinct and difficult to compare with sales of other office buildings, when estimating value.

This makes the Market Data Approach generally inapplicable, *except for purposes of estimating land value, and gauging the office rental market.*

In the evaluation of an office building, the *Cost Approach* lends better support to the Income Approach than Market Data, because the Cost Approach leads the appraiser to a close examination of construction details, and the age, condition and and anticipated life of the property, hence the life of the income stream. The ratio of effective age of the building to life expectancy is crucial.

The *Income Approach* is the chief guide to value and is the proper test of an office structure's ability to throw off a worthwhile investment yield over a long period of time.

Since the market value of an office building depends to a great extent upon the *present worth of its future earnings,* the appraiser must rationally anticipate such earnings and estimate how long they will endure, if he is to calculate their present worth in money.

Capitalization rates on office buildings will vary with circumstances. Yield percentages will differ. Choice of capitalization rate and method is the appraiser's critical *fourth step* in evaluating an office building.

Capitalization Methods. Depending upon the *quality and durability* of income (see Chapter V) flowing from the property you are appraising, you can elect to follow either of the following courses of capitalization:

1. Use the straight-line depreciation plus capitalization-rate method of capitalization when you anticipate that the net income before depreciation *will decline* regularly each year in the future.

2. But if the net income before depreciation is expected to be level or better and is *of a contract nature,* say with a bank on the ground floor; if the financial stability of the upper floor office tenants is substantial and the leases extend over a period of at least *twelve years,* then the Inwood premise may be used. This premise is used only on prime office buildings with rated corporations as tenants on long-term leases. (See Chapter V, page 79.)

TECHNIQUES FOR ESTIMATING VALUE OF LAND AND IMPROVEMENTS IN OFFICE BUILDING APPRAISAL

Procedure for Estimating a Separate Land Value Under the Office Building

As the *fifth step* in office building evaluations, it is best to estimate land value, particularly where Market Data on nearby vacant land is sufficient.

On occasion such Market Data may be scarce, but the appraiser may know from the outset the value of the building, particularly if the structure is new, or recent, and the builder's costs are competitive and at hand. In that case, the appraiser would set up his Cost Approach first, and find his land value using the Land Residual Technique. This process was demonstrated in Chapter VI, page 97, in the Model Appraisal. It is a valid application to land under office buildings.

Methods of evaluating land. Land value may be estimated by: (1) Recent sales of nearby vacant land; (2) Recently executed land leases; (3) The Land Residual Technique. (For explanation of this technique, see Model Appraisal, Chapter VI, page 93.) This chapter will emphasize the first method, recent sales of nearby vacant land, with adjustments of comparables as described in Chapter VI, page 92.

Procedure for Estimating Value of the Improvements in Office Building Appraisals

Residual techniques under the Income Approach. An older property may be leased for rentals that, capitalized, prove investment or market value greater than Depreciated Reproduction Cost could show, which is contrary to the fact that on new or recent buildings the Cost Approach is usually the upper limit of value.

Therefore, we will turn to other means of finding the value of office building improvements, when the value of the land is already known through Market Data. These means are provided by the Building Residual Technique under the Income Approach. This is the *sixth and final step* in the appraiser's road to valuation of an office structure.

In the following Model Appraisal of a middle-aged downtown office building, the *Building Residual Technique* is employed as stronger proof of value than the Cost Approach shows. (Nevertheless, the Cost Approach has contributed much to the appraiser's knowledge of the construction.)

MODEL APPRAISAL OF OFFICE BUILDING: USING COST APPROACH IN SUPPORT OF THE BUILDING RESIDUAL TECHNIQUE UNDER THE INCOME APPROACH

The following is an appraisal of an office building in the interior of a downtown block in a city in the Northeast. The structure has an established character as a lawyers' building, with a prominent bank as tenant on the ground floor with basement vault, but the age of the building and its mechanical equipment has limited rental returns on the upper floors. Such properties, with proper improvements, generally represent highest and best use of the land.

Purpose and Function of the Appraisal

Fair Market Value for condemnation by Urban Redevelopment Agency.

Valuation Premise

City population is 250,000, surrounded by easy-access suburbs within 15-mile radius aggregating a population of 368,500.

Subject property is aging, with functional inutilities on the upper floors, but is strategically located in the prime downtown block.

Market Survey and Property Analysis (abbreviated)

City and area economic prospects are bright. Trend is toward population increase in the area, and expanded commercial and industrial activity in the city, stemming from micro-market outburst of growth in local banks, insurance and utility companies, plus limited macro-market demand from incoming concerns from other cities in the fields of law, insurance, engineering, shipping, medical research and manufacturing, most of which require modern office facilities with parking. *Tenant-profile*: Typical office tenant in this city requires 1,000 s.f., air-conditioned, with 5 parking spaces and cleaning services included in a 5-10-year lease. He is a professional, employs 5 others, and is currently paying $6. p.s.f. for older, less attractive space. More than 100 such tenants are looking for new space.

Macro-market Study

Government is by Mayor and City Council. Elected officials are progressives who pioneered redevelopment in this part of the nation, as leaders of a growing cultural and industrial city with a large university and medical school at its center. The city is an important communications and shipping center with rail-head and marshalling yards. The harbor is deep water, and raw materials from world ports are brought here.

City unemployment is less than 3% of the adult population.

Defense contracts account for less than 15% of the total annual industrial output, locally.

Micro-market Analysis of the District and Block

The district, block and subject site constitute the prime downtown professional service core of the city. On this block, immediately to the east of subject is another older bank building on the corner, also being taken by the Redevelopment Agency to increase plottage for a new and higher structure with parking. To the west in this order are city hall, U.S. post office, police headquarters, the federal courthouse, the power and light building, and the main office of the telephone company.

One block to the east is a large, regional shopping center, with 80-store mall connecting two major department stores, linked to the municipal parking garage.

The district, block and subject are most auspicious for bank and office use, and the demand for both new and older office space is brisk.

Property Analysis and History

Following a recitation of grantor, grantee, date of transfer with volume and page from the land records, and type of deed with metes and bounds, tax information, zone and zone requirements, the property may be analyzed as follows:

The Site

Frontage extends 64.30′ on the northerly side of Federal Street, by 200′ average depth abutting city hall on the west. The topography is flat and on level with street. Subsoil is impacted gravel over hardpan and rock. (Available utilities, street improvements, public transportation, etc., included here.)

The site is within three blocks of entrance and exit ramps at junction of interstate highways. It is two blocks from the railroad station and bus depot, and two miles from the airport.

Improvements

The site is improved with a 14-story, masonry-on-steel bank and office building with basement bank vault and boiler-room. Structure was built in 1920. Lobby modernized in 1955. Two passenger elevators and one freight elevator, operated by car switch control. Cab modernization in 1955. Air-conditioning above the bank level by individual room units only, at tenant expense. The land area is 12,800 square feet, of which the basement excavation is 11,133 square feet. On the ground level, the building's exterior is 12,267 square feet. At the second floor level and straight up, the tower is set back, so that exterior floors above the first have 6,600 square feet each.

Justification of Land Values

Five recent sales of comparable land in the same zone of the business district are cited here. After study and analysis with careful adjustments as to time elapsed since date of sale, location, plottage, shape and corner influence, these sales indicate a value to subject of $40. per square foot.

Therefore, 12,800 sq. ft. × $40. = $512,000. stated as:

Estimated Value of the Land

Five Hundred Twelve Thousand Dollars
($512,000.00)

Building Description, Area and Condition

The exterior floor areas are as follows:

Basement	11,133 square feet
First Floor (fully occupied by bank)	12,267 square feet
Second Floor through 14th floor, each @ 6,600 sq. ft. × 12 =	79,200 square feet
Total	102,600 square feet

(A detailed description of the building, floor by floor, including electrical services, basement mechanicals, roof construction, elevator, motor room, etc., would follow here. Ceiling heights, type of partitioning, corridor width and length, lavatory equipment, itemized piece by piece, must be indicated. Physical and functional depreciation must be carefully noted.)

Cost Approach

Building:

Using the cost index of an approved valuation service, the following square foot reproduction cost of building is developed:

102,600 square feet @ $20.34 =	$2,086,884.
Add—Basement office (bank) 5,600 square feet @ $10.65 + 26¢ for heat adjustment = $10.91 × 5,600 square feet =	61,096.
Basement—Storage and heating $7.98 + heat adjustment of $1.19 = $9.17 × 5,533 square feet =	50,737.
	$2,198,717.

$2,198,717. × 1.08 (local multiplier) equals $2,374,614.

Estimated Reproduction Cost of Building—$2,374,614.

Bank Premises:

The costs of the improvements in the bank-leased premises in 1955 were $200,000. and included copper-framed plate glass windows, marble flooring, vaults, trim, safe deposit boxes, dome, lighting, etc. that became part of the real estate.

Original Cost—1955 . . . . $200,000.

Adjustment Factor	
Average 1968 = 3.68	
$200,000 × 3.85 =	$770,000.
Deduction for Vault Doors	75,000.
Estimated Reproduction Cost	$695,000.

Explanation of Depreciation

Building:

The physical depreciation as observed includes painting, decorating, pointing, roofing, electrical equipment and lighting fixtures, plumbing and plumbing fixtures, floor covering, window frames and sash, heating plant. The functional depreciation includes wash basins and toilet facilities for different sexes on alternating floors.

The physical depreciation is calculated on a ratio of effective age to life expectancy.

The maintenance has been good. There are no evidences of neglected or deferred maintenance, due to the renovations necessary to keep the property attractive to tenants. The effective age is estimated at 33 years, and the life expectancy at 99 years, or 33/99ths which equals 33% physical or $651,862.00.

Functional—installing male, or female, lavatories on floors and nine (9) stall type urinals.

30 Water closets—Floor type—White 3 per unit, each @ $340. (Flush valve)	$10,200.
9 urinals @ $516.67 each unit =	4,650.
40 sinks (wash basins, 4 per lavatory) 24″ × 20″ @ $325.00	13,000.
	$27,850.

Time location multiplier—1.10
1.10 × $27,850. = $30,635.00

Estimated Functional Depreciation . . . . (Cost to cure toilet inadequacies on alternate floors)	$30,635.00
Estimated Total Depreciation of Building . . . . ($651,862.00 + $30,635.00)	$682,497.00

Bank Premises:

Estimated Life Expectancy	50 years	
Estimated Effective Age	30 years	
Estimated Depreciation (30/50ths)	60%	
Estimated Depreciation ($695,000. @ 60%)		$417,000.
Estimated Depreciated Cost		$278,000.

The physical depreciation is as observed. Consideration was given in estimating depreciation to painting, marble floor, wear and tear, window frames and sills, metal dome, and contemporary style, design and layout. The estimate was based on a ratio of effective age to life expectancy.

Summary:

	Reproduction Cost		*Depreciation*		*Depreciated Cost*
Building	\$2,374,614.	−	\$682,497.	=	\$1,692,117.
Bank Premises	\$ 695,000.	−	\$417,000.	=	\$ 278,000.
Add Land					\$ 512,000.
					\$2,482,117.
			Rounded to		\$2,482,100.

Estimated Market Value of the Property by Cost Approach
Two Million Four Hundred Eighty-two Thousand One Hundred Dollars
(\$2,482,100.00)

Income Approach

Synopsis of Lease Agreement between Bank and Owner

Area: Entire first floor except foyer, elevator, hall, shaft and stairway. Also basement under first floor, approximately 56′×100′, or 5,600 sq. ft.

Term: Ten years from September 1, 1959.

Annual Rent: \$17,500.

Lessors Pay: Water, heat, skylight repairs, keep lobby floor clean, clear snow; toilet and pipe (plumbing) repairs, sidewalk cleaning, elevator hoistway door repairs, and liability insurance thereon.

Lessees Pay: Glass on premises, painting, repairs of interior, and removal of rubbish. Pays for gas, electricity, and public liability insurance, \$50,000 per person and \$100,000 for one accident, and bank clearing services.

Taxes: Lessee pays on fixtures, safes and vaults.

Herewith are statements of income for the years commencing January 1, 1963 to December 31, 1968 and Rent Rolls of tenants for the same years as supplied by rental and management agents for the subject property.

Rental Income—1968	\$261,600.41
Miscellaneous Rental Income	60.00
Other Income—Vending Machines	6,178.92
Insurance Rebates	23.00
Income Credits Due to Errors, etc.	100.55
Income Telephone Pay Stations	53.83
Total	\$268,016.71

(Earlier years inserted here)

A statement of rental loss due to vacancies, for the years 1963, 1964, 1965, 1966, 1967, is listed as follows:

Office Number	*Date of Vacancy*	*Monthly Rent*	*Months Lost*	*Annual Rental*	*Total*
401	10/31/67	$165.	12	$1,980.	$1,980.
402	10/31/67	$160.	12	$1,720.	$1,790.
403	10/31/67	$120.	12	$2,440.	$1,440.

etc., (list is foreshortened in this example)

Total Annual Rental Income Loss Due to Vacancies ..... $39,372.
Total Vacancy Loss, 1963 to 1968, incl. .... $76,411.

Note: Owing to the shadow of condemnation, which has been widely publicized in the city for the past three years, existing leases do not reflect the general increase in rental values in the district in the past four years. Therefore, I will estimate current stabilized economic rentals for subject property by going into the market for comparable space in the district. These are as follows:

Ground Floor Space Comparables:

Five rentals of similar nearby ground level space are cited here. After adjustment in detail, they indicate an annual rental value of $8.50 per square foot for subject.

Office Space Comparables:

Five rentals of similar upper floor space are cited here. After adjustment in detail, they indicate an annual rental value of $5.00 per square foot for upper floors in subject building.

Basement Comparables:

The same comparison is made for finished basement retail space in the district, indicating a value of $4.25 per square foot for subject.

Explanation of Stabilized Economic Rentals:

After a study and analysis of the various foregoing rentals I have stabilized the economic rents for the subject property as follows:

Basement .... $4.25 per square foot
Bank Space .... $8.50 per square foot
Third through 14th floors .... $5.00 per square foot

With subtractions on the first floor for the space devoted to the corridor, elevator and stairway, and ditto for the second through fourteenth floors. Also deducting floor space in the upper structure for each floor on which there are not male and female wash room and toilet facilities provided, for which I have made a provision for functional depreciation using the Cost-to-Cure Method.

The Building Residual Technique is used in the Income Approach to estimate value.

Calculations:

Basement—Bank space—5,600 square feet @ $4.25 per square foot=	$23,800.
First Floor—Bank Space—less foyer, elevator and stairway spaces. 11,098 square feet @ $8.50 per square foot=	94,333.
Second floor to 14th floor (net rentable) 60,000 square feet @ $5.00 per square foot=	300,000.
Gross Income	$418,133.
Vacancy and rent loss—5%	20,906.
Effective Gross Income	$397,227.

Effective Gross Income		$397,227.
Expenses (1968):		
Tenancies, building maintenance and reserves	$20,000.	
Fuel	5,500.	
Janitors & Elevators Operators	35,000.	
Water	1,500.	
Electricity	13,500.	
Management	9,500.	
Miscellaneous	3,500.	
Insurance	5,000.	
Taxes	32,500.	
Elevator Service	1,500.	
Total:		$127,500.
Net Income:		$269,727.
Interest imputable to Land ($512,000×7.75%)		39,680.
Interest to Improvements		$230,047.

Therefore, $230,047÷11.75%=	$1,957,846.
Add Land	512,000.
Total	$2,469,846.
Rounded to	$2,470,000.

Estimated Market Value of the Subject Property by Income Approach

Two Million Four Hundred Seventy Thousand Dollars
($2,470,000.00)

Explanation of Expenses:

The 1968 expenses are taken from the ledger with additions and adjustments based on increased costs of materials, utilities and labor. The taxes have been adjusted to reflect an estimated adjusted assessment based on market value of the land as estimated in this appraisal. A knowledgeable purchaser would make a study of other properties on this street and adjust his expenses against the property based on an anticipated realistic adjustment of the land assessment.

Explanation of Capitalization Rate:

A responsible investor would expect to be able to procure a mortgage of 65% of the value of the subject property at an interest

rate of	7.5 %
the product of which is	4.87%
and Equity of 35% at 8% return	2.80%
Total	7.67%
Say	7.75%

On improving a building the age and type of the subject, an informed investor would expect a recapture of investment in 25 years, or at the rate of 4% per annum; then,

Interest on Land	7.75%
Interest and Recapture on Improvement	4.00%
Total	11.75%

Conclusion:

Cost Approach. The Cost Approach usually reflects the upper limit of value. I consider it a useful tool in giving support to the Income Approach on which I am placing reliance for my value conclusion. On an investment property such as the subject, I consider the Income Approach processed to a value conclusion as the most reliable indicator of value.

Market Data Approach. It is impossible to find an office building of similar design, construction, materials and usage, on a parcel of land and in a location that would be considered of comparable quality to the subject. Therefore, I considered this approach inapplicable.

Income Approach. I consider this approach the most reliable indicator of value.

Estimated Market Value by Market Data Approach .... Land Only
Estimated Market Value by Cost Approach .... $2,482,100.
Estimated Market Value by Income Approach .... $2,470.000.

Estimated Market Value of the Property

Two Million Four Hundred Seventy Thousand Dollars
($2,470,000.00)

IX

How to Appraise Apartment Houses

The term "apartment house" covers such a variety of forms of multi-family dwellings, that we must at once narrow the range to be examined here. Our aim is to choose a median which is in between the modest suburban garden-apartment walk-up and the mammoth, downtown 50-story deluxe apartment complex of the big city. Further, the examples stressed here must demonstrate procedures applicable to both ends of the range in a locale at the perimeter of, say, a medium-sized city, where land values might be average for the nation. Therefore, this chapter will be confined to the middle-income, modern, high-rise apartment house which is built, owned, managed, bought or sold as investment property.

Introduction

Location is of prime importance to the value of an apartment house, particularly as it relates to the attractiveness of the immediate environment and the city or town in which it stands. Micro-market data emphasis in the appraisal of an apartment house is, therefore, placed on the site and neighborhood. But the economic well-being of the area is also important and macro-market statistics on area population and city employment are vital, up to a distance of an hour in commuting time.

A properly located and successfully rented apartment house, is likely to be found in a residential zone of good quality, where public transportation is at hand, not too far from schools, churches, and cultural and recreational facilities, and in a neighborhood where stores, restaurants, banks and professional services are nearby. Off-street private parking or garaging on at least a one-for-one allotment basis is a must for apartment dwellings; and in most municipalities this minimum, or a two-for-one allotment is required by zoning.

The appraisal of an apartment house may be based on plans for a proposed structure on a given site as a feasibility study to test highest and best use of the land; or it may be a report on a finished building for mortgage refinancing, with or without a long-term financial history. In any case, rents can be "stabilized" for the subject property by comparison and adjustment with other apartment rentals in the area.

If the subject apartment house is proposed and in the planning stage, a design and tenant profile should be developed before the architect reaches the stage of working drawings. The profile may be based on comparative properties in the area, and/or a questionnaire based on a direct-mail sampling of apartment-dwellers in the locale. Even in the appraisal of an existing apartment house, a tenant profile is important to the owner who may be guided by it in making future alterations, and to the mortgage lender who may be asked for refinancing. This profile should reflect effective demand, the type of units and number of rooms called for, and design preferences in both the micro-market and macro-market. Such a profile might appear in the market survey as follows:

Tenant and Design Profile

(On the basis of 200 neighborhood prospects surveyed)

Element	*Aggregate*
Average Family Size:	2.06 persons; 36% require 1-BR; 24% 2-BR; 24% 3-BR; 16% Efficiencies
Average Age of Family Head:	48 years; 75% are 40 to 65 years.
Families with children:	36%
Occupational Activity:	18% professional; 49% executive, 26% retired; 7% other.
Places of Work:	61% downtown business core; 22% north side of city; 10% south side: 7% other.
Commutation to Work:	79% automobile; 21% bus.
Commutation Time to Work Less than 30 minutes:	83%; and 17% less than one hour.
Former Domicile:	61% from nearby communities.
Type of Former Dwelling:	59% Single family; 41% apartment.
Average Anticipated Tenancy and Attainable Rent per Room:	10 years; $100. per room per month.
Summation and Recommendation:	Location is ideal, and justifies de luxe high-rise with pool, sauna and other amenities, 158 units.

DOMINANT ASPECTS OF VALUE IN APARTMENT HOUSES

After location, the functional design of the apartment building is of maximum importance to its value. Living space should be roomy, and well-closeted, with neatly arranged kitchens and bathrooms, and with exterior exposure and balcony wherever possible. Architectural expertise in the arrangement of the living quarters, and central placement of lobby, elevators, corridors and laundry rooms so that these services are readily accessible to tenants is vital. Certain amenity factors, such as prestige, security and satisfaction in the home, bear a value to apartment buildings, just as they do to individually owned residences.

The mechanical equipment of the building—heating, lighting, air-conditioning, elevator-capacity, plumbing, wiring, and fire-proofing—bears heavily on rental return.

Management is of equal importance to value in an apartment building. Tenants pay for comfort and safety and quiet enjoyment of the premises, and if they are not provided with responsible maintenance the income from aggrieved tenants will be erratic, if not halted altogether, with less desirable tenants replacing those moving out. The aspects which characterize the property as excellent or poor in design and maintenance dominate the quality of tenant the building attracts, hence the quantity and quality and durability of the building's income.

The appraiser's *initial step* in evaluating an existing or proposed apartment building is to process its actual or hypothetical income. He decides upon capitalization method, rate and valuation technique only after examining the quality of the subject's income stream, basing his conclusions on the dominant aspects of value that created the situation, namely the ease or difficulty with which the owner has collected his rents, filled his vacancies, reduced his turnover and kept his expenses in line. A properly designed, functional and well-maintained apartment building reassures the appraiser.

Market Survey and Property Analysis

The *second step* the appraiser takes in evaluating a proposed or existing apartment house is to gather and correlate data which exposes the likelihood of success or failure in renting up the building at a given location. He relates this information to his analysis of the subject property in this manner:

1. *Prospects.* Macro-market influences of area economic situation, measured against the micro-market demand for apartment space in the city. In measuring local economic conditions, the following factors must be scrutinized:

a) Population of the municipality and the area within a 15-mile radius. Forms of transportation within the municipality and to and from subject location. Chief forms of employment within the locale, and estimate of present and future employment levels.

b) The amount and substance of commerce and industry in the area, and its contribution to the growth of the locale. The city's importance as an industrial, commercial or cultural (university) center.

c) The planning and zoning practices, the tax policies, and local ordinances affecting the property and the neighborhood must be noted.

d) Cultural and recreational facilities provided, including theaters, museums, libraries, parks, sports centers and clubs.

e) Seasonal conditions and the prevailing climate.

2. *Market Analysis of the neighborhood.* Micro-market data concerning the immediate vicinity of the proposed or existing apartment building should be set forth as follows:

a) Assuming that highest and best use of the site is an apartment building, with public transportation and automobile parking at hand, and shopping not far away, is the neighborhood quiet, orderly and sedate? Is accessibility to the neighborhood easy and attractive? Are there evidences of traffic congestion, air pollution or other inharmonious elements?

b) Describe trends in the neighborhood. What is family income level here? What is average family size and composition? Is police and fire service at hand? Are medical services adequate? Is garbage removal service frequent and efficient?

c) Are churches of several denominations nearby? Are there both elementary and high schools, public and parochial?

d) Do the amenities of the neighborhood far outweigh any drawbacks? Is the trend for the neighborhood upgrade, static or downgrade? Is the site the best available in the neighborhood?

3. *Property analysis and history.* Specific details of the property under appraisement must be clearly delineated: (a) Recitation of the title, including metes and bounds, assessments and tax levy; (b) Zone requirements; (c) Description of the site topography and subsoil conditions, plottage and shape of the land area, together with list of utilities on site or available; (d) The type of construction, use and condition of the proposed or existing building and its machinery, together with site improvements, planned or existing, such as paved parking, fencing, and outdoor floodlighting; (e) Each floor of the building must be measured and described; (f) A summary of the development of the property, if existing, with a five-year history of income and expense, and type of management and maintenance attending the property; (g) The anticipated useful life of the property must be estimated and allowances made for depreciation and obsolescence.

If the building is proposed or in the planning stage, the appraiser must project income and expenses for five years from his knowledge and experience in new apartment house construction, and recommend management and maintenance procedures for the proposed building that are both practical and economic.

4. *Comparable land sales and apartment leases.* The appraiser must list in detail verified data concerning land sales and leases of apartments in buildings similar to the subject property, in the locale of the subject property. These comparables should be inspected and similarities or differences described, as compared to subject land or apartments, summing up the property analysis.

THE APPROACHES TO VALUE

The appraiser's *third step* in apartment house appraisal lies in his choice of Approaches.

Every apartment house has its own peculiarities in terms of location, land area and income flow, not to mention age, design and services. Thus its nature tends to make it distinct and difficult to compare with sales of other apartment buildings, when estimating value.

This makes the Market Data Approach generally inapplicable, *except for purposes of estimating land value, and gauging the apartment rental market.*

In the evaluation of an apartment building, the *Cost Approach* lends better support to the Income Approach than Market Data, because the Cost Approach leads the appraiser to a close examination of construction details, and the age, condition and remaining economic life of the property. However, Reproduction Cost less depreciation only sets an upper limit of value. The real test is investment value.

The *Income Approach* is the investor's guide to value, which can rest upon the proper capitalization of net income, less the cost of curing whatever deferred maintenance there may be.

Since the market value of an apartment building depends to a great extent upon the *present worth of its future earnings,* the appraiser must rationally anticipate such earnings and estimate how long they will endure, if he is to calculate their present worth in money.

Capitalization Rates and Methods. Capitalization rates on apartment properties will vary with circumstances. Choice of capitalization rate and method is the appraiser's critical *fourth step* in evaluation of an apartment property.

Depending upon the *quality and durability* of income flowing from the property you are appraising, you can elect to follow either of the following courses of capitalization:

1. Use the straight-line depreciation plus capitalization-rate method of capitalization when leases are short-term and the net income before depreciation is therefore uncertain for each year in the future. This method is demonstrated in connection with the Building Residual Technique in the Model Appraisal of an apartment house at the end of this chapter.

2. But if the net income before depreciation is expected to be level or better and is *of a contract nature,* say, on long-term leases with security deposits from tenants of financial stability, and there is a long waiting list of tenant applicants for apartments so located that extended popularity is implicit, then the *Property Residual Technique* in conjunction with the Inwood or Hoskold premises can be used as a truly sound means of appraising investment realty. This technique treats the worth of the property as an undivided entity during the entire economic life of the building, at the end of which the land reverts to its virgin state as vacant and is evaluated as a reversionary interest.

TECHNIQUES FOR ESTIMATING VALUE OF LAND AND IMPROVEMENTS IN APARTMENT HOUSE APPRAISAL

Procedure for Estimating a Separate Land Value Under the Apartment Dwelling

The Land Residual Technique is best used on a new project where the cost of the apartment building is a known factor. In that case, the appraiser would set up his

Cost Approach first and find his land value as demonstrated in the Model Appraisal. It is a valid application to land under apartment buildings. Estimating land value is the appraiser's *fifth step* in apartment property evaluation.

Procedure for Estimating Value of the Improvements In Apartment House

If the appraiser has established his land value via ample Market Data, particularly in the case of an older building, then the Building Residual Technique is the best avenue to value of the improvements.

If the value of the building turns out to be near its depreciated cost, then the appraiser should turn back to the Land Residual process in capitalization of net income.

If the worth of neither land nor building is known, then either the building's value for depreciation purposes must be assumed or land value must be assumed for reversionary purposes only, and the Property Residual Technique is employed. When the appraiser has chosen his basic residual technique, his sixth and final step is estimating value of the improvements.

In the following Model Appraisal of a four-year-old, eight-story apartment building, the straight-line method of capitalization is employed as the most common in apartment house valuation, where short leases generally prevail. The capitalization rate has been composed under the Band of Investment Theory.

MODEL APPRAISAL OF APARTMENT HOUSE USING COST APPROACH IN SUPPORT OF THE BUILDING RESIDUAL TECHNIQUE UNDER THE INCOME APPROACH

The following is an appraisal of a modern apartment house in a college neighborhood at the perimeter of a city in the Northeast. The structure has an established identity as an apartment building for business and professional people and faculty from the college. However, leases are short term, and competitive apartments are under construction nearby. Such a property, used as a college dormitory, would represent highest and best use of the land, at this location.

Purpose and Function of the Appraisal

Fair Market Value for sale to the college as dormitory.

Valuation Premise

City population is 300,000, surrounded by easy-access suburbs within 15-mile radius aggregating a population of 450,000.

Subject property is modern in every aspect, with ample parking, and is strategically located on downtown and crosstown bus routes offering transportation every fifteen minutes.

Market Survey and Property Analysis (Macro-market)

Prospects for city and area are promising. Trend is toward population increase in the area, and expanded commercial and industrial activity in the city, stemming from outburst of growth in local banks, insurance and utility companies, plus demand from incoming concerns in the fields of law, engineering, shipping, insurance, medical research and manufacturing, most of which require residential facilities for their employees at moderate cost. Several bus lines serve the city in all directions, and two of these stop directly in front of subject location. Taxi service at subject location is prompt. Arterial routes by automobile to all parts of the city are at hand.

The city has twelve public parks (one of which is about a block from subject location). It also has five museums, six public library locations, and a legitimate theater traditionally given to Broadway try-outs. There are two municipal golf courses, a municipal ice-skating rink, and three public swimming pools. Clubs and civic and fraternal associations are numerous. Temperature climate is enjoyable most of the year, although winter months are apt to be harsh.

Market Analysis of the Neighborhood (Micro-market)

Neighborhood is urban residential and is characterized by the presence of the state college, with campus adjacent easterly to the subject.

Available utilities include water, gas, electricity, and sanitary and storm sewers, all connected to the subject site.

Frontage is a hard-surfaced macadam artery, with sidewalks, curbs, fire hydrants and street-lights.

Such community services as stores, churches and schools are in convenient proximity to the subject property. Public transportation is available at the subject property. A shopping center and cinema are less than ¼ mile west of the subject.

The neighborhood is most auspicious for high-rise apartment use, and the demand for modern apartments at moderate rentals is brisk, but the rental market is tempered by the fact that 3,500 rental units are now under construction in the area, and supply may overtake demand in the near future. (Tenant profile follows here. See page 133.)

Property Analysis and History

Following a recitation of grantor, grantee, date of transfer with volume and page from the land records, and type of deed with metes and bounds, tax information, zone and zone requirements, the property may be analyzed as follows:

The Site

Enjoying a frontage of approximately 350 feet, the property has an average depth of 235 feet and a rear boundary running 419.85 feet. Total area is approximately 86,000 square feet or two acres, of which 50,000 square feet is paved, outside of the building area, with bituminous asphalt and marked for parking of 92 automobiles. An open culvert runs along the southerly boundary of the property. Landscaping includes an abundance of trees and shrubs made up of pine, oak, maple, flowering dogwood upright and spreading, and rhododendron. Grass turf borders and islands are well maintained.

Justification of Land Values

All five comparable land sales submitted fall within a narrow range. However, Sale No. 4 comes nearest to the subject in comparable plottage, neighborhood and location, and has the lowest adjustments. Land Value indicated is $2.75 per square foot. Therefore:

86,000 square feet @ $2.75 per square foot = $236,500.00

Improvements

The property is improved with an eight-story brick-on-steel apartment building housing 91 units. The building is about four years old, in excellent condition, with first-class maintenance. The building which adjoins is architecturally sympathetic to the state college buildings.

Building Description, Area and Condition

Condition: Excellent

Age: Four (4) years; commenced renting early in 1964.

Modernization: Modern in every detail. Central air-conditioning, janitor services, master TV antenna, bath and kitchen venting system, incinerator, ranges, refrigerators, dishwashers, garbage disposal units. Coin-operated laundry in the basement. Air-conditioning, ranges and refrigerators plus dishwashers are furnished to the tenants.

Basement: Steel I-Beam 18″; steel bar joists; concrete poured on corrugated plate forms. Concrete, wire lath and plaster ceilings. Beam and joists are fire-proofed with sprayed asbestos coating.

Foundation: Poured concrete, 18″ thick.

Exterior Walls: Brick

Roof: Built-up tar and gravel; copper flashing; bonded for 20 years.

Gutters and Leaders: Interior drains, copper and iron.

Incinerators: One (1)

Exterior Floor Area: 12,095 square feet

Chimney: One (1)—Double flue.

Heat: Two (2) oil-fired Superior Rotary Burners and Superior Boilers, Burns Bunker No. 4 pre-heated by gas; re-circulating hot water heat vented through Carrier fan-packaged room vents. Air-condition by Central Chiller System.

Plumbing: Copper and brass. Ninety-one (91) stainless-steel kitchen sinks; ninety-two (92) porcelain toilets, bathtubs and washbasins. Chrome taps and faucets. Ninety-two (92) Kelvinator kitchen sink garbage disposals, ninety-one (91) Kelvinator dishwashers, refrigerators and ranges.

Living Units: Ninety-two (92) units including the superintendant's apartment, with license and permit to build two more in the basement. One (1) apartment has 3 bedrooms, and 2 baths.

Rooms: Three hundred forty-two (342)

Bedrooms: One hundred fifteen (115)

Bath Finish: Ceramic tile wainscot and floor, plaster above. Ninety-two (92) bathrooms.

Interior Walls: Concrete block, plastered.

Interior Floors: Concrete in the basement, all floors are hardwood except for the lobby which is terrazzo. The basement floor is concrete with asphalt tile covering in the basement corridors.

Ceilings: Plaster

Effective Age: Four years (4)

Estimated Remaining Economic Life: Fifty (50) years

Cost Approach

Building:

Using the cost index of an approved valuation service, the following square foot reproduction cost of building is developed:

$28.06 × 12,095 square feet =		$339,386.00
4th, 5th, 6th and 7th floors + 1% each floor = 114.44 × 12,095 =	$1,384,152.00	
Basement $6.40 × 12,095 =	77,408.00	
Total	$1,461,560.00	
$1,461,560.00 × 1.02 = $1,490,781.00		$1,490,781.00
		$1,830,167.00

Yard Improvements

50,000 square feet, bituminous asphalt paving @ 26¢ per square foot =	13,000.00
1,000 feet ± 1′6″ curbing @ $2.00 per lineal foot =	2,000.00
	$1,845,167.00
Depreciation—7.5%	138,387.00

Depreciated Value of Building and Site Improvements		$1,706,780.00
Extras		
Dishwashers, garbage disposal units, ranges and refrigerators=	$40,397.00	
Less Depreciation	2,163.00	
Total.		38,234.00
		$1,745,014.00
Add Land		236,500.00
Estimated Market Value by Cost Approach		$1,981,514.00

Explanation of Depreciation

The improvements are about four (4) years old and the care, maintenance and upkeep have been very good. The observed physical depreciation includes painting and decorating, roofing cover, boiler, paving and fair wear and tear.

There is no observable functional depreciation, and I have not been able to find any economic depreciation or influences that could cause such depreciation within the foreseeable future.

Summary

	Depreciation	*Depreciated Value*
Apartment Building and Site Improvements		
$1,845,167.00	$138,387.00=	$1,706,780.00
Appliances		
$40,397.00	2,163.00=	38,234.00
Estimated Market Value by Cost Approach		$1,981,514.00
	Say	$1,982,000.00

Market Data Approach

After a thorough search I was unable to locate sales of comparable properties in the area.

Income Approach

Rent Roll (Foreshortened example)

Apt. #	*Tenant's Name*	*Monthly Rental*	*Lease Dates from:*		*to:*
Basement	Ash	$140.00	Month	to	Month

1A	Buck	$134.00	10/1/67		9/30/69
1B	Cole	$150.00	Month	to	Month
1C	Dee	$181.00	11/1/67		11/30/69
1D	Earl	$215.00	2/28/67		2/28/68

Explanation of Adjusted Income

Comparable Apartment Rentals

Tower Apartments

Studio apartments to $149.00 per month.
One (1) bedroom apartments to $199.00 per month.
Two (2) bedroom apartments to $299.00 per month.

Parking rentals are additional and range from $9.00 to $20.00 per month depending on location. These rates are for uncovered areas.

Crown Apartments

Studio apartments to $179.00 per month.
One (1) bedroom apartments to $215.00 per month.
Two (2) bedroom apartments to $352.00 per month.

Parking averages from $24.00 to $26.00 per month in covered and enclosed parking spaces.

The Actual Annual Gross Rental Income for Subject Property is $175,680.00.

Thirteen (13) apartments are on a month-to-month basis.
Six (6) apartments are vacant.

Thirty-nine (39) apartments are short-term leases expiring in 1968 or have already expired, and the balance of 33 apartments have leases averaging about 18 months from January 1, 1968. There are no longer term leases.

In the opinion of this appraiser, a stabilized economic rental for the subject would be as follows:

		Annual
22	one-bedroom apts. @ average of $150.00 per month=	$ 3,300.00
45	two-bedroom apts. @ average of $215.00 per month=	9,675.00
8	three-bedroom apts. @ average of $250.00 per month=	2,000.00
16	four-bedroom apts. @ average of $280.00 per month=	4,480.00
1	superintendent's apartment @ $130.00 per month=	130.00
	Total	$19,585.00

On December 6, 1967 the Department of Housing and Urban Development authorized an increase in the average gross rental to $19,345.63 or $232,150.00 per annum.

I am, therefore, accepting the Federal Housing Administration figures of $232,150.00 per annum, to which I have added an additional $2,900.00 rental per annum for two (2) additional apartments in the basement, for the construction of which permit has been issued.

Total Estimated Gross Annual Rental

Two Hundred Thirty-five Thousand Fifty Dollars—$235,050.00

Explanation of Adjusted Expenses

The care and maintenance of the building and grounds has been exceedingly good due to the necessity of presenting an attractive image to prospects. I have accepted the records of the owner's accountant as the stabilized expenses in this appraisal.

Capitalization Rate

I have selected a straight-line method of capitalization to reflect the short terms of the leases and the instability of the income stream.

I have used the Band of Investment Theory of Capitalization:

First Mortgage—80% @ 6.5% =	5.20%
Equity—20% @ 9% =	1.80%
Total	7.00%

Estimated Remaining Economic Life—50 years
Recapture Rate—2.0%

Interest to Land and Buildings—	7.00%
Recapture Rate—	2.00%
Interest and Recapture—	9.00%

The Building Residual Technique is used in the Income Approach to estimate value.

Calculations:

Estimated Gross Annual Income		$235,050.00
Vacancy and Rent Loss (Actual)		7,050.00
Effective Gross Income		$228,000.00
Expenses:		
Taxes	$37,386.00	
Fuel, Oil and Gas	4,503.00	
Janitors, Wages, Apts., Grounds, Maintenance and Supplies	8,150.00	
Electricity	5,440.00	
Water	2,110.00	

Elevator Maintenance	1,376.00	
Insurance (Fire and Liability)	4,754.00	
Rubbish and Snow Removal	830.00	
Reserves:		
Painting and Decorating	3,560.00	
Roof	203.00	
Boiler	645.00	
Ranges, Refrigerators, Dishwashers and Garbage Disposals	2,163.00	
Management	1,175.00	
Total		$ 72,105.00
Net Income to Land and Improvements		$155,805.00
Interest to Land ($236,500.00 × 7%)		16,555.00
Interest to Improvements		$139,250.00
$139,250.00 ÷ 9% =	$1,547,222.00	
Add Land	236,500.00	
Total		$1,783,722.00
Rounded to		$1,784,000.00

Estimated Market Value by Income Approach

One Million Seven Hundred Eighty-four Thousand Dollars ($1,784,000.00)

Analysis, Correlation and Conclusions

The Cost Approach reflects the upper limit of value. It is a useful guide to reproduction value, not necessarily market value.

I have selected the Income Approach in this appraisal as the best indicator of investment value, or the market price which a sophisticated investor would pay for the property.

Estimated Market Value by Market Data Approach	Land Only
Estimated Market Value by Cost Approach	$1,982,000.00
Estimated Market Value by Income Approach	$1,784,000.00

Estimated Market Value of the Property

One Million Seven Hundred Eighty-four Thousand Dollars ($1,784,000.00)

X

How to Evaluate a Motel

In this era of revolutionary business change and competition, the hospitality industry has changed its milieu. In the past five years, somewhere around 35 percent of the nation's hotel guests have been lured away from hotels to motels, so-called. At the same time, the "motel" has changed its size, location and services more closely to resemble a downtown inn with drive-in and parking facilities, and hotels have frequently added auto parks to qualify as "motor-lodges."

Introduction

The blend will henceforth in this chapter be called a *motel,* and the type described will be in excess of 100 rooms (national average), downtown, at an intersection of strategic highways near an airport, with banquet facilities and parking for 150 cars or more. It will be in part high-rise, because downtown land is dear. It will be a highly sophisticated in-town evolution of the countryside, 50-room motel of twenty years past.

Even in the large cities, the new motel plant has replaced the aging hotel. Chicago has seen an invasion of some 300 motels in the past decade. The East is catching up with the West and South with increasing numbers.

As long as the economic and profit performance of motels justifies the investment of new capital, the onrush of urban motels will continue, obliterating the old-fashioned hotel as we knew it.

The motor-hotel industry depends upon travel. Travel is occasioned by: (1) business activity; (2) government activity; (3) vital happenings in individual or family affairs; (4) leisure time and discretionary income for vacations, exploring and touring.

The velocity of these four elements in travel movement varies at different times and in different directions. But it is a force of constant expansion with population growth, spreading wherever airlines and new highways and a viable economy allow it to penetrate.

Valuation of a motel may be based on plans for a proposed structure on a given site as a feasibility study to test highest and best use of the land; or it may be a report of a going hostelry with a financial history. In either case, value criteria must employ all three (if possible) approaches to value, with data emphasis on the locale and site, and the competition in the area. Comparisons with competitive motels must be based on physical attractiveness of the property, convenience of the location, ingress and egress, and equipment and furnishings.

Dominant Aspects of Value in Motels

The trend in the motel business, after ups and downs in the sixties, is toward stability and security. This location-oriented business is receiving more serious attention as an investment and mortgage loan outlet than at any time since the first tourist courts appeared along the highways of the country shortly before World War II.

The variety of tourist courts and downtown motels is emerging as four well-defined types:

1. The suburban motel, such as the Marriott, in Alexandria, Virginia.
2. The strategic highway motel at an intersection or cloverleaf of major arteries, such as the new Holiday Inn at the cloverleaf of the Connecticut Thruway and the Routes 25 and 8 Expressway in Bridgeport, Connecticut.
3. The resort motel, which is raising havoc with older existing resort hotels, such as the Balmoral, in Miami, Florida.
4. The downtown motel, such as the Sheraton in Dallas, Texas.

The aspects that dominate value in a new motel (or an older unprofitable one) are as follows:

a. *Room sizes.* The motel customer now requires larger rooms and often housekeeping facilities as well. Former room sizes of less than 200 square feet are now obsolete. Today's travelers get 250 square feet without a kitchenette and approximately 360 square feet with housekeeping facilities.
b. *Number of units.* Motels are becoming larger; 100 units or more is the rule for chain management.
c. *Area for expansion.* The new motel pattern also includes room for expansion (especially high-rise). Enough land initially is acquired so the motel can grow with success and with the growth of the community (for instance, the Hilton Motel in San Francisco). The new units frequently constitute a completely separate building from the original.
d. *Public facilities.* Sufficient public space is now a must for the new motel which caters to businessmen as well as tourists. The old rule of 100 square feet per room of public space (meeting rooms and conventions) is now increased to 200 square feet per room. The growth in public space in motels has been so

great that competition is becoming a major factor, as is the ability to obtain trained personnel. Furthermore, the competition is not merely within the community, but also is intercity, state and national. That is another reason why the motel chains have an edge over the single ownership operations; the chains can offer a choice of cities and, more recently, of countries.

e. *Height increase with land costs.* Of necessity, the height of a motel is a function of land costs, e.g., the Holiday Inn in midtown Manhattan must be high-rise to justify land costs.

f. *Architecture and design.* Modern design must incorporate features for built-in operating economy. Gadgetry which is expensive to maintain is out. Plumbing and other utility lines must be available for easy repair. This means they must be accessible without the need to tear down a wall which puts rental space out of use for significant periods of time. Floor and wall redecoration is standardized and simplified. Furniture and fixtures must be durable as well as aesthetic, and be resistant to ordinary wear and tear. Single kitchens should be used to service all of the eating facilities in the motel, with, at most, serving pantries on other floors.

Dramatic design helps too. For example, the Regency Motel in Atlanta, Georgia, considered one of the most beautiful in the country, is built in a square enclosing an old Roman court, with outdoor cantilevered elevators at the four inside corners. A motel must provide a special ambiance to build a steady return of guests more than once charmed.

Today's motel should return 14 percent on a free and clear basis (i.e., operating income as a percentage of total investment). Financing today is available to 75 percent of value and at an interest rate of about 8¼ percent. Recognizing the increased stability in the industry, lenders will extend 20-year terms which may still require a balloon at the end, in order to prevent a negative cash flow to the investor.

Demand for hospitality space remains relatively constant. Growing demand caused by increased travel is offset by speedy air transport that eliminates much of the former need to be away from home for extended periods. A motel should not be built unless there presently is a greater demand than can be supplied in the community.

The appraiser's *initial step* in evaluating an existing or proposed motel is to process its actual or hypothetical income, gross to effective gross to net. He decides upon capitalization method, rate and valuation technique only after examining all the circumstances surrounding his subject's location, competition, design and service, basing his conclusions on the dominant aspects of value that contribute to its operation.

Market Survey and Property Analysis

The *second step* the appraiser takes in evaluating a proposed or existing motel is to gather and correlate data which points up the likelihood of success or failure in operating a motel in the locale. He relates this information to his analysis of the subject property in this manner:

1. *Prospects.* Macro-market trends and travel patterns in the nation, region and

area, measuring against the micro-market demand for a motel in the locale. In measuring regional vs. local economic conditions, the following factors must be scrutinized:

a) Highway arterial system feeding the locale and the site; the business, tourist and sport travel using these arteries; and the nearest airport facility.

b) Chief forms of employment within the locale, and the amount of local commercial patronage on which the motel can count.

c) The amount and substance of industry in the region and its contribution, if any, to the commerce of the locale. The area's atmosphere as an industrial, commercial or resort center, with all three described if necessary.

d) The planning and zoning practices, the tax policies, and local ordinances affecting the property and its district must be stated clearly. Ingress and egress permits from and to frontage highways are vital.

e) Assuming that highest and best use of the site is a motel, with good roads, and automobile parking on site, surrounded by banks, shops, restaurants and other conveniences, where will the patrons for the proposed or existing motel come from? State the likely competition to be met from motels nearby.

2. *Property analysis and history.* Specific details of the property under appraisement must be clearly delineated: (a) Recitation of the title, including metes and bounds, assessments and tax levy; (b) Zone requirements; (c) Description of the site topography and subsoil conditions, plottage and shape of the land area, together with list of utilities on site or available; (d) The type of construction, use and conditions of the proposed or existing building and its furniture and equipment together with site improvements, planned or existing, such as paved parking, swimming pool, other recreational facilities; (e) Each floor of the building must be measured and described; (f) A summary of the development of the property, if existing, with a five-year history of income and expenses, and type of management and maintenance attending the property; (g) The anticipated useful life of the property must be estimated and allowances made for depreciation and obsolescence.

If the building is proposed or in the planning stage, the appraiser must project income and expenses for five years from his knowledge and experience in new motel construction, and recommend management and maintenance procedures for the proposed building that are both practical and economic.

3. *Comparable land sales and leases.* The appraiser must list in detail verified data concerning land sales and leases similar to the subject property, in the locale of the subject property. These comparables should be inspected, and similarities or differences described, as compared to subject land and/or buildings, summing up the property analysis.

THE APPROACHES TO VALUE

The appraiser's *third step* in motel appraisal lies in his use of all three approaches: Cost, Income and Market Data.

Usually valuation of a motel is first gauged by its *Depreciated Cost,* with land, site improvements, furniture equipment and houseware added. An approved cost index service will provide square foot or cubic foot multipliers for a variety of classes of motels.

The Income Approach first totals earnings from all activities of the hostelry. From this gross, the appraiser subtracts operational expenses, replacement reserves, accelerated depreciation of furnishings and equipment, and recapture of the investment in the construction over its anticipated economic life. The bottom line is *net income* which is accordingly capitalized into value.

Capitalization rate under the Income Approach should be banded on the basis of money market conditions, the readiness of mortgage funds and the interest rate that will draw equity capital. Selection of capitalization rate is the appraiser's critical *fourth step* in evaluating a motel. The reciprocal of the capitalization rate may be used to simplify computations in applying the Property Residual Technique under the Income Approach (see Model).

The Market Data Approach can be applied to motels, on a selling-price-per-unit basis, where recent sales of motels similar to the subject have taken place. The comparables can be taken from distant points, as long as type of operation and room rates are close.

TECHNIQUES FOR ESTIMATING VALUE OF LAND AND IMPROVEMENTS IN MOTEL APPRAISAL

Procedure for Estimating a Separate Land Value Under the Motel

As the fifth step in motel evaluations, it is necessary to estimate land value. Market Data on sales of vacant land is usually abundant, since land sales do not have to be close by, but similar in respect to area, location, highway conditions and topography.

Procedure for Estimating Value of the Improvements in Motel Appraisals

Property Residual Technique Under the Income Approach. A sound motel may develop net income that, capitalized, proves investment or market value greater than Depreciated Reproduction Cost can show. It may also show capitalized value greater than Market Data indicates.

Therefore, the Income Approach is generally the best proof of investment value, with close support from the Market Data Approach. But the Cost Approach, when the building is new or proposed, is an important documentation of the construction of the improvements and should not be obviated. Estimating value of the improvements is the *sixth and final step* on the appraiser's road to valuation of a motel.

In the following Model Appraisal of a proposed downtown motel building, the Property Residual Technique is employed for value conclusion with the Cost Approach and Market Data Approach in close support. Since the value of the land has been established via Market Data, the Property Residual Technique under the Income Approach solves the remaining questions concerning market value, namely the value of the improvements with interest and recapture imputable to land and building.

MODEL APPRAISAL OF MOTEL USING ALL THREE APPROACHES IN SUPPORT OF THE PROPERTY RESIDUAL TECHNIQUE UNDER THE INCOME APPROACH

The following is an appraisal of a proposed motel on leased land in a downtown area of a city in the Northeast.

Purpose of Appraisal

The purpose of this appraisal is to estimate market value of a proposed motel complex and the land upon which it will be situated at 100 Main Street, City, as of January 15, 1970.

Property Appraised

All rights inherent in the fee are appraised.

Valuation Premise

City population is 275,000, surrounded by easy-access suburbs within 15-mile radius aggregating a population of 500,000.

Subject property is strategically located in the prime downtown block, at cloverleaf intersection with major highways.

Market Survey and Property Analysis (abbreviated)

Macro-market economic prospects are bright. Trend is toward population increase in the region, and expanded commercial and industrial activitity in the city, stemming from outburst of growth in local banks, insurance and utility companies. Hospitality demand from flourishing concerns in the fields of electronics, engineering, insurance, medical research and manufacturing, most of which require modern motel facilities with parking, for convention and banquet occasions, and for constant overnight visits from government officials and out-of-town businessmen. Resort patronage in the summer-time is steady, stemming from wayfarers en route from all parts of the nation to northern New England and Canada.

Micro-market Study

Locale

The property being appraised is located on the westerly side of Main Street (Route 19) just southerly of a full cloverleaf interchange with Route

10, a portion of a limited access highway extending between Boston, Massachusetts and New York City. Main Street is a four-lane thoroughfare leading into Worcester, Massachusetts. The area is a high-density manufacturing belt, with unemployment at less than 2%. There are two major universities within a half-hour's driving time.

Route 4, a limited access highway westerly of and parallel to Main Street, extends between Hartford and towns and cities in the Northeast industrial corridor. Business travel in this area is constant and growing. Summer tourist and winter ski travellers also patronize the area in growing numbers.

The property being appraised consists of land which is now a rarely used portion of a shopping center parking lot. The shopping center includes a discount store, food mart, and six satellite stores.

Southerly of the property being appraised are located several gasoline service stations, retail stores, quality restaurants, banks, offices, and a medical center.

A chemical plant, about one-half mile north of subject, is a major manufacturer, employing approximately 15,000 persons.

The center of the city is slightly in excess of one-half mile northerly of the property being appraised and the center of the City of Hartford is about five miles away southeasterly.

The locale is most auspicious for a modern motel operation which, in spite of older nearby competition, would be heavily patronized by the growing business community and tourist in-flow.

Bradley Field, an international jet-port, is 10 miles to the northeast from subject site.

The redevelopment district of subject city is bounded to the east by Main Street which is improved in this section primarily with retail stores on the ground floor and offices on the upper floors.

Competition

The following motels and hotels were considered competitive with the highest and best use of this property.

Northerly:

Across Main Street—

National Motor Lodge—88 guest rooms plus conference room, pool; adjacent restaurant under separate ownership. Service and food, poor. Rates average $12. per day (single), $16. (double). Older furnishings. Average occupancy about 75 percent. Not equal to subject's proposed deluxe appointments.

Main Street:

One mile—

The Tarkington. Same side of street. 97 guest rooms plus conference room, pool. Cramped parking. Restaurant—small and inferior in service. Rates $11. per day (single), $15. (double). Occupancy rate, 80 percent.

I-92:

Three miles—

Travelon Motor Lodge. 80 guest rooms, small meeting room, pool. Inferior to subject location. Adjacent restaurant—separate management. Rates average $14. per day (single), $16.50 (double). Average occupancy about 90 percent. Planning to add 48 rooms, banquet hall and cocktail lounge, spring 1969.

I-92:

Four miles—

Caravan Motor Lodge. 100 guest rooms, pool, restaurant and cocktail lounge. Inferior location. Rates $10. per day (single), $14. (double). Average occupancy 80 percent.

Planned Motels:

A Ramada Inn is planned at the intersection of interstate 92 and Jones Avenue, about 6.5 miles northerly of the subject.

A 14-story Holiday Inn containing 375 rooms with full banquet facilities is scheduled to begin construction during the spring of 1970; this facility will be constructed near the center of the City of Hartford, about 7 miles from subject property.

Property Analysis and History

Following a recitation of grantor, grantee, date of transfer with volume and page from the land records, and type of deed with metes and bounds, tax information, zone and zone requirements, the property may be analyzed as follows:

Site Description

The site is irregular in shape with 449.1 feet of frontage on the westerly side of Main Street, and 420.12 feet of frontage on Union Square which forms the easterly boundary. Total land area is 95,000 square feet or 2.346 acres. The site is generally level and at the grade of Union Square and approximately one foot below the grade of Main Street. All public utilities are available to the site.

Highest and Best Use

The highest and best use of the subject property is to be improved with a motel with conference room and restaurant, as proposed. There are two other motels in the city, but discussions with knowledgeable people in the city indicate that there is a definite need for a new facility.

Site Improvements

The proposed site improvements will include bituminous concrete paving of much of the site except that portion which will be occupied by the building's storm drains, light standards and landscaping. Parking will be provided on the site for 150 cars. There will be an enclosed walk leading from the motel to the adjoining municipal parking garage.

Justification of Land Values

There have been no recent sales of land in the downtown business district outside the redevelopment area. This is due to the activities of the Redevelopment Commission which has acquired a large portion of the central business district for a renewal program. A thorough investigation of land transactions was made including discussions with prominent real estate brokers, town officials, Redevelopment Commission officials and a search through town records.

The following sales were used as a guide in estimating the value of the subject land if unrestricted by controls imposed by the Redevelopment Commission:

Sale No. 1 S/s West Main Street

Grantor: People's Bank & Trust Co.
Grantee: Union Federal Savings and Loan Association
Recorded: Volume-423, Page 622
Date: February 29, 1967
Zone: Same as subject
Sale Price: \$150,000. + \$40,000. demolition, fill and other site work = \$8.43 per square foot
Lot Size: 109.25 front feet; 22,546 square feet
Topography: Sloping

(Four other sales are listed as above)

Sale No. 1 was adjusted upward for time, as the sale took place about 2 1/2 years prior to the date of appraisal. An upward adjustment was also made for location, as the subject property is situated in a more desirable commercial location. A downward adjustment was made for size, as the sale land area is much smaller than the subject. Usually a large tract of land will sell at a lesser unit price than a smaller tract, all other factors being similar.

Sales Nos. 2, 3, 4 and 5 were adjusted upward because the sale properties are situated in a much less desirable location than the subject, which is within close proximity to the 100% business location and at the edge of an urban renewal area. A downward adjustment was made for size.

Land sales within the urban renewal area do not reflect current market value because the sales are based upon prices established in the past. The sale prices also reflect controls imposed upon the various parcels and the fact that all parcels should be sold over a relatively short period of time. Sale prices in the redevelopment area vary from $1.75 per square foot to $6.50 per square foot. The subject land was purchased August 20, 1969 at a price of $1.75 per square foot.

Based upon the above sales analysis, the subject land is estimated to have a value of $8.00 per square foot subject to no restrictions and controls by the Redevelopment Commission.

Upon consideration of controls and restrictions exercised on this land and considering that the land will be improved with a motel with conference area and restaurant, land value is estimated at $4.00 per square foot.

Then: 95,000 × $4.00	=	$380,000.
Estimated Value of Land, rounded	=	$380,000.

The land will be leased to the building corporation for 99 years at an annual rent of $18,000.

Description of Buildings

Motel

A part 6-story and part 1-story motel and conference room.

Floor Plan

First Floor:	16 guest rooms, cocktail lounge, lobby, registration desk, work area and manager's office. A large meeting room is connected to the main motel structure by a corridor.
Second through Sixth Floor:	24 guest rooms each.
Total:	136 guest rooms.

(At this point the appraiser will describe construction details of exterior and interior walls, floors, roof, conference room, bath and toilet areas, elevators, heating and air-conditioning, basement and other features. He will also detail the construction of the restaurant, kitchen and swimming pool, and any other improvements, such as tennis courts, putting green, etc.)

Cost Approach

Motel

Source of Cost Data: Cost Index Service—Section 12, page 14
Excellent. Class C Motel.

9,806 square foot floor area = 6-story section
5,769 square foot floor area = 1-story section
489 lineal feet perimeter = 6-story section
400 lineal feet perimeter = 1-story section

Base Square Foot Cost $21.87
Number of Stories Multiplier 1.03
Floor Area—Perimeter Multiplier .959
Refined Square Foot Cost $21.61
$21.87 × 1.03 × .959

Cost of Square Foot Items:

9,806 sq. ft. × $21.61 × 6 stories =	$1,271,446.
Balconies: 10,120 sq. ft. × $7.13 =	72,156.
Elevator Addition =	89,820.
Basement: 1,260 sq. ft. × $2.88 =	3,659.
Total	$1,437,081.

Current Cost Multiplier 1.00
Local Multiplier 1.07
Replacement Cost: 1,437,081. × 1.07 × 1.00 = $1,537,677.

Meeting and Waiting Areas

Base Square Foot Cost $21.87

Story Height Multiplier 1.06
Floor and Perimeter Multiplier 1.047

Refined Square Foot Cost:
$21.87 × 1.06 × 1.047 = $24.28

Cost of Square Foot Items:

5,769 sq. ft. × $24.28 =	$140,071.
Less Common Wall:	1,260.
Total	$138,811.

Current Cost Multiplier 1.00
Local Multiplier 1.07

Replacement Cost: $138,811 × 1.07 × 1.00 = $148,528.

Pool Area and Enclosed Walk

Base Square Foot Cost $21.87

Floor Area and Perimeter Multiplier 1.124
Story Height Multiplier 1.03

Refined Square Foot Cost $21.87 × 1.124 × 1.03 =	$25.38
Less Lack of Interior Finish	4.09
Final Square Foot Cost	$21.29

Cost of Square Foot Items

3,296 sq. ft. × $21.29 =	$70,171.
Pool 902 sq. ft. × $9. =	8,118.
Total	$78,289.

Local Multiplier 1.07
Current Cost Multiplier 1.00

Replacement Cost

$78,289.×1.07×1.00=	$83,769.

Restaurant

Source of Cost Data: Cost Index Service
Section 13, Page 8
Excellent Class C Restaurant

4,998 square feet floor
333 lineal feet perimeter
10-foot average story height

Base Square Foot Cost $31.02
Story Height Multiplier .945
Floor Area—Perimeter multiplier 1.048
Refined Square Foot Cost
$31.02×.945×1.048=$30.71

Cost of Square Foot Items	
4,998 sq. ft.×$30.71=	$153,489.
Less Cost of Common Wall	−2,492.
Total	$150,997.

Current Cost Multiplier .99
Local Multiplier 1.07
Final Replacement Cost

$150,997.×.99×1.07=	$159,951.

Site Improvements (from pro forma)

Bituminous Concrete Paving and Curbs	$12,000.	
Landscaping	24,000.	
Site Work and Drainage	64,000.	
Total		$100,000.

Building Equipment (from pro forma)

Furniture, restaurant equipment and miscellaneous equipment	$425,000.

Summary

Motel	$1,537,677.
Conference Room and Waiting Room	148,528.
Enclosed Pool	83,769.
Restaurant	159,951.
	$1,929,925.

Total Buildings:

Site Improvements	100,000.
Building Equipment	425,000.
Land Value	380,000.
Total:	$2,834,925.

In the Addenda of this report are sheets supplied by the owner showing the anticipated construction costs of the improvements. Total anticipated cost excluding land and financing charges is $3,150,225.

The estimated cost by use of a Cost Index Service was used as the basis for the Cost Approach.

Value Indicated by the Cost Approach, rounded= $2,835,000.

Income Approach

Projected Gross Income per 365-day year

Guest Rooms: 136 at $15. average room rate daily 80% average occupancy			$595,680.
Food			640,000.
Beverages			125,000.
Other			5,000.
Potential Gross Income			$1,365,680.
Cost of Goods Sold			
Rooms 16%		$218,509.	
Food and Beverages 40%		546,272.	
Total		$764,781.	
Deductions from Income:			
Administrative and General=		$88,769.	
Advertising and Business Promotion 2%=		27,314.	
Heat, Light and Power 3%=		40,970.	
Maintenance and Repair 3%=		40,970.	
Total		$198,023.	962,804.
House Profit			$ 402,876.
Property Taxes 3%	$40,970.		
Insurance	6,828.		
Land Rent	16,000.		63,798.
Net Income:			$ 339,078.

Income Explained

Room income is based upon 136 guest rooms being rented at an average rent of $15. per day at 80% occupancy. This office has made numerous studies of hotels and motels in the State and the above projection is feasible for this property.

A Caravan Motor Lodge located in East Dingletown with 88 guest rooms, a conference room and pool has an average occupancy of 75%. Room rates are $12. per day single and $16. per day double.

The Royal Plume Motor Lodge in Sawyer's Hill at the intersection of Route 92 and Route 10 has 96 guest rooms, banquet facilities and a pool. Room rates are $13.50 per day for single occupancy and $16.50 per day for double occupancy. Average occupancy at this facility is 95% to 98%.

The Hotel Dashmore in downtown New Haven has 304 guest rooms, a small pool, banquet facilities and several dining areas. The average room rate is $20.50 per day. Occupancy has been running at a level of 73%.

The projection for food is based upon a pro forma supplied by the property owner. Typically, income from food is 35–40 percent of gross income. However, because this facility is in the center of the business district and there is no comparable facility, the estimate from the owner's pro forma statement has been accepted.

The projected income from beverages and other sources is in line with national averages and known operating percentages of specific properties.

Expenses Explained

Expense estimates are based upon studies contained in "Economic Factors and Case Studies in Hotel and Motel Valuation" published by The American Institute of Real Estate Appraisers.

Valuation Process by the Property Residual Technique

Continuing studies of the motel industry have shown that motels similar to that being appraised will usually sell at 8 to 8½ times net earnings. Because of the deluxe quality of subject, I choose the higher range.

Then: $338,898 × 8.5* = $2,880,330.

Value Indicated by Income Approach, rounded = $2,880,000.

*8.5 × the net earnings is the reciprocal of 11.7% capitalization, which is the combined interest and recapture rate for land and improvements. If the anticipated life of the improvements is 33 years, then 3% is allocated to recapture, and 8.7% is the interest to land and improvements.

Market Data Approach

Research of the market for sales of large, modern, chain type motels through the State was conducted. Many transactions investigated were between related corporations and the indicated consummations did not represent true arm's length transactions. There were only three known arm's length sales involving modern motels in the area.

Sale No. 1

Address:	Hart's Crossing
Grantor:	E. George Plank
Grantee:	Dozy Enterprises, Inc.
Recorded:	Volume—203, Page—8
Date:	September 26, 1966
Sale Price:	$936,000. = $18,000/unit
Units:	52, plus 4-room manager's apartment
Age:	1965
Facilities:	Meeting room for 30–35 persons, pool, billiard room, no restaurant.
Remarks:	Each unit in this motel contains two rooms. A restaurant is adjacent to this motel.

Sale No. 2

Address:	Mt. Tom Park
Grantor:	ABC Corporation
Grantee:	Alex Smith *et al.*
Recorded:	Volume—91, Page—311
Date:	September 29, 1967
Sale Price:	$1,910,000. of which 8.5% represents value of lease of Texaco service station which was leased separately. $1,910,000×91.5%=$1,747,650. or $19,418. per unit.
Units:	90
Age:	1965
Facilities:	Pool and restaurant
Remarks:	The subject property has chain franchise subject to three separate net leases totaling $103,820. per year. Indicates overall rate of 9%.

Sale No. 3

Address:	U.S. No. 1, Wakesville
Grantor:	XYZ Corporation
Grantee:	Samuel Brown
Recorded:	Volume—201, Page—169
Date:	June 15, 1969
Sale Price:	$2,500,000. = $20,000/unit
Units:	125
Age:	1967
Facilities:	Restaurant, meeting area, pool. Equal to subject property in luxury appointments, but inferior to subject in location.

Remarks: Property was sold subject to foreclosure. Sale property now has Tilton Inn franchise.

Sale No. 1 was adjusted upward because the sale property did not include a restaurant and the building was constructed about 1965 compared to the proposed motel which will be new.

Sale No. 2 was adjusted upward to reflect the difference between the sale buildings, constructed about 1965, and the proposed subject buildings which will be new.

Sale No. 3 was adjusted upward because the sale buildings were constructed in 1967 and the sale property was sold under duress.

Based upon analysis of these sales and considering other sales throughout the State, the subject property is estimated to have a value of $21,000. per unit by comparison.

Then: 136 units × $21,000 = $2,856,000.

Value Indicated by Market Data Approach . . . . $2,856,000.

Correlation and Final Value Estimates

Value Indicated By Cost Approach . . . . $2,840,000.
Value Indicated By Income Approach . . . . $2,880,000.
Value Indicated By Market Data Approach . . . . $2,856,000.

The value indicated by the Income Approach was selected as the most reliable approach because motel type properties are usually purchased for their income-producing ability. This value estimate is considered conservative for the following reasons:

1. There is a definite lessee's interest in the land which will be more in evidence with completion and operation.
2. Because the owning corporation will own the buildings only and pay rent for the land, there is advantageous tax shelter.
3. The advantage of the land lease becomes evident when it is realized that a 99-year lease tends to equal the fee.
4. Cash flow is realized in a direct ratio to reflect no land investment for purchaser, i.e. lease equity with increased leverage.

The value indicated by the Cost Approach is lower than that indicated by the Income Approach. The builder's costs are higher than those applied in this report which may reflect his degree of amenity value and consequent higher cost of quality items intended.

Estimated value of the improvements, if completed in a good and workmanlike manner within reasonable time in accordance with plans and specifications which form a part of this report, is, as of September 25, 1970:

Two Million Eight Hundred Eighty Thousand Dollars
($2,880,000.00)

XI

How to Evaluate Leaseholds and Leased Fees

An unencumbered property *in fee simple* is historically known, in law, as a *freehold,* in which the owner has full right of use and enjoyment. *A lease is a contract* by which an owner conveys an interest in his property, usually for a term of years at a specified rent. When a freehold is leased, *it changes status,* and becomes encumbered to the extent of the rights conveyed in the lease. *Subleases* are further encumbrances on the property.

Introduction

When the value of leased property is to be estimated, two or more interests are in question, designated as follows:

1) The owner, as lessor, retains a *leased fee interest.*
2) The direct tenant, as lessee, owns rights to a *leasehold estate equity,* which is an encumbrance on the owner's title in fee simple.
3) If the direct tenant has, in turn, *subleased* to others, the interest of the direct tenant becomes a "sandwich lease interest," because it is now *sandwiched* between *the interest of the owner* and the *interest of the sublessee.*

A sublessee's interest is always taken into account in condemnation proceedings. Indeed, his share of just compensation may approximate that of the direct tenant.

For instance, a former trolley-car terminal, once converted by the direct tenant into a commercial laundry, had again been converted by a subtenant to use as a Cadillac agency showroom and service shop near the downtown core of an urban area. Now it was taken in condemnation by the Redevelopment Agency. The condemnors and the owner were willing to settle for $395,000. The direct tenant had a 21-year lease with three years remaining from the date of the taking. The annual rental was $9,500, net to the owner. The direct tenant had sublet (to the Cadillac dealer) at annual rental of $40,000, plus tax escalator and maintenance. The subtenant had invested $150,000 in the property, revamping the showroom, expanding the service garage, and paving, lighting and fencing the parking lot.

Neither lease nor sublease contained a clause cancelling the lease in case of condemnation, so the claims of both the "sandwich tenant" and the sublessee had to be deducted from compensation to the owner.

The "sandwich tenant" was entitled to the value of the difference between his rent payable ($28,500) and his rent receivable from the subtenant ($120,000), coming to $92,500. (He had amortized his improvements to the building, during the ten years he used it as a laundry and dry-cleaning plant.)

The subtenant's claim included moving costs for cars, spare parts and service equipment to a new location, the re-establishment of equipment in place, and unamortized leasehold improvements, in all totalling $100,000.

After weeks in court, the subtenant was awarded $85,000 as just compensation, which, along with sandwich tenant's $92,500, had to be taken from the owner's total of $395,000. So the owner received net, only $217,500.

In this case, the "sandwich tenant" had received the bonus in the lease, $92,500, for having been able to rent to a subtenant at a much higher figure than his own contract with the owner had stipulated. (The owner would have received the bonus if there had been a cancellation clause in his lease to the direct tenant.)

Dominant Features in the Valuation of Leaseholds

The theory of leasehold valuation has developed over a period of two thousand years in Europe and Britain, where it was introduced by the Romans, who had taken it from the Greeks. Long experience in the market place here has made it clear to owners and lessees, their attorneys and appraisers, and the courts, that there are *two hinges* on which value swings in leasehold appraisals:

1. Leasehold value is established by *rental market* conditions, or through a capital investment by owner or lessee, and by a combination of each of these factors.
2. Leasehold value is enhanced when the *market rental* (economic rent) becomes greater than the contract rent; or when the lessee constructs an improvement or makes a substantial capital investment in rehabilitating an existing structure.

This creates the framework of the "two property concept," familiar to many appraisers, which holds that when there is a lease favorable to the owner, then the owner has, in effect, two properties: the leased fee interest (the real estate itself), and *the bonus in the lease.*

The reverse situation will be true when the direct tenant obtains a lease to his own advantage; which is to say, at a rental lower than the market rent, or when because of improvements made by others, he is getting the *bonus.* This situation was dramatized on the foregoing page in the story of the "sandwich tenant" in condemnation.

There is a bonus submerged somewhere in every contract between humans. In the leasehold contract, the bonus must be revealed by the diligent appraiser seeking to estimate fair market value.

Types of Leases

There are five types of commercial property leases in general use today, made for brief or long-term periods. They are as follows:

1. The straight, fixed-sum net lease, with in-advance monthly rental payments, is the most common form in commercial use.
2. The graded lease, with periodic "step-ups" in rental payments, is sometimes made where tenant's start-up cost is heavy, but his future is assured.
3. The percentage lease, usually applied to retail gross sales, annually, sometimes with monthly minimum guarantee.
4. The security-advance lease, sometimes applied to special new construction, with the tenant advancing rent for a year or more in order to gain long-term advantages in the lease.
5. The revaluation lease, where revised rentals are established by arbitration. This is the weakest form of lease, holding perils for both owner and tenant. Lending institutions sheer away from it.

Reversionary Right (Repossession)

The owner's interest in the leased fee consists of his right to collect the stipulated rental from the tenant monthly, quarterly, or other period of time, in payment for his release *of the use* of the premises, which he nevertheless continues to own *in fee simple*. In this title, he also retains the right to repossess the premises at the expiration of the lease, which is legally known as his *reversionary right*. Unless otherwise specified in the lease instrument, this right gives the owner recapture title to all physical improvements on the premises, even if he must pay the expiring tenant a depreciated part of their cost.

The Tenant's Rights

The lessee's primary interest in a commercial leasehold is his right to transact business on the premises in a profitable enterprise, which entitles him to the excess of any net gain over expenses for the duration of the lease, after payment of rent to the owner. The tenant is also entitled to rental income from the property ensuing in leases to subtenants, which is the right to the difference between the contract rent payable to the owner and any higher market rentals current at the time of valuation. Further, the tenant retains an interest in the market value of any improvements to the property which he may have created during the term of the lease. While he must leave these improvements attached to the property at the end of the lease, he will be compensated for their depreciated cost unless the provisions of the lease instrument state otherwise.

In evaluating the leasehold, the appraiser must estimate the present worth, or market value, of rental increment, if any, above the contract rent, and the lessee's interest in any improvements, being guided by the provisions of the lease.

The value of a leasehold is that amount of money for which a tenant can sell his leasehold in the prevailing market.

Provisions of the Lease Instrument

The *first step* in the evaluation of a leasehold requires that the appraiser shall obtain and carefully study all the provisions of the lease instrument. These may be highlighted as follows:

1. *Term of lease and renewal options.* A long-term lease generally has greater value to a tenant than a short-term would afford. It is a hedge against inflation. It gives the tenant time to amortize expensive improvements. It is insurance against the "penalties of success," i.e. burdensome rental increases, constantly stepped up. And options to renew the lease at the same, or slightly increased rental, add to the value of the leasehold.

2. *Rental.* To return to the "two hinges on which value swings in leasehold appraisals," "*Leasehold value is established by rental market conditions . . . Leasehold value is enhanced when the market rental becomes greater than the contract rent.*" When the contract rental is higher than the current market rental, the value of the leasehold is depressed.

3. *Condemnation.* This all-important clause can be written to protect both owner and tenant in the event of eminent domain proceedings against the property. Its absence as a provision can be damaging to the owner's leased fee interest, and highly speculative in value to the leasehold.

4. *Termination.* Specific language as to the owner's obligations to reimburse the lessee for depreciated value of improvements which the lessee may have installed, together with a statement of the lessee's obligations to the owner as to condition of premises to be quitted, disbursement of any security deposit, and other matters pertinent to expiry of the lease, will add to the value of the leasehold.

5. *Purchase option.* The right to purchase the property at a set price can be an important provision in a long-term lease, particularly where it will be exercised after the owner's tax shelter in depreciation has run out, and where the tenant benefits by insuring permanence to his place of business and recapture of his investment in improvements.

Other provisions of a commercial lease, such as clauses for assignment of the lease, tax participation, maintenance and building improvement, insurance, forfeiture in event of default by lessee, mortgages on the leasehold, and use of the property, are equally important to both owner and tenant, and vital to evaluation of the leasehold.

The Special Effects of Sale and Leaseback

A popular gambit in financing sound commercial properties on a long-term basis is the sale and leaseback transaction, whereby a user-owner will sell his property to an investor, simultaneously taking back a lease on the premises which guarantees income to the investor for many years. It is a good move for an owner-user whose property has outrun its depreciation factor.

When the contract rental from such a lease is under the prevailing rental market, the leasehold may have great value. When the rental is greater than actual market, the leasehold may be valueless, and purely a paper-transaction as a tax benefit to the seller.

If the lease contains a recapture clause, giving the property back to the seller-lessee after a period of years, the Internal Revenue Service will view the sale and leaseback as a mortgage in disguise. To be valued as a true leasehold, the seller-lessee must maintain an enduring arm's-length position with the buyer. (See Chapter XIII, page 188, for details.)

Leasehold and Property Analysis

The *second step* the appraiser takes in preparing evaluation of a leasehold is to condense the provisions of the lease in their significant aspects, with a detailed statement of rental income, and the details of any subleases involved. The format of the report is developed in the investment-analysis manner:

Market Survey and Property Analysis

1. *Identification.* A complete legal description of land and (proposed or existing) buildings is set forth. Terms of the lease are stated in connection with description of the property. And the following macro-market influences should be noted:

a) Type of city government, and its effectiveness politically and economically, together with a synopsis of the city's reasons for being (i.e. importance as a rail-head, communications center, harbor and/or airport facility). Indications of growth or decline in such facilities.

b) Population of the city. Forms of transportation within the city and to and from the suburbs and other cities. Chief forms of employment within the city.

c) Principal industries within the city, their growth patterns, and public utilities that serve them. The amount and substance of industry in the area, and its contribution, if any, to the commerce of the city. The city's atmosphere as an industrial, commercial or cultural (university) center, with all three described if necessary.

d) The planning and zoning practices, the tax policies, and local ordinances affecting the property and its district must be stated clearly.

2. *Micro-market Data of the Commercial District and Block.* Factual data concerning the immediate vicinity of the proposed or existing property and leasehold should be set forth as follows:

a) Highest and best use of the property should be sharply emphasized. If a change in highest and best use is recommended, it may render present improvements valueless. State the rent per square foot in competing properties nearby. Note number of vacancies.

b) Describe trends in the district and block. Is the district growing or decaying? Is redevelopment underway? Is the block the best one in the district? How far away is city hall, the public library, hospitals, medical clinics, the newspaper plant, public utility offices? Is the district served by main highways, and a sensible traffic pattern? Is it readily accessible to other important districts within the city?

3. *Description of the Improvements.* Specific details of the property under appraisement must be clearly delineated:

a) The building's layout, design and construction, together with assessments and tax levy.

b) Zone requirements.

c) Description of the site topography and subsoil conditions, plottage and shape of the land area, together with list of utilities on site or available.

d) Use and condition of the proposed or existing building and its machinery, together with site improvements, planned or existing, such as paved parking, fencing, outdoor floodlighting.

e) Each floor of the building must be measured and described.

f) A summary of the development of the property, if existing, with a five-to-ten year history of income and expense, and type of management and maintenance attending the property.

g) The anticipated useful life of the property must be estimated and allowances made for depreciation and obsolescence.

4. *Method of Evaluation.* Usually the property is first evaluated in fee simple, as if there were no lease involved. Then the value of the leasehold is separately estimated by capitalization of net income, and this amount is subtracted from the value of the whole property. The difference is the value of the leased fee, (or lessor's interest). But the reverse is operable: the value of the lessor's interest may be estimated and subtracted from the value of the whole, to produce the value of the leasehold. Choice of method should be made clear.

5. *Feasibility Reports.* If the building is proposed or in the planning stage, the appraiser must project income and expenses for five years from origination of the proposed lease, and recommend management and maintenance procedures for the proposed building that are both practical and economic.

6. *Comparable Land Sales and Leaseholds.* The appraiser must list in detail verified data concerning land sales in the area. If sales prices of other comparable leaseholds can be obtained, these should be exhibited. These comparables should be inspected and similarities or differences described, as compared to subject land or space, summing up the property analysis.

THE APPROACHES TO VALUE

The appraiser's *third step* in leasehold appraisal lies in working up his Approaches, as to both the property as a whole, and the leasehold.

The Market Data Approach may be useful only *for purposes of estimating land value and gauging the rental market.*

In the evaluation of both leasehold and property as a whole, the *Cost Approach* may lend better support to the Income Approach than Market Data, because the Cost Approach leads the appraiser to a close examination of construction details, and the age, condition and anticipated life of the property, hence the life of the income stream. The ratio of effective age of the building to life expectance is crucial.

The *Income Approach* is the chief guide to value and is the proper test of the lessee's ability to deliver a worthwhile investment yield over a long period of time.

Since the market value of a leasehold depends absolutely upon the *present worth of its future earnings,* the appraiser must tabulate such earnings from the provisions of the lease, if he is to calculate their present worth in money.

Capitalization rates will vary with circumstances. Yield percentages will differ. Choice of capitalization rate and method is the appraiser's critical *fourth step* in evaluating a leasehold.

Capitalization Methods. Depending upon the *quality and durability* of income (see Chapter V, page 55) flowing from the property under appraisement, one can elect to follow either of the following courses of capitalization:

1. Use the straight-line depreciation plus capitalization-rate method of capitalization when you anticipate that the net income before depreciation *may decline* regularly each year in the future.
2. But if the net income before depreciation is expected to be level or better and is *of a contract nature,* with rated tenants and the leases extended over a period of at least *twelve years,* then the Inwood premise may be used. This premise is used only on prime properties with rated corporations as tenants on long-term leases. (See Chapter V, page 56.)

TECHNIQUES FOR ESTIMATING VALUE OF LAND AND IMPROVEMENTS IN LEASEHOLD APPRAISAL

Procedure for Estimating a Separate Land Value in a Leasehold Estate

As the *fifth step* in leasehold evaluation, it is best to estimate land value, particularly where Market Data on nearby vacant land is sufficient.

On occasion such Market Data may be scarce, but the appraiser may know from the outset the value of the building, particularly if the structure is new or recent and the builder's costs are competitive and at hand. In that case, the appraiser would set up his Cost Approach first and find his land value using the Land Residual Technique. It is a valid application to land under a leasehold.

Methods of evaluating land. Land value may be estimated by: (1) Recent sales of nearby vacant land; (2) Recently executed land leases; (3) The Land Residual Technique. This chapter will emphasize the first method, recent sales of nearby vacant land, with adjustments of comparables.

Procedure for Estimating Value of the Improvements in Leasehold Appraisals

Residual Techniques under the Income Approach. An aging leased property may produce a rental that, capitalized, proves investment or market value greater than Depreciated Reproduction Cost could show.

Therefore, one can employ other means of finding the value of building improvements when the value of the land is already known through Market Data. These means are provided by the Building Residual Technique under the Income Approach. This is the *sixth and final* step on the appraiser's road to valuation of a leasehold.

In the following Model Appraisal of a property leased as a full liquor restaurant, the *Building Residual Technique* is employed as stronger proof of value than the Cost Approach could show. The whole property is evaluated first, as in fee simple. Then, the equity in the leasehold is evaluated as part of the whole, or freehold, using the Discount Tables. Since the property is being condemned by the Highway Department, the bonus payable under the lease over 11½ years would have to be compensated in a single lump sum to the lessee. Therefore, the Table representing Present Value of a single payment of $1. at a future date, for computing the present value of a reversion, is the Table selected.

MODEL APPRAISAL

Factual Data and Important Conclusions

Date of Appraisal	February 24, 1970
Owner	ABC, Inc.
Location	399-411 Beltone Avenue, City
Zoning	Business #1, for 150′ depth. Under Zoning Regulations of the City, Chapter 21, Section 2, Paragraph (C) 1; entire land may be used for Business #1 use.
Present Use	Restaurant, with lease term remaining 11½ years.
Highest and Best Use	Present use for Restaurant on 16,700 sq. ft. of land (Parcel "A") and any Business #1 use for excess 60′ width ×150′ depth (9,000 sq. ft.) adjoining land (Parcel "B").
Macro-market Data	Subject is located in the north end section of the City. Beltone Avenue is a heavy traffic route for travel between city and suburbs. The area is commercial, light industrial and residential, mixed. Area is thriving.
Micro-market Data	Subject site is located on the west side of Beltone Avenue. The terrain is level and the soil is good. Neighborhood patronage is constant and historic.

Utilities	Electricity, water, gas, septic system, paved street, bus service on Beltone Ave.
Land Valuation	*Parcel "A"*—Total area of 16,700 square feet, 16,500 level, valued at $5.00 per square foot, including permit to operate full liquor restaurant, *$82,500.00.* *Parcel "B"*—Added parking lot area of 9,000 square feet, 8,640 square feet level, valued at $4.00 per square foot —Say, *$34,500.00.* Total Land Value =*$117,000.00.*
Indicated Values—*Parcel "A"*	Building Residual Technique Under Income Approach. . . . $113,500.
Parcel "B"	Land only (via Market Data Approach). . . . . 34,500.
	Total Value . . . . $148,000.

Final Estimate of Value, Whole Property as in Fee Simple . . . . $148,000.

Less:

Leasehold interest of XYZ, Inc., Restaurant Lessee, as part of $148,000.00 valuation:

Economic Rental	$7,500.00 per year	$625.00 per month
Actual Rental	$3,600.00 per year	$300.00 per month
Bonus Position in Leasehold	$3,900.00 per year	$325.00 per month

At 8 percent discount rate for a period of 138 months remaining of XYZ's Lease, the value of one dollar paid on February 24, 1970 is . . . 0.642772

Computed as follows:

$325.00 per month × 138 months × 0.642772 (11½ years) $28,828.32
Say $29,000.00

Leasehold Estate Equity= $148,000.00
−29,000.00

Value of the Reversionary or leased fee, interest $119,000.00

Note

Your appraiser used 8 percent interest rate throughout this report based upon the interest rate existing as of the date of this report, February 24, 1970.

Reference made to Discount Tables, *McMichael's Appraising Manual,* Fourth Edition, page 98.

FINAL ESTIMATE OF VALUE

After a study of the data and information secured during this appraisal, it is your appraiser's opinion that the Fair Market Value of subject property, as of the date February 24, 1969, is the sum of

One Hundred and Forty-eight Thousand Dollars
($148,000.00)

Special "built-in" restaurant improvements permanently affixed to the realty are included and listed separately in this report.

Note: If the court should accept values estimated in this appraisal, the owner, ABC, Inc., will be awarded $148,000, out of which he must pay $29,000 to the lessee, XYZ, Inc.

XII

Appraising Gasoline Service Stations

Gasoline service stations are commercial "special purpose" properties. They are similar to other types of retail property only as far as the importance of location is concerned. In every other regard, they are valued by criteria unique to their kind.

Introduction

The format for investment analysis of this type of income-producing property may be set up in the same investigative manner as for other commercial appraisals, i.e. Market Survey and Property Analysis, with comparables. But the approaches to value deviate from those applied to the usual income unit, and the data under the Market Survey is peculiar to gasoline stations alone.

Contrary to the laws of valuation affecting almost all types of income (or investment) property, the Market Data Approach is usually the soundest indicator of value in a gasoline service station. Land is the core of service station value. The buildings, tanks, pumps and other incidentals are in the category of site improvements, and may be easily replaced, without disturbance to the business.

Unlike other retail properties, gasoline station locations are not tested by regional or national market surveys. Location is of prime importance to the value of a station, but only as it relates to the immediate traffic artery and the highways feeding the neighborhood in which it stands. Data emphasis in the appraisal of a service station is, therefore, placed on its residential or commercial neighborhood, traffic flow, visibility, and convenience of access. A strategic right-hand corner at a busy intersection is of prime note.

A strategically located and successfully operated gasoline station will generally be found on such a corner in an established neighborhood, convenient to a dense population of homes, apartments, factories, shops and professional services. Economic level of the neighborhood is not of great importance, since low level wage earners have long proved to be heavier gasoline consumers than the affluent. They also purchase tires, batteries and accessories (TBA) more often and in greater profusion than the wealthy, who instead trade in their nearly new cars more often. The personality of the station manager and his attendants is of great importance to station prosperity.

The appraisal of a service station may be based on plans for a proposed structure on a given site as a feasibility study for a petroleum company; or it may be a report for an investor on a going business, with or without a long-term financial history. In any case, rents can be "stabilized" for the subject property by comparison and adjustment with other service station rentals in the city.

Unique aspects of value in gasoline stations. The special features of location in service station valuation make it essential that a site have qualities more adaptable to this use than any other nearby, because competition can be deadly. In nearly all municipalities now, restrictive zoning tends to insure the site, by prohibiting other stations from adjacency, sometimes putting competition as far as a mile distant. These restrictions place a special value on acceptable sites. The value of the permit is in itself a factor in land valuation.

The approved site should have a minimum frontage of 150 feet on the primary street and be not less than 100 feet in depth. It will need this minimum requirement for parking customers' cars before and after service functions, particularly where there is shopping nearby. Setback requirements almost everywhere place the building and pumps 30 to 40 feet back from entrances on primary streets. The turn-in-and-out radius requires longer frontages than formerly.

The grade of the site must be level with the street. Visibility from the highway should be clear up to 300 feet from the entrance, and convenience of access arranged at a gentle angle. The "best" corner varies, depending on traffic flow. If most of the traffic flow is turning right at the corner, the near corner is best. The far corner may be preferable where the heaviest flow is straight ahead. Generally, a corner traffic light is beneficial.

The appraiser's *initial step* in evaluating an existing or proposed station is to sense its actual or hypothetical income-producing ability to do business. Skill in service station appraisement rests chiefly on familiarity with the local market and the practices of the petroleum industry, not on estimates of gallonage, which are at best unreliable. Value of land for service station use is determined by the operator's capacity to pay rent for such use, after deducting an adequate living for himself. The income approach alone does not provide this test, and Market Data becomes most important.

Market Survey and Property Analysis

The *second step* the appraiser takes in evaluating a proposed or existing service station is to gather and correlate data which exposes the likelihood of success or failure of the station at a given location. He relates this information to his analysis of the subject property in this manner:

Macro-market

1. *The Area.* Using a road map, the appraiser circumscribes the area, pinpointing the subject and several comparable use stations. The area that this map covers will depend on population density, the size and number of arteries over which traffic flows to the subject, and factors affecting the future of subject property as follows:

a) A description of the artery on which the subject fronts; an approximation of the traffic flow, noting which is the busiest side of the street.

b) Population within a two-mile radius and the number of competing service stations serving this area. (If the city is a metropolis with population of a million or more, a one-mile radius will be sufficient.)

Micro-market

2. *The Locale.* The number of residential inhabitants of the locale. The substance of industry near the site, and its customer contribution, if any, to the subject station. The locale's atmosphere as an industrial, commercial or residential neighborhood, with the influences of all three on the subject site, carefully noted.

c) The planning and zoning practices, the tax policies, and local ordinances affecting the property and its district must be stated clearly.

d) State highest and best use of the site, and note value of the permit to the land.

e) Describe trends in the neighborhood. Is the district growing or decaying? Is redevelopment underway? Is the location the best one in the district? How far away is the residential area, schools, shopping facilities? Is the neighborhood served by main highways and a sensible traffic pattern?

3. *Property analysis and history.* Specific details of the property under appraisement must be clearly delineated:

a) Recitation of the title, including metes and bounds, assessments and tax levy;

b) Zone requirements;

c) Description of the site topography and subsoil conditions, plottage and shape of the land area, together with list of utilities on site or available;

d) The type of construction, use and condition of the proposed or existing building and its equipment, together with site improvements, planned or existing, such as paved parking, fencing, outdoor floodlighting;

e) The building must be measured and described;

f) A summary of the development of the property, if existing, with a five-year history of income (or gallonage) and expense, and type of management (company-owned, or leased) attending the property;

g) The anticipated useful life of the property must be estimated and allowances made for depreciation and obsolescence.

If the building is proposed or in the planning stage, the appraiser must project income and expenses for five years from his knowledge and experience in new service station construction, and recommend leasing provisions for the proposed building that are both practical and economic.

4. *Comparable land sales and station leases.* The appraiser must list in detail verified data concerning land sales, and sales and leases of service stations similar to the subject property, in the locale of the subject property, (unless subject is on a limited access expressway, in which case a distant comparable could be used). These comparables should be inspected and similarities or differences described, as compared to subject land or station facilities, summing up the property analysis.

THE APPROACHES TO VALUE

The appraiser's *third step* in service station appraisal lies in his choice of Approaches.

Usually a service station is similar to some others in its locale, in terms of location, gallonage and TBA sales, not to mention age, construction and services, or rental to its operator; thus, its character tends to make it comparable to sales or leases of other stations, when estimating value.

This makes the Market Data Approach generally the strongest indicator of value in the appraisal of service stations.

In the evaluation of service stations, the *Cost Approach* is likely to set an upper limit of value. The Cost Approach is a frame of reference to construction details, and the age, condition and anticipated life of the improvements, but these are replaceable without interrupting the income stream from the use of the land. It can be used as a guide, however.

The *Income Approach* is conjectural because it rests on a gallonage rate or rental that fluctuates constantly in the trade, 2%—2½ %—2-3/4%. Gallonage sales are frequently puffed up by merchandising contests and "give-aways," etc. Nevertheless, the Income Approach should be included to prove the appraiser's thorough examination of every aspect of value. The Income Approach will probably prove the lower extreme in value estimate.

Capitalization rate and method. Selection of capitalization rate and method is the appraiser's critical *fourth step* in evaluating a gasoline service station. A capitalization rate for a gasoline station is usually between 8% and 10%. Depending upon the *quality and durability* of income flowing from the property you are appraising, you can elect to follow either of the following courses of capitalization:

1. Use the straight-line depreciation plus capitalization-rate method of capitalization when you anticipate that the net income before depreciation *will decline* regularly each year in the future.

2. But if the net income before depreciation is expected to be level and is *of a contract nature,* say an absolutely net lease with a major oil company for a period of at least *fifteen years,* then the Inwood premise may be used. This premise is used only on prime, company-managed service stations with rated oil companies as tenants on net, long-term leases.

TECHNIQUES FOR ESTIMATING VALUE OF LAND AND IMPROVEMENTS IN GASOLINE SERVICE STATION APPRAISAL

Procedure for Estimating a Separate Land Value Under the Service Station

As the *fifth step* in service station evaluation, it is necessary to estimate land value, and this must be done via Market Data on sales or leases of comparable sites. The value of the land is paramount in service station evaluations.

The data gathered on other sites is closely compared with the subject site. If a comparable site has been used for purposes other than a service station, a permit value (of say 50¢ per square foot) should be added to subject, if its permit to sell gasoline has been issued. Where gasoline stations have recently been erected subject to long-term lease, the sale of the land just before execution of the lease makes excellent comparative data. The appraiser, nevertheless, should familiarize himself with all of the terms of the lease, which may have been made only as a financing gambit to help the operator and owner to set up the project.

Frequently, service stations are purchased by institutional owners (banks, insurance companies, pension funds) and leased to oil companies. (See Model Appraisal following, where this is the case.) There may be re-purchase agreements in these leases which invalidate them as arm's length transactions, so the appraiser must look in such cases only to the original acquisition cost of the site, before the lease was made.

Procedure for Estimating Value of the Improvements in Service Station Appraisals

The Cost Approach with reservations. Since land is the prime producer and the chief element of value in service stations, the improvements are simply window-dressing-with-plumbing, to be added to the value of the land. The *sixth and final step* lies in estimating the value of these improvements.

The attractiveness of the building and appropriate fittings in the service areas are more important to value than a mathematically correct estimate of reproduction cost less depreciation.

However, a recitation of costs in a service station should include site improvements, amenities and utilities. Cost of clearing and levelling the site and paving the area must be itemized. Lighting, wiring and piping, concrete mats around the pump island, pumps and storage tanks, office, service bays, and toilets must be accounted for. Obsolescence must be duly noted, because inefficiencies do not help *sales or services.*

In the following Model Appraisal of a middle-aged urban service station, the *Market Data Approach* is employed as stronger proof of value than either the Income or Cost Approach shows. (Nevertheless, the Income and Cost Approaches have contributed much to the appraiser's sense of the marketability of the property in comparison with others.)

MODEL APPRAISAL OF GASOLINE SERVICE STATION: USING THREE APPROACHES IN SUPPORT OF MARKET DATA

The following is an appraisal of a gasoline service station and motor repair garage in a business zone at the highly populated edge of an industrial city where the locale is mixed, (apartment house residential, secondary shopping and factory-oriented).

The station fronts on the main artery to and from downtown at a busy intersection, but the threat of condemnation has stunted its growth.

Purpose and Function of the Appraisal

Fair Market Value for condemnation by State Highway Department.

Valuation Premise

100,000 people live within a two-mile radius of subject. There are fourteen gasoline stations in this area.

Subject property is aging, with functional inutilities, but it is strategically located on a busy artery in a neighborhood in which it might have prospered, prior to the shadow of condemnation.

Market Survey and Property Analysis (Macro-market)

Economic prospects in the region and area are mixed. Trend is toward population increase but cut-backs in defense contracts have raised unemployment level in the city to 6%, reducing industrial activity in the area.

Micro-market

A new State expressway is scheduled to eliminate the entire block on which the subject is located, transecting overhead the street on which subject fronts. The cloud of condemnation, widely publicized in the past four years, has caused neighboring residents and businesses to move out, with a subsequent damage to growth of gallonage and TBA sales at subject location.

The subject neighborhood is urban. All public utilities are available to the neighborhood and are connected. There are sidewalks with curbs, street lights and hydrants.

There are two elementary schools within walking distance. A junior high school and a senior high school are located nearby. Churches serving all denominations are within walking distance or a very short drive by car. Lower income apartment dwellings are numerous in the neighborhood, mostly inhabited by factory workers employed in plants within a two-mile radius. A community shopping center is located two blocks south of the subject.

The neighborhood consists of commercial buildings which are in need of repair with interior and exterior decorating abundantly evident. Owners have made no effort to maintain them, due to impending condemnation.

There has been in recent times a noticeable introduction of inharmonious elements in this neighborhood, some of which may be characterized as human delinquency or "skid-row" occupancy of dilapidated vacant store structures.

Highest and Best Use

Highest and best use would be for intensive retail use such as service station, dairy bar, or other similar business.

The present use conforms to zoning as permitted by the Zoning Board of Appeals.

Property Analysis and History

Following a recitation of grantor, grantee, date of transfer with volume and page from the land records, and type of deed with metes and bounds, tax information, zone and zone requirements, the property may be analyzed as follows:

Description of Property Before and After Taking

Before

The subject is located on the east side of the main artery at the junction of three avenues. It has an area of 0.32± acres, a frontage of 106± feet, a corner depth of 140±′, and is used as a service station site and a repair garage area. It is improved with a service station and a corrugated metal garage.

Site Improvements

7,900 square feet of amesite, one 4′ × 20′ × 10″ concrete pump island.

After

Total take—no remainder.

Justification of Land Values

Five recent sales of comparable land in the same zone and locale are cited here. After study and analysis with careful adjustments as to time elapsed since date of sale, location, plottage, shape and corner influence, these sales indicate a value to subject of $2.50 per square foot. The value of the permit at subject site is estimated at plus 50¢ per square foot, therefore,

13,813 sq. ft. × $3.00/s.f. =		$41,439.00
Land Improvements		
Paving—7900 sq. ft. @ 12¢ × 378.4 (local index) equals	$3,587.23	
Depreciation 50% (observed)	1,793.61	
Depreciated value of paving		1,793.61
Pump Island—Nominal		100.00
Underground storage tanks installed (See cost index)		
4 1000-gallon tanks @ $380 $1,520.		
1 500-gallon tank @ $200 . . . . 200.		
Value of Tanks installed . . . $1,720.		
These tanks have an estimated depreciation of 60% based on 25-year life. Depreciated 1,032.		
Estimated Value of Tanks		688.00
Estimated Value of Land & Land Improvements		$44,020.61
Rounded to		$44,000.00

Building Specifications and Condition

The subject building is a commercial gasoline service station 42′ × 26′ 10″ in size. It is a two-bay building of concrete blocks with baked-enamel metal panels on front. The office space is partitioned off with concrete blocks. Its condition is good.

This station is 14 years old. Its estimated remaining economic life is 20 years. Its effective age is 10 years, as it has been well maintained and is in better condition than most other commercial buildings in the neighborhood. The floor is concrete.

The office portion is raised six inches above the remainder. A men's two piece toilet is off the back wall of the office. The women's two piece toilet is reached by a door on the south side of the building. The interior walls and ceiling are unfinished.

There is one chimney in the southeast corner of the building.

The building is heated by a suspended warm-air, oil-fired furnace. The station operator states that this was the original heating unit in the building. The plumbing is brass and copper.

At the rear of the service station lot there is a 24′ × 24′ prefabricated corrugated metal building with a steel frame. It is in poor condition and is used as a repair shop. The sheathing is rusted through in places.

Cost Approach

Source, Cost Service Manual:

Wall type #7—1200 square feet

Base Unit $5.39
Local index 381.7 (local) 1963
Total Base Cost: $20.57 per square foot

Therefore:

1127 square feet @ $20.57=$23,182.39

Lump sum additions:

24×24 corrugated metal
building—nominal 700.00

Total Replacement Cost....	$23,882.39
Less Depreciation..................................	9,552.96
Estimated Value of Service Station	$14,329.43
Say.....................	$14,300.00

Explanation of Depreciation

Physical—Normal wear and tear as observed during inspection.

Functional—Older style station, too small for location in area of a 5-way intersection; needs larger and more modern selling area, special washing area, etc.

Economic—Due to deterioration of neighboring properties and influx of inharmonious neighbors.

Total Depreciation—Service Station...................... 40%.

Summary

Service Station	$23,182.	— $9,273.	=$13,909.	
Rear Building	700.	— 280.	= 420.	
			$14,329.	
Total Structure	—Say,................		$14,300.	
Land Value			44,000.	
			$58,300.	Say, $58,000.

Market Data Approach

Five recent comparable sales of operating gasoline service stations are cited here.

These range in price from $52,000 to $85,000 and four are superior to the subject, one inferior. The inferior station was 30 years old on an inside lot.

The most similar comparable is one which sold for $61,000, and this is equal to subject in location, but slightly larger in building and land area. It is equal to subject in gallonage, but has better repair facilities. Accounting for these differences, the appraiser may compare sale against subject as follows:

Address:	440 Blank Street
Grantor:	ABC Repairers, Inc.
Grantee:	DEF Oil Co. (Arm's length)
Recorded:	Volume-1219 Page-216
Date of Sale:	May 9, 1968
Sales Price:	$61,000 (Verified by Grantee)
Lot Size:	130′ frontage and corner depth 110′
Zone:	Business #1—Station is company managed, no lease.

Sale building—a three bay station similar to subject in construction and design. It is built of concrete block with a brick and metal front. It has a concrete floor and a flat tar and gravel roof. It contains 1300± square feet of area. Included in this is an office and display area.

The station has one pump island with two pumps. Income is derived from a good repair and TBA business as well as gasoline and oil products.

Comment:

The sale is located near the downtown business area in a superior location. The subject is on a main thoroughfare further out of town. The sale building has 1300± square feet of area, the subject 1127± square feet. The sale building has three bays, the subject two bays. At time of sale the comparable pumped 25,000± gallons of gas per month; the subject averages 25,000±. The subject sells less in TBA than the comparable sale and has smaller repair facilities.

Adjusting for these factors, the sale indicated a value of $5,000 less for the subject, or $56,000.

Estimated Market Value by Market Approach

Fifty-six Thousand Dollars
($56,000.00)

Income Approach

The XYZ Life Insurance Company leased the land and building to the PQR Refining Company for a period of 20 years and 124 days starting August 11, 1950 and ending December 31, 1970. Tenant is to pay all taxes and utility charges and keep the property in good repair.

The PQR Refining Company as "tenant" is to pay the XYZ Life Insurance Company as "Owner" the sum of $1215.81 semi-annually during the term of the lease.

The PQR Refining Company as "Lessor" subleased the property to

John Doe, Jr. for a period of 8 years from October 1, 1960 to September 30, 1968. It was not renewed because of the impending highway taking. (This is also known as a "sandwich lease.")

Under this lease, the sublessee pays the utility charges. The lessor shall pay the taxes and any repairs that are not due to the negligence of the lessee. This appraiser was informed that the franchise rental is 2¢ per gallon.

The amount of gallonage pumped during the last five years as furnished by the PQR Refining Company was as follows:

1965	236,759 gallons
1966	274,224 gallons
1967	287,752 gallons
1968	316,022 gallons
1969	326,476 gallons

Explanation of Adjusted Income

The above gallonage figures show an increase each year during the last five. Therefore, the economic rent is based on 330,000 gallons at the present time. Income from the sale of tires, batteries and accessories, and repair services were not furnished, and have been offset to the credit of the operator.

Explanation of Adjusted Expenses

Expenses assignable to the lease are insurance, repairs and taxes. A management figure of 5 percent is assessed. Taxes are known, but insurance and repair figures were not furnished. Insurance was adjusted at $200 and repairs at $500.

Explanation of Capitalization Rate

The capitalization rate is made up of the interest and recapture.

The interest is figured at 7 percent by the band of investment theory as follows:

2/3 of 6% mortgage	=	4%
1/3 of 9% equity	=	3%
Interest Rate	=	7%

The remaining economic life of the building is 20 years. In order to recapture the value of the building a rate of 5 percent must be returned each year. Then,

Capitalization Rate is:

Interest	7%
Recapture	5%
	12% Capitalization Rate.

Calculations

Gross Income—$330,000 @ 2¢ . . . . $6,600.

Expenses

Taxes	$1,284.79		
Insurance	200.00		
Repairs	300.00		
Management	330.00(5%)		
	$2,114.79	—Say,	2,115.
	Net Income		$4,485.
Income Imputable to the Land			2,901. ($41,439 @ 7%)
Income to Building			$1,584.

Then, the value of building equals

$1,584. capitalized @ 12%	$13,200.	
Add Value of Land	41,439.	
	$54,639.	Say, $54,600.

Indicated Value of the Property by the Income Approach—$54,600.

Analysis, Correlation and Conclusions

Indicated Value by the Cost Approach . . . . $58,000.
Indicated Value by the Market Data Approach . . . . $56,000.
Indicated Value by Income Approach . . . . $54,600.

The three approaches indicate a range in estimated value for the subject from a low of $54,600 to a high of $58,000. The Market Data Approach indicates a value of $56,000, which I have chosen *as value conclusion.*

The Cost Approach shows the upper limit of value.

The Income Approach, I have placed as the lower limit because it is based on conjectural factors such as gallonage at the low rental of 2¢ per gallon.

Limiting Conditions

1. That estimates or opinions furnished by others are considered correct and reasonable, but are not guaranteed.

2. That title to the property is good and that the property is free and clear of liens and easements.

3. That the property has not been surveyed to ascertain whether the physical improvements are properly placed upon it.

4. That the legal description furnished is correct.

5. That separate values given the land and the building in this report must be used together and in their entirety when representations are made as to the appraiser's findings.

Salvable Items

Two sinks, two toilets, four 1,000-gallon tanks, and one 500-gallon tank.

Non-compensable Items

The following items have been considered but are regarded as non-compensable by the State government, and therefore were not included in my final estimate.

1. Increased traffic
2. Diversion of traffic
3. Loss of rights of access on new location
4. Loss of business
5. Tenant relocation
6. Moving personal property

XIII

How to Appraise for Commercial Mortgage Financing

The appraiser writing a report for the purpose of estimating fair market value, as a function of obtaining mortgage financing for his subject, is panning for gold in the fascinating millstream of money supply and demand. He must protect both prospective borrower and lender from drowning in the eddies and cross-currents, and surges and shallows of currency flow, time and rate, so that subject property is not overburdened with debt beyond salvation.

Introduction

Generally, borrowers do not want to lose their properties, and lenders have no desire to foreclose. Most institutional lenders are not property managers or real estate traders. They are in the "money game" to make money on their loans, and they don't like losers. Both borrower and lender will pay close attention to the appraiser who can reveal substance in a property which spells out a winner for both sides.

If the property lacks such substance, the appraiser will acquit himself honorably by informing his borrower of this position at the outset, and earn the respect of lenders by so doing. But if the property is a consistent income-producer, properly managed and maintained, lenders will be attentive to its appraisal.

The prospective lender must be told in the appraisal the amount of debt that the property can pay its way out of, over a set term of years, at a fixed rate of interest. Such a burden on the property usually eats up the greater part of its value, so the question looms "What is a safe maximum mortgage loan?"

Out of the burning experience of the Great Depression, sound amortization rules have developed: Most institutional lenders are bound by law to make mortgage loans of no more than two-thirds to three-fourths of a commercial property's fair market value for a term of not more than 25 years. Savings banks are usually held to 66-2/3% of value, but insurance companies often go as high as 75%. FHA and VA insured mortgages on residential properties often go to 90% and some government-backed industrial mortgages exceed the 75% limit, but on commercial properties an equity position of 25% to 35% is the rule.

It is this equity which provides the borrower's net income, after debt service; and it is this equity which is saleable and for which a market exists, that keeps the borrower's interest in managing the property alive and well. An equity position of 35% in a good commercial property is strong and saleable, as the Model Appraisal at the end of this chapter will demonstrate. The equity position must not be destroyed by an amortization schedule that is too rapid, or by an interest rate that devours it.

Dominant Requirements in Appraisal for Mortgage Loan Aims

The appraiser must have complete financial disclosure and a candid statement of aims from the subject's owner before he can determine what financing is suitable for and available to him. He must have a history of the borrower's income and expense ratio for the subject property, and he must be able to project *future benefits of ownership* of the subject property, for this is the bond, *the common interest,* between borrower and lender. If the property's anticipated earnings are soundly based, the lender can arrange a schedule of periodic amortizations of his loan to insure his margin of security against future decline in value from all causes. This amortization works to the benefit of the borrower, too, because his equity builds as his indebtedness declines, which tends to offset deterioration from all causes. The appraiser should set the limit on the interest rate his owner can afford to pay, in the summary of his report.

Data Requirements

The appraisal of a property offered as mortgage security should contain the same data that a fair market value report for any other function would be built upon. The type and amount of data required will depend upon classification of the property under appraisement. Retail stores would require the type of data outlined in Chapter VI; gasoline stations require special data as detailed in Chapter XIII, office buildings as in Chapter VIII, and so on.

However, the appraiser's feel for his borrower's property and his knowledge of institutional lending practices should be related. Whether the appraiser has been retained by the borrower to analyze the property and recommend a lender, or has been paid by the lender to screen the borrower and his property, the appraiser should be aware of compatible options in the mortgage market-place.

Requirements of the Mortgage Market

An appraiser of commercial properties must maintain an up-to-date file of local, big-city and national lenders, and should acquaint himself with the mortgage officers of such institutions. If he's working in Columbus, Ohio, the mortgage appraiser should be in touch with lending markets in Chicago, New York and Los Angeles, as well as in his hometown.

He should also know the individuals in his immediate community who sometimes privately finance real estate transactions.

The alert mortgage appraiser keeps informed as to these facts about lenders:

1. *Types of loans the lender is accustomed to making.* Some big lenders make loans on all types of properties—residences, farms, shopping centers, motels, apartment houses, office buildings and industrial properties. Others restrict themselves to specialties for which they are particularly geared. Many small savings banks lend only on residential properties. Some insurance companies lend only on apartment houses. Some savings and loan associations finance churches, apartment houses and even college fraternity and sorority houses, as well as apartment houses.

2. *Limits of size of loan the lender can legally make.* Generally, the lender is limited by law to lending a percentage of deposits on hand. The lender spreads this percentage among as many sound borrowers as possible, lending between 65 and 75% of appraised evaluation on any one given property.

3. *Territorial limits for the lender.* A life insurance company lends on a regional, or even nationwide basis. Banks usually restrict themselves to their municipal or county areas, but large ones sometimes lend statewide and even in neighboring states. It is the same with savings and loan associations.

4. *Rate of interest.* Rates vary with locale, type of property, term of the loan and quality of the security. They also fluctuate, depending on the prime interest rate.

5. *Cost to the borrower to obtain the loan.* In tight money markets, lenders often charge "points," i.e., 1%, 2% or 3% as a surcharge.

Types of Mortgage Financing

Commercial property mortgage financing can be divided into the following classifications:

a) *Conventional financing.* The simplest kind of mortgage loan is the modern mortgage loan which enables a borrower to purchase his place of business or investment property with a nominal amount of cash, usually about 35% of appraised evaluation, and to pay for the mortgaged portion in monthly amounts. This makes the mortgage payments comparable to rent, fitting the investor's budget. The monthly payments liquidate the indebtedness over a definite period, say 10 to 25 years, so that the property becomes clear of indebtedness and free of encumbrance, or "free and clear." (See Model Appraisal following.)

b) *Interim financing, or construction loan.* This is a short term loan, usually from one to three years duration, which allows a builder to pay interest only through the period of construction before he derives income from his property. It is payable in full when the construction is finished and ready for permanent mortgage financing on a long-term, amortizing basis. Interim financing is most frequently provided by mortgage companies, banks and trust companies, and savings and loan associations. Interim financing is sometimes made a primary part of a long-term loan, and is then called construction and permanent financing.

c) *Project financing.* This entails the financing of large-scale building projects by means of a Blanket Mortgage with the advancement of funds from lender to borrower on a staged basis as construction is completed, with permanent financing built into the agreement. For instance, a builder acquires and develops a major condominium or cooperative apartment project on a large parcel of land. He then builds on the same land a shopping center, costing several million dollars. Nearly all of the costs will have to be paid before the units are sold and paid for. The lender advances the money to the builder to meet these bills. As each unit is sold, the lender takes over permanent mortgage financing for the buyer, who retains ownership of the leased stores, after all the apartments have been sold.

This type of financing stabilizes the developer, protects all interests, and makes possible a better quality of construction.

d) *Purchase money financing.* This is a type of mortgage created by the buyer giving the seller a mortgage on the property in part payment of the purchase price. It can be a first mortgage, but most frequently is a second, put on after an institutional lender has committed to a first. It cuts down the amount of cash the buyer must come up with.

e) *Junior financing.* This is a term applied to a mortgage subordinate in lien to an existing first mortgage. Such mortgages are known as second mortgages. In some circumstances, a third mortgage may be made, subordinate in lien to the first and the second, but even a second mortgage involves risk to the mortgagee (lender) and higher interest and discount fees for the mortgagor (borrower).

f) *Leasehold financing.* This is favored by owners of valuable land who wish to create profitable estates without paying burdensome profit taxes imposed upon a sale. By leasing land for an extended period of time, generally 99 years, with an obligation on the part of the tenant to improve the land with suitable buildings, the owner puts into valuable use land that he may not be financially able to improve himself. A *long-term land lease constitutes practically a 100% loan to the lessee,* who is thereby enabled to employ all his available funds for construction of a building or buildings on the leased premises. The owner is spared the usual problems of management. The tenant pays taxes and insurance, and looks after production and maintenance of improvements, periodically paying his land rent to the owner. Dating back to the Roman Empire, and used extensively in the British Isles and the cities of Europe, this is a form of financing favored by owners of land in downtown business districts of large cities.

g) *Sale-and-leaseback financing.* This is an arrangement that companies which own land and buildings use to raise capital to finance expansion or to provide additional working capital. For example, corporate headquarters property is sold to a life insurance company or tax-exempt institution which simultaneously enters into a Lease Agreement whereby the seller retains possession of the property as tenant and continues to use it as before. The tenant pays rent to the buyer and assumes the obligation to maintain the property and pay taxes and insurance.

Sale-and-leasebacks have certain qualities, distinguished from ordinary mortgage-debt borrowing, which are attractive to a borrower, yet provide for the investor those elements of equity ownership and related depreciation deductions so popular in current money markets.

The benefits of a sale-and-leaseback transaction to a borrower are described in the following summary from Volume II, Number 3 of *Mortgage Marketing Trends,* published by ICA Corporation, Philadelphia mortgage bankers:[1]

> 1. The rental payments made by the Seller-Tenant are fully deductible, permitting him a unique opportunity to "depreciate" land value in some sale-leaseback transactions.
> 2. Rental deductions are allowable in full for the term of the lease, regardless of the depreciable value of the property.
> 3. Working capital is retained, and possibly increased, rather than being tied up in a long-term, fixed-asset investment, with perhaps beneficial results upon the subsequent debt picture of the Seller-Tenant.
> 4. Sale-and-leasebacks provide flexible financing on a piecemeal basis for multi-outlet marketers, with leases and premises tailored precisely to the needs and capacities of the Seller-Tenant.
> 5. Sale-and-leasebacks often induce a lender to advance a larger amount of money for the transaction, as the lender is actually a purchaser of the fee simple title to the property, and thus not limited by loan-value ratios.
>
> The foregoing is not entirely the land of milk-and-honey for the Seller-Tenant in a sale-leaseback transaction, since there are bound to be certain disadvantages depending upon the Seller-Tenant's desires and current financial position. Some of the obvious disadvantages are:
>
> 1. Loss of the fee simple title to the premises, presuming there is no repurchase option, and consequently, the loss of a possible increase in value of the real estate, over the term of the lease.
> 2. Loss of depreciation deductions. Under the applicable provisions of the Tax Reform Act of 1969, this loss of depreciation, and particularly the early depreciation deductions for newly constructed property, may become less significant.
> 3. Increase in cost of funds received per dollar, as compared to a straight mortgage loan, for Seller-Tenants of less than prime responsibility financially.
>
> Generally, a prospective Borrower (Seller-Tenant) may compute the cost of a sale-and-leaseback transaction by himself as follows:
>
> (Rental + loss of title or reversion) − (tax savings of rent deductions + use value of unrestricted working capital).
>
> For comparison, the cost of the usual mortgage financing transaction may be roughly figured as follows:
>
> (Amortization + loss of use value of working capital invested) − (tax savings of Interest and Depreciation deductions = value of retained fee simple).

Pension Funds and Mortgage Investment Trusts

The special effects of certain sophisticated and innovative methods of financing real estate, combining complementary characteristics of pension funds with one of the new types of finance vehicles, the mortgage investment trust, will not be elaborated on here, because the subject would entail a book in itself.

Suffice it to say that most mortgage investment trusts operate solely in the field of construction financing, with special capacities to originate and manage short-term

[1]Reprinted by permission of Investment Corporation of America, 215 South Broad Street, Philadelphia 19107.

investments directly, and/or with others. While some mortgage investment trusts invest part of their assets in guaranteed FHA/VA mortgages, their most profitable harvest is in the short-term construction loan area. Before making the construction loan, mortgage investment trusts (MITs) demand take-out commitments by a permanent lender who will assume the long-term loan after project completion. These take-outs are usually from conventional sources such as banks and life insurance companies, and sometimes pension funds.

Commencing the Appraisal for Mortgage Determination

The appraiser's *initial step* in evaluating an existing or proposed commercial property as a mortgage-finding function is to process its actual or hypothetical income. He decides upon capitalization method and valuation technique only after examining the subject's income stream, arriving at a rate determination based on the quantity and quality of income that he finds consistent in the property. Management is also closely scrutinized for skill in keeping income and expenses in proper perspective.

A well-designed, properly maintained, functionally apt property in a good locale is a fitting prospect for adequate mortgage financing. The credit of its owner-user and/or its tenants will have to be screened and weighed, the length of leases noted, and the prospects of the community or district measured to determine the quality of the income flowing from the property. These items having been set forth, the appraisal for mortgage function is underway.

Market Survey and Property Analysis

The *second step* the appraiser takes in evaluating a proposed or existing property for mortgage aims is to gather and correlate data which exposes the likelihood of safety or bankruptcy in mortgaging the subject. He relates this information to his analysis of the subject property in this manner:

Macro-market Study

1. *Prospects.* Trends of regional and area economic situations, measured against the demand for the use of his subject. In measuring area and municipal economic conditions, the following factors must be scrutinized:

a) Type of city government, and its effectiveness politically and economically.

b) Population of the city itself and of suburbs within a 15-mile radius.

c) Principal industries within the city itself, their growth patterns, and public utilities that serve them.

Micro-market Study

2. *Market Analysis of the Commercial District and Block.* Data concerning the immediate vicinity of the proposed or existing property should be set forth as follows:

a) Assuming that highest and best use of the site is the stated use, with public transportation and automobile parking at hand, surrounded by commercial uses complementary or auxiliary to the subject, where will the tenants for the proposed or existing use come from? State the rent per square foot in competing buildings nearby. Note number of vacancies.

b) The planning and zoning practices, the tax policies, custom, and local ordinances affecting the property.

c) Where is the demand for stated use coming from? State the scope and intensity of this demand, or reasons for lack of it.

d) Describe trends in the district and block. Is the district growing or decaying? Is redevelopment underway? Is the block the best one in the district? Is the district served by main highways and a sensible traffic pattern? Is it readily accessible to other important districts within the city?

3. *Property Analysis and History.* Specific details of the property under appraisement must be clearly delineated: (a) Recitation of the title, including metes and bounds, assessments and tax levy; (b) Zone requirements; (c) Description of the site topography and subsoil conditions, plottage and shape of the land area, together with list of utilities on site or available; (d) The type of construction, use and condition of the proposed or existing building and its machinery, together with site improvements, planned or existing, such as paved parking, fencing, outdoor floodlighting; (e) Each floor of the building must be measured and described; (f) A summary of the development of the property, if existing, with a five-to-ten year history of income and expense, and type of management and maintenance attending the property.

If the building is proposed or in the planning stage, the appraiser must project income and expenses for five years from his knowledge and experience in new construction, and recommend management and maintenance procedures for the proposed building that are both practical and economic.

4. *Comparable Land Sales and Leases.* The appraiser must list in detail verified data concerning land sales and leases of office space for buildings similar to the subject property, in the locale of the subject property. These comparables should be inspected and similarities or differences described, as compared to subject use, summing up the property analysis.

THE APPROACHES TO VALUE

The appraiser's *third step* in a mortgage-suitability appraisal lies in his choice of Approaches.

If his subject is different from any other in terms of location, tenant mix and income flow, not to mention age, style and services, the Market Data Approach may be inapplicable, *except for purposes of estimating land value and gauging the rental market.* In this case, the appraiser may substitute a Gross Income Multiplier (see Model Appraisal following) as a check point under the Income Approach.

In appraising for mortgage aims, the *Cost Approach* is not likely to add great importance to the picture, because it is the income stream and the marketability of the property which is under closest inspection. If the building is new, cost might be included to show that the owner has not overextended. But in older buildings, as long as maintenance is good, capitalized net income is probably going to show much higher value than the Cost Approach.

The *Income Approach* is the chief guide to value and is the proper test of the subject's ability to throw off a worthwhile investment yield over a long period of time.

Since the market value of an income property depends to a great extent upon the *present worth of its future earnings,* the appraiser must rationally anticipate such earnings and estimate how long they will endure, if he is to calculate their present worth in money.

Capitalization rates on office buildings will vary with circumstances. Yield percentages will differ. Choice of capitalization rate and method is the appraiser's critical *fourth step* in evaluating his subject.

Capitalization Methods. Depending upon the *quality and durability* of income flowing from the property you are appraising, you can elect to follow either of the following courses of capitalization:

1. Use the straight-line depreciation plus capitalization-rate method of capitalization when you anticipate that the net income before depreciation may not increase regularly each year in the future, but nevertheless has stable qualities over a period of years.

2. But if the net income before depreciation is expected to be level or better and is *of a contract nature,* and if the financial stability of the tenants is substantial and the leases extend over a period of at least *fifteen years,* then the Inwood premise may be used. This premise is used only on prime properties with rated corporations as tenants on long-term leases. (See Chapter V, page 56.)

TECHNIQUES FOR ESTIMATING VALUE OF LAND AND IMPROVEMENTS IN MORTGAGE APPRAISAL

Procedure for Estimating a Separate Land Value Under the Subject

As the *fifth step* in mortgage suitability appraisals, it is best to estimate land value, particularly where Market Data on nearby vacant land is sufficient.

On occasion such Market Data may be scarce, but the appraiser may know from the outset the value of the building, particularly if the structure is new or recent and the builder's costs are competitive and at hand. In that case, the appraiser would set up his Cost Approach first and find his land value using the Land Residual Technique.

Methods of evaluating land. Land value may be estimated by: (1) Recent sales of nearby vacant land; (2) Recently executed land leases; (3) The Land Residual Technique. This chapter will emphasize the first method, recent sales of nearby vacant land, with adjustments of comparables.

Procedure for Estimating Value of the Improvements in Mortgage Appraisals

Residual techniques under the Income Approach. An older property may be leased for rentals that, capitalized, prove investment or market value greater than Depreciated Reproduction Cost could show, which is contrary to the fact that on new or recent buildings the Cost Approach is usually the upper limit of value.

Therefore, we will turn to other means of finding the value of the improvements when the value of the land is already known through Market Data. These means are provided by the Building Residual Technique under the Income Approach. This is the *sixth and final step* in the appraiser's road to valuation for mortgage functions.

In the following Model Appraisal of an aging block of single-story retail stores (sometimes called a tax-payer), the *Building Residual Technique* is employed as stronger proof of value than the Cost Approach could show.

MODEL APPRAISAL OF RETAIL BLOCK TO DETERMINE SAFE EXTENT OF MORTGAGE LOAN: USING THE BUILDING RESIDUAL TECHNIQUE WITH GROSS INCOME MULTIPLIER AS A CHECK

Letter of Transmittal

June 6, 1969

Mr. John Smith, President
Savings & Loan Association
City

Re: Appraisal of Real Estate
Commercial Property
50-96 Main Street
City

Dear Mr. Smith:

At your request we examined the captioned property for the purpose of estimating its market value in fee simple, toward adequate long-term mortgage financing.

Based on my investigation, the market value, as of May 31, 1969, was:

One Hundred Thirty-two Thousand ($132,000) Dollars

Contained in my Appraisal Report following, you will find some factual and descriptive data upon which our final market value was partially predicated.

Respectfully submitted,

____

Appraiser

APPRAISAL REPORT

Purpose of Appraisal

The purpose of this appraisal is to estimate the market value of the property herein described, and its function is to study the propriety of an available mortgage from a local savings bank.

The rights being appraised are in fee simple, as of May 31, 1969.

Definition of Market Value

Market Value, as used in this appraisal, is the highest price in terms of cash, or on terms reasonably equivalent to cash, which a property will bring if exposed for sale on the open market by an informed seller, with a reasonable time to find a purchaser, buying with full knowledge of all the uses and purposes to which it is adapted and for which it is capable of being used, with neither the buyer nor seller being under compulsion to buy or sell.

Market Survey and Property Analysis (Macro-market)

Metropolitan area is a flourishing urban hub in a major industrial region. City government is aldermanic, progressive, and has accomplished much in terms of downtown urban renewal, major belt expressways, and "Model Cities" programming. Prospects for further industrial and commercial growth are bright, with 1,500 acres surrounding the railroad marshalling yards laid out for development. Chief industry is transportation equipment. City population is 220,000; trade area including suburbs within a 15-mile radius is 400,000. Airport is equipped for jet service to major cities in the nation. Retail sales in the trade area exceeded $380,000,000 in 1968. Unemployment rate is 2.8%.

Description of Commercial District (Micro-market)

Main Street at this location is comprised of diversified businesses and enjoys an active market. It runs north and south, on two bus service routes. To the east and west are single and multi-residential properties. We see no trend other than normal which might effect real estate values adversely or otherwise. It has always been a good renting area for business.

Subject property is located advantageously at a point half-way between the downtown core and the northern suburbs. There are no store vacancies in the district, which supplies ancillary retail staples to a well-to-do residential population at a heavily traveled intersection of four compass directions. Average retail facility in the district is rented for $2.00 per square foot, indicating that subject might attain this, with modernizations. Traffic is two-way, and count is 19,000 cars per day, both ways. Business trend is up-grade.

Zoning

Main Street in this area is zoned for a depth of 100 feet, including the subject property which is zoned Business No. 1. The immediate areas to the east and west are primarily in a Residence "C" zone which permits one, two and three family dwellings. There are also some apartments and multi-family houses together with a few commercial uses in the neighborhoods off Main Street. Residential trend is up-grade, with large, new middle-income apartment projects in the district approved for construction.

Utilities

All utilities are available and connected to the premises, including sanitary sewers.

Property Analysis and History

The property under appraisement was purchased from the ABC Estate by the XYZ Management Corporation on December 31, 1962 for a reported price of $125,000. Volume 1285, Page 659 of the City Land Records.

Present title owner—James Roe
Quit Claim Deed from XYZ Management Corporation.
March 15, 1963—Volume 1306, Page 818 City Land Records.
North—115 feet
East—220 feet
South—105 feet on Bank Street
West—220 feet on Main Street
Contains 24,000 square feet. (See property map in Addenda.)

Analysis of Site and Improvements

The property being appraised consists of a one-story brick and frame building with eleven stores situated on a corner plot.

Tax Assessment (Grand List of 1968)		
Land	—	$23,300.
Building	—	$31,260.
Total	—	$54,560.

Tax Rate—47.9 Mills Annual Taxes—$2,614.

Site Data

The plot is located at the northeast corner of Main Street and Bank Street. The land is level with the street grades. There are sidewalks and curbing. The building occupies about 62% of the plot. There is access to the rear of the buildings over the remainder portion.

Building

Exterior dimensions total 16,401 square feet, of which 15,328 square feet is net rentable. One-story brick and frame construction. Built in 1923.

Flat roof. Eleven stores with full basements. Also, one small store between the subject and the building to the north. While the building was designed for eleven stores, there are only eight tenants. Some occupy more than one store. All have central heating and toilet facilities. Functional utility is standard for this type of facility.

The exterior needs pointing, painting and some repairs. A new roof has been applied since the purchase by the present owner.

The interiors are a mixture of finishes and are in fair condition. New store fronts might improve rental returns.

In my opinion it will be necessary to do some of the above-mentioned work in order to maintain the present rent schedule and retain the tenants. It is also possible to make some alterations and receive higher rentals. This, however, would be a matter of negotiation between the owner and the individual tenant.

Market value estimate is predicated on the existing conditions and actual rent productivity at the present time, with forecast of increasing value to subject land, regardless of the age of the buildings. If the amount of the mortgage loan approximates the present value of the land, such a loan would appear secure.

Highest and Best Use

The highest and best use of the property is that particular legal use that will support the highest market value of the land, provided the land is suitable for that use and that there is a likely demand for that use within the reasonably near future.

It is our opinion that the highest and best use for the subject property is its present use with a modern building of the same general nature, vertically expanded.

The building is old. A study should be made as to the cost of a new structure and the rent potential, to see if it would be advisable at this time to make better use of the land, perhaps high-rise, with professional offices overhead.

Valuation Process

In appraising the market value of real estate, three basic approaches are generally recognized:

1. The Cost Approach
2. The Income Approach
3. The Market Data Approach

The Cost Approach is a method of estimating market value by using a reproduction cost of the structure new, less accrued depreciation, plus the value of the raw land and any other site improvements thereon.

The Income Approach is concerned with the present worth of all future benefits. By the measurement of the income stream and capital recapture, these are capitalized into value by the use of a capitalization rate. The selection of the capitalization rate is made from the existing market and is done by a comparison with investments of similar or nearly similar character.

The Market Data Approach is a method of estimating market value by considering recent sales of similar or nearly comparable properties and making certain adjustments for differences between them and the subject property, in order to arrive at a market value by the process of comparison. The sales are analyzed for the purpose of estimating a price which the prudent buyer would be willing to pay for the subject property, by comparison with prices paid for similar properties.

Although only one approach is designated by name as market orientated, all three are directly connected to the market.

Each of these approaches has its ultimate significance and their prime importance is dependent on the type of property being appraised and the purpose for which it is being made.

Land Valuation

A study of six comparable land sales in the area and other similar neighborhoods leads us to conclude a land value for the subject of $3.50 per square foot.

Land area—24,000 square feet at $3.50= $48,000.

Land Value - $84,000.

1. *Cost Approach*

Because the building is old and not likely to be reproduced on today's market, it is difficult to figure depreciation with any degree of accuracy; I am not using the Cost Approach to value.

Furthermore, the prudent buyer rarely considers this method of valuation when purchasing this type of property.

2. *Income Approach*—Rent Schedule—Current Year

No.	*Tenant*	*Monthly Rental*	*Sq. Ft. Area*	*Rental Sq. Ft.*	*Annual Rental*	
50	Interior Decorator	$150.	1,228	$1.46	$1,800.	*

56	Lamp Shop	$300.	2,560	$1.41	$3,600.	NL
66	Beauty Salon	$150.	1,184	$1.52	$1,800.	*
68	Restaurant	$350.	4,440	$0.95	$4,200.	*
82	Appliances		(included below)			
88	Fur Shop	$100.	814	$1.47	$1,200.	**
90	Printers	$115.	1,110	$1.24	$1,380.	NL
92	Appliances	$250.	2,912	$1.03	$3,000.	***
96	News Shop	$ 40.	480	$1.00	$ 480.	NL
	Signs (4 on roof) (Billboard)	$ 50.	600	$1.00	$ 600.	NL
		$1,505.	15,328	$1.19 Avg	$18,060.	

NL—No Lease.
Leases expire *Sept. 30, 1975; **April 30, 1978; ***Dec. 31, 1979

Rental at 92 (includes store at 82): It does not include the concrete block addition in the rear, used by the Appliance Dealer, which we understand is owned by him and extends over onto his property in the rear. All square foot areas have been approximated but are believed to be substantially correct, though not exact.

The annual gross rental income was increased by the present owner since the date of his purchase, December 1962, when gross rents were $16,500. Rents have increased slightly each year since, but will peak out if store fronts are not modernized. Owner says he will implement these modernizations next year. His management of the property is conscientious.

The Building Residual Technique is applied thus:

Annual Gross Rental Income		$18,060.
Estimated vacancy allowance, 5%—called		900.
Annual Effective Gross Rental Income		$17,160.
Estimated Annual Expenses:		
Real Estate Taxes	$2,700.	
Fire and liability ins.	900.	
Water	160.	
Reserve for repairs and Replacements	1,000.	
Total		$ 4,760.
Net income from property		$12,400.
Income attributable to land:		
$84,000 @ 7½%		6,300.
Income attributable to building		$ 6,100.

Net income $6,100 capitalized at 12½%

indicates a value of $48,800 for the building.

Land value	$ 84,000.
Building	$ 48,800.
Indicated value by Income Approach	$132,800.

Called—$133,000.

Interest and Capitalization Rates

The "Band of Investment" theory was used to conclude our interest rate for the subject property.

Mortgage Money available—65% @ 7½%	4.87
Equity Money available —35% @ 8%	2.80
Interest Rate	7.67%

Because of the age and condition of the building, we rounded out our rate to 7½%.

The Capitalization Rate is as follows:

Capital recapture of Investment—20 years	5%
Interest Rate	7½%
Capitalization Rate	12½%

Alternate Approaches: Gross Income Multiplier.

By using an overall rate of 9½% which is generally considered by the investor, we get the following value: net income from property—$12,400 capitalized at 9½% indicates a value of *$130,500.*

Commercial properties of this type sell from 6.5 to 8.5 times the annual gross income. This factor is called a Gross Multiplier. After considering the location, the physical features of the subject property, and its age and condition, we feel a gross multiplier of 7 to 7.5 is applicable.

Annual Gross Income—$18,060×7 =$126,420.
Annual Gross Income—$18,060×7.5=$135,450.

Indicated Value—$131,000.

By the foregoing methods of the income approach to value, we find the range to be from $130,500 to $133,000.

We have concluded a fair market value by this approach to be $132,000.

Final Indicated Market Value—$132,000.

As stated in our "Band of Investment" theory, the buyer of this property would look for a return of 8% on his investment.

Estimated Value—$132,000.
Mortgage available—$86,000 (65% at 7½% interest for 15 years)

Net income before debt service	$12,400.
Debt service (Amortization and Interest)	9,500.
Return on equity of $36,000.	$ 2,900.

This shows an 8% return on the equity investment, which has a ready market. This is a fair return, justifying market value of $132,000. It should be noted that the recommended amount of the mortgage loan exceeds land value by only $2,000. Such a mortgage would be most conservative, and bears a reasonable burden on the income.

3. *Market Data Approach*

I could not find improved property sales in this area or any similar area with a sufficient degree of similarity as to age, tenant mix and location, to be considered comparable. For this reason I did not use this approach to value.

Correlation and Conclusion

1. Cost Approach	Not applicable.
2. Income Approach	$132,000.
3. Market Data Approach	Not applicable.

For the subject property, with the building thereon, we have concluded a value of $132,000. This figures $5.49 per square foot of land area including the land.

It is our opinion that this is a fair and just value for the property "as is."

FINAL MARKET VALUE ESTIMATE

(Real Estate Only)
as of May 31, 1969
$132,000.00

Notes:

1) The "Lender's Market" of 1969–70 brought changes in the "standard" capitalization rates applied by lenders to retail properties earlier in the sixties. When interest rates climbed to a range between 8.5 and 10.5 percent, a cap rate of 8.5 percent seemed imperative as applied to 15–20 year leases from national chain tenants in shopping centers, such as Sears, Penney and Kress. For secondary tenants in shopping centers, i.e. chain stores with net worth of less than six million, a 9.5 percent cap rate has lately been applied. For still smaller chains and local tenants, a 10.5 percent cap rate is being used. These are overall rates, including depreciation.

2) Even with a quoted "prime rate" of 8.5 percent, most lending institutions have been making loans with 9.5 percent to 13 percent interest, with few customers qualifying as "prime." Therefore the "prime rate" could be stated as 3 percent. If no one qualifies as a prime borrower, it makes no difference. With the new federal laws, the

banks can pay their depositors a higher rate of interest, and recently there has been talk of the banks lowering their "prime rate." This does not signify that money will flow to borrowers in abundance, only that more banks may follow the trend of some by doing more business, but making less profit.

XIV

What to Look For in Condemnation Proceedings

Chapters VII, VIII, XI, and XIII of this book have presented Model Appraisals *in narrative form* of properties being taken, under power of eminent domain, in condemnation proceedings, by various agencies of city, state or federal governments. These appraisals were worded as if written for attorneys *representing owners,* where the narrative form is acceptable, and often requested. Chapter VII, on shopping center evaluation, demonstrated "The *Partial* Take" procedure earlier discussed in Chapter V in the section on "Before" and "After" values, as written in narrative for the owner.

Consequently, this chapter will dwell on "The *Total* Take," and will use the "49-Point Form" which is compulsory when writing appraisals for federal agencies, and in states where federal funding is involved in state acquisitions. This time, we will be appraising for the *condemnor,* rather than the owner.

The *49-Point Form* has much to be said for it. Chiefly, it eliminates any possibility of oversight or forgetfulness on the part of the appraiser or the government, which sometimes happens in *narrative* reports. Further, it rules out redundancies, and funnels the appraiser's concentration. Some appraisers now use it in all types of appraisal function, on both sides of the eminent domain procedure, and it is perfectly acceptable, even preferred by most of the courts of the nation.

Introduction

Generally, there are two appraisals required by federal, state, or municipal agencies in the condemnation of private property that is to be used for public improvements such as expressways, parks and public buildings. Two more are usually sought by the attorneys representing the condemned property owner in opposition to the taking authority.

So there are likely to be at least four distinct and different reports for a judge, referee, committee of judges, or jury to study before settling on one of them as most approximate to fair market value.

One of the reasons for so many testimonials in condemnation proceedings is that the property in question is being seized or confiscated, if you will, by a power taking it from an *unwilling* seller, which defies the very definition of Fair Market Value (where there must be a *willing* seller and a knowledgeable buyer operating under no *undue pressure*).

The Fifth Amendment of the U.S. Constitution concludes ". . . nor shall private property be taken for public use without *just compensation.*"

The Fourteenth Amendment emphasizes this with: " . . . nor shall any state deprive any person of life, liberty, or property without *due process of law,* nor deny to any person within its jurisdiction the equal protection of the laws."

The U.S. Constitution, however, does not go on to define "just compensation," but leaves it to be given meaning by judges in federal and state courts.

In attempting to define *just compensation,* one must note the jurisdiction under which a case is to be tried, since definitions of value and the right of an appraising witness to prove value vary in different states. There are many conflicting views as to what constitutes market value where an *unwilling* seller is forced to part with property that may have priceless sentimental value attached, or may be his irreplaceable place of business, indeed his livelihood. Most often, judicial opinion equates market value with market price, and with discretion adds something for emotional upset and damages to business as usual, "to make whole" indemnity to the condemnee. So the appraiser appears in court with his opinion of market value, and the judge or jury takes it from there.

Five elements to look for, which make up the basis for compensation when real property is condemned under eminent domain, are:

1. Market value of the land actually condemned.
2. Severance damage, if any, due to the remainder.
3. Market value of the total, or any part, of the improvement condemned.
4. Cost of proper restoration of any remainder of such an improvement.
5. Consequent damages to the improvement owing to impaired economic utility or injury to its rental value. (See Partial Take of the Shopping Center parking lot and consequent Lease Damages, in Model Appraisal, Chapter VII).

Dominant Requirements in Appraisal for Condemnation

Familiarity and practice in the applications of severance damages, and "Before" and "After" appraisal methods in Partial Takings are requisite to the appraiser approaching condemnation evaluation.

A knowledge of the "Before" and "After" methods of approaching easements, and *Offsetting Benefits in Condemnation,* are also of paramount importance as dominant requirements in condemnation appraising.

These subjects have been carefully explained in Chapter V, and will not be more than recalled here. Treatment of the Leasehold and Leased Fee in condemnation has been explained and demonstrated in the Model Appraisal in Chapter XI, and it would be redundant to elaborate on it again.

In summary, however, there are three premises of valuation to look for in each of the five elements of compensation listed on the foregoing page. They are:

1. *Severance damages,* developed by use of the "Before" and "After" appraisal methods, amounting to three distinct appraisals: (a) The entire property before the taking; (b) The part to be taken; (c) The remainder.
2. *Offsetting Benefits in Condemnation.*
3. *Easements:* "The difference between the value of a tract of land and its value with an easement imposed thereon, is *the value of the easement.*"

Data Requirements

The appraisal of a property taken in condemnation must contain the identical data that a fair market value report for any other function would be built upon. The type and amount of data required will depend upon classification of the property under appraisement, be it retail store, apartment house, offices, shopping center, vacant land, or special purpose.

Market data as to land sales, improved properties, comparable rentals, and income and construction will be particularly stressed in the courtroom. Whether testifying for owner or taking agency, the appraiser will be closely cross-questioned on verified data, which should be documented in detail and related to the subject property with logic and clarity. The "49-Point Form" will narrow the range of these questions to absolute principles, so it is well for every appraiser to familiarize himself with its content, even when in opposition to the government.

Commencing the Appraisal of Property in Condemnation

The appraiser's *first step* in evaluating a commercial property taken in condemnation is to process its actual income, if any, on scratch sheets, postponing his entries on the "49-Point Form" until his supporting information has been solidified. With these figures in mind, he can work back and forth through the problem of value. (If there is no income, in the case of vacant land or an empty store, income must be hypothecated on the basis of highest and best use as compared to similar occupied income-bearing property.)

The appraiser decides upon valuation technique and capitalization method only after processing the subject's actual or hypothecated income stream, arriving at a rate determination based on the quantity and quality of the income that he finds inherent in the property, or similar income properties.

In the condemnation of commercial property, that is to say, *investment property,* it is the earnings or Income Approach that will prove value, and the appraisal must begin and end in that channel, adequately supported by other data.

HEADINGS OF THE 49-POINT FORM AS COMPARED TO THE NARRATIVE STYLE

Market Survey and Property Analysis

The *second step* the appraiser takes in evaluating a condemned property is to gather and correlate data which exposes the market strengths and weaknesses of the property in its locale. Using the *49-Point Form,* he relates this information to his analysis of the subject property in the same way as though he were writing a narrative report, except that he follows the form, point-by-point, with his 49 paragraph headings already made for him by his government reviewers.

The *49-Point Form,* as will be observed in the following Model Appraisal, begins with thorough identification and description of the project-taking, together with estimate of its value, on the first page. Although this order may be different from the appraiser's narrative habit, the same factors must be weighed as in any narrative report, and the appraiser, of course, cannot complete the first page of the 49-Point Form until he has been to the end of the 49-Points and back again. The 49-Point Form does not have headings entitled "Market Survey" or "Property Analysis." Nevertheless, these studies are part of the screen through which the 49-Point Form sifts information, and the data the appraiser must collect is no less than would be required in a narrative report.

It may be helpful, therefore, to recommend the following order of data collection when working with the 49-Point Form:

Micro-market Study

1. *Property Analysis and History.* Identification of the property under appraisement must include: (a) Recitation of the title, including metes and bounds, assessments and tax levy; (b) Zone requirements; (c) Description of the site topography and subsoil conditions, plottage and shape of the land area, together with list of utilities on site or available; (d) The type of construction, use and condition of the proposed or existing building and its machinery, together with site improvements, planned or existing, such as paved parking, fencing, outdoor floodlighting.

2. *Highest and Best Use.* What is the demand for present use? Is a change of use indicated? State the scope and intensity of this demand, or lack of it.

3. *Market Analysis of the Neighborhood.* Data concerning the immediate vicinity of the condemned property should describe trends in the district and block. Is the district growing or decaying? Is redevelopment underway? Is the block the best one in the district? Is the district served by main highways and a sensible traffic pattern? Is it readily accessible to other important districts within the city?

4. *Income and Construction Data.* (a) A summary of the development of the property, if existing, with a five-to-ten year history of income and expense, and type of management and maintenance attending the property; (b) The anticipated useful life of the property must be estimated and allowances made for depreciation and obsolescence.

Macro-market Study

5. *Municipal Statistics.* (a) Type of city government and its effectiveness politically and economically; (b) Population of the city itself and of suburbs within a 15-mile radius; (c) Forms of transportation within the city and to and from suburbs and other cities; (d) The amount and substance of industry in the area and its contribution to the commerce of the city. The city's atmosphere as an industrial, commercial or cultural center, with all three described if necessary.

6. *Comparable Land Sales and Office Leases.* The appraiser must list in detail verified data concerning land sales and leases of space for buildings similar to the subject property, in the same city as the subject property. These comparables should be inspected and similarities or differences described, as compared to subject land and improvements, summing up the property analysis.

THE APPROACHES TO VALUE

The appraiser's *third step* in condemnation appraisal lies in his choice of Approaches.

If his subject is different from any other in terms of location, tenant mix and income flow, not to mention age, style and services, and its character tends to make it distinct and difficult to compare with sales of other buildings, the Market Data Approach may be inapplicable, *except for purposes of estimating land value and gauging the rental market.* If, however, Market Data is ample, it should be used as a check on the Income Approach.

In appraising for condemnation, the *Cost Approach* may lend close support to the Income Approach because the Cost Approach leads the appraiser to a close examination of construction details, and the age, condition and anticipated life of the property, hence the life of the income stream. The ratio of effective age of the building to life expectancy is crucial.

The *Income Approach* is the chief guide to value and is the proper test of an income property's ability to throw off a worthwhile investment yield over a long period of time.

Since the market value of a condemned income property depends to a great extent upon the *present worth of future earnings* it might have produced, the appraiser must rationally anticipate such earnings and estimate how long they would have endured but for condemnation, if he is to calculate their present worth in money.

Capitalization rates on condemned properties will vary with circumstances. Yield percentages will differ. Choice of capitalization rate and method is the appraiser's critical *fourth step* in evaluating condemned income property.

Capitalization Methods. Depending upon the *quality and durability* of income flowing from the property you are appraising, you can elect to follow either of the following courses of capitalization:

1. Use the straight-line depreciation plus capitalization-rate method of capitalization when you anticipate that the net income before depreciation will not increase regularly each year in the future, but nevertheless may have stable qualities for a few years.

2. But if the net income before depreciation is expected to be level or better and is *of a contract nature,* say with a bank on the ground floor; if the financial stability of the tenants is substantial and the leases extend over a period of at least *twelve years,* then the Inwood premise may be used. This premise is used only on prime properties with rated corporations as tenants on long-term leases.

TECHNIQUES FOR ESTIMATING VALUE OF LAND AND IMPROVEMENTS IN CONDEMNATION APPRAISAL

Procedure for Estimating a Separate Land Value Under the Condemned Building

As the *fifth step* in condemnation evaluations, it is best to estimate land value, particularly where Market Data on nearby vacant land is sufficient.

On occasion such Market Data may be scarce, but the appraiser may know from the outset the value of the building, particularly if the structure is new or recent, although this would be rare in condemnation and the builder's costs are competitive and at hand. In that case, the appraiser would set up his Cost Approach first, and find his land value using the Land Residual Technique.

Methods of evaluating land. Land value may be estimated by: (1) Recent sales of nearby vacant land; (2) Recently executed land leases; (3) The Land Residual Technique. (For explanation of this technique, see Model Appraisal, Chapter VI.) This chapter will emphasize the first method, recent sales of nearby vacant land, with adjustments of comparables as described in Chapter VI, page 89.

Procedure for Estimating Value of the Improvements in Condemnation Appraisals

Residual techniques under the Income Approach. An older property may be leased for rentals that, capitalized, prove investment or market value greater than Depreciated Reproduction Cost could show, which is contrary to the fact that on new or recent buildings, the Cost Approach is usually the upper limit of value.

Therefore, we will turn to other means of finding the value of condemned improvements, when the value of the land is already known through Market Data. These means are provided by the Building Residual Technique under the Income Approach. This is the *sixth and final step* in the appraiser's road to valuation of condemned structure.

In the following Model Appraisal of an old downtown retail store, office, and apartment building, the *Building Residual Technique* is employed as stronger proof of value than the Cost Approach shows. (Nevertheless, the Cost Approach has contributed much to the appraiser's knowledge of the construction and condition.)

---

1. *PROPERTY OWNER*

Appliances Inc.

2. *PROJECT NUMBER*

   Federal #595, Open Space Acquisition—#1040

3. *PROPERTY ADDRESS*

   #95-103 Blank Avenue, City

4. *ADDRESS OF OWNER*

   Mr. John Doe
   #195-103 Blank Avenue, City

5. *DESCRIPTION OF PROJECT AND CONSTRUCTION DETAILS*

   Federal Courthouse Plaza.
   Being acquired for a mall and sitting park adjacent to the new federal courthouse.

6. *DATE OF INSPECTION*

   May 10, 1968

7. *ESTIMATE OF MARKET VALUE AS OF MAY 10, 1968*

   Two Hundred Twenty Thousand ($220,000) Dollars

8. *TYPE OF TAKING*

   Total

9. *TYPE OF PROPERTY*

   Commercial

10. *TOTAL LAND AREA*

    5,900 square feet

11. *TOTAL AREA WITHIN TAKING*

    5,900 square feet

12. *TOTAL LAND AREA REMAINING*

    None

13. *NUMBER OF STRUCTURES*

    One

14. *LEGAL DESCRIPTION*

Grantor	—XYZ, Inc.
Grantee	—Appliances, Inc.
Type of Deed	—Administrators Deed
Date of Deed	—October 1, 1945
Volume—866	—Page—546
Revenue Stamps	—$30.25
Price stated in deed	—None

    Description—
      North—56.70 feet—Blank Avenue
      East—96.08 feet—Dome Realty

South—1.50 feet—Joseph Smith
East—19.55 feet—Joseph Smith
South—45.08 feet—Joseph Smith
West—120.75 feet—Homer Jones

15. *TAX INFORMATION*

Assessment—List of 1967

Building—$21,560.	Special Assessment:
	None to my knowledge
Land—$71,390.	
Total—$92,950.	Special Taxes:
	None to my knowledge
Tax Rate—	$45.60 per thousand
Annual Taxes—	$4,239.

16. *TITLE HISTORY*

There has been no transfer of title to this property or any portion thereof within the past five years.

17. *PURPOSE OF VALUE TO BE ESTIMATED*

The government desires to acquire this property in conjunction with other contiguous parcels to provide a mall (or plaza) in the manner proposed, to be located west of the site upon which the erection of a federal courthouse is contemplated. This is part of a project which will embrace an entire block bounded by Main Street, Blank Avenue, Asylum and Chapel Streets.

The purpose of this appraisal is to estimate the market value of the property herein described.

The function of this report is to assist in determining just compensation under the laws of eminent domain, as a result of the total take of the property under appraisement.

18. *TYPE OF TITLE ON WHICH MARKET VALUE IS ESTIMATED*

Fee Simple, as of May 10, 1968

19. *PRESENT USE*

Retail stores, offices and apartments.

20. *ZONE*

Business No. 1

21. *ZONE REQUIREMENTS*

Minimum Area	—900 square feet
Minimum Frontage	—None
Minimum Depth	—None
Front yard building line depth	— 8 feet
Side yard measurement	—None

Rear yard measurement	—10 feet
Maximum Building Coverage	—80%
Maximum Building Height	—20 stories or 250 feet high
Uses Permitted Under Present Zoning	—Commercial. Residence as prescribed for Residence "C" zone.

22. *HIGHEST AND BEST USE*

The highest and best use of the property is that particular legal use that will support the highest market value of the land, provided the land is suitable for that use and that there is a likely demand for that use within the reasonable near future.

With the existing improvement, I believe the highest and best use of the property is its present use. However, the building is old and, in addition to physical depreciation, it does suffer considerable functional obsolescence, except for the stores. For this reason I am of the opinion that the highest and best *re*-use of the *land* is for the proposed mall (or plaza) in connection with the proposed new courthouse.

23. *NEIGHBORHOOD DATA*

The subject property is located in the heart of the downtown shopping and banking district. All utilities are available and streets are paved. There are sidewalks and curbing.

Micro-market Study

District is urban cosmopolitan and characterized by the presence of banks, municipal offices, county courthouse, and a redeveloped downtown core embracing major department stores and other retail shops, and a modern hotel and good restaurants. Intercity bus service is available one block from subject, and a railroad station is three blocks east. Retail trade is brisk.

Macro-market Study

The new Spruce Street redevelopment project is nearby. The city has plans to rehabilitate the old central business district to coordinate its activities and environs with the new plaza thereby enlarging the downtown business area. The city's principal industries are electronics, chemicals, aircraft parts and insurance.

Population of the city proper is 189,000. Population of the trade area (15-mile radius) is 325,000. Unemployment is 2.9 percent.

24. *SITE IMPROVEMENTS*

Some asphalt pavement on side and rear of building. Good level plot, almost completely covered by the structure.

25. *DESCRIPTION OF PROPERTY BEFORE AND AFTER TAKING*

The property consists of a three- and one-story brick and granite building with a one-story projection across the front. Built about

75 years ago, the ground floor stores have been modernized. The upper portion has been only partially remodelled. See Paragraph #27 for further details.

It is located on the southerly side of Blank Avenue between Main and Broad Streets in the downtown shopping and banking district.

All utilities are connected to the premises.

Building area —10,700 square feet.
Land area — 5,900 square feet.

This is a total take so there will be no remainder property.

26. *JUSTIFICATION OF LAND VALUE*

On the following pages will be found five property sales which I have analyzed to arrive at final land value estimate for the subject property.

Comparable Sale No. 1

Location:	480 Main Street, City
Date of Sale:	January 12, 1968
Grantor:	A. B. Thomson
Grantee:	D. E. Falk
Volume/Page:	1556/358
Revenue Stamps:	$59.40
Verified Price:	$57,700.
Lot Size:	85 × 107± Average
Square Feet:	9,125
Price Per Square Foot:	$6.32 plus cost of demolition
Zoning:	Business #1 front 100 feet
Utilities:	All
Remarks:	Price was $54,000 plus extraordinary legal fees of $500 plus $3200 commission paid by buyer. Total sales price—$57,700. Old building demolished.

(Four other sales in this form follow here.)

Land Valuation Analysis (Elements of Adjustment)

Time	—	Increase or decrease in land value from date of sale to date of appraisal.
Location	—	Adjusted to density of market activity and use.
Marketability	—	Shape and size of plot, topography, street frontages and corner influence.

Sale	*Time*	*Loca-tion*	*Market-ability*	*Plottage*	*Adjust. Factor*	*Price Per Square Foot*	*Adjusted Value to Subject Property*
1	+2	+30	+25	0	157	$ 6.32	$ 9.92
2	+4	+15	+10	−25	104	$10.20	$10.61
3	+4	+5	−10	0	99	$11.25	$11.14
4	+4	+5	−10	−25	74	$15.31	$11.33
5	+2	+5	−25	−25	57	$19.40	$11.06

Sale No. 3 is closest to the subject property and has corner influence. It is not involved with the increment of plottage value. This, in my opinion, is the most comparable, but due consideration must be given to the other sales, as one sale does not establish value.

On analysis, I have concluded a land value for the subject property of $11.00 per square foot.

Land Area—5,900 square feet at $11—$64,900.

FINAL LAND VALUE ESTIMATE—Called—$65,000.

Valuation of Site Improvements

There are no site improvements.

Estimated raw land value	—$65,000.
Estimated site improvements	—None
Total	—$65,000.

27. *BUILDING SPECIFICATIONS AND CONDITION*

Type — Three- and one-story brick and granite construction with a one-story projection across the front.

Age — About 75 years. Remodelled in 1960. New store fronts and remodernization. One-story projection in front. Metal fire escape installed at rear of building. Access to rear is by a narrow passway along the easterly boundary.

Basement — *Under the main building.* There is no basement under the one-story addition. Concrete floor. Half this area is finished and used by Appliance Store. Concrete block walls separate the areas. The finished part is divided into five sections. Sheetrock walls and ceilings. Asphalt tile floor on concrete. There are two stairways which serve Appliance Store and Finance Company respectively. 400 amp electric service for each store. Offices and apartments have separate meters. Steam, oil-fired heating system for first and second floors. 1000-gallon underground fuel tank. The third floor apartments have space heating units. Ceiling height about 8 feet.

First Floor —	*Two stores*—1. Appliance Store: Area approximately 3,300 square feet. In addition to the store space there is a private office used by owner. Plastered walls and ceilings, except for the rear addition which has painted concrete blocks. Two toilets (men's and women's), metal toilet stalls, tile floors and wainscoting. Plate glass front windows and returns. 2. Finance Company store has approximately 1,250 square feet. Asphalt tile floors. Plaster walls and ceilings. Stairway to storage area in basement. Private toilet.
Second Floor —	*Private entrance* in ground center of building. Wood stairway. Plaster walls and ceiling. Asphalt tile floor. *Six offices of various sizes.* Two toilets (men's and women's).
Third Floor —	*Three five-room apartments,* each with bathrooms equipped with toilets and old-fashioned bathtubs. Each apartment has a gas-fired space heating unit. Plastered walls and ceilings. Common wood flooring. Rear access to fire escape from each apartment.
Conditions —	This property has been very well maintained and at the time of my inspection was in very good condition. To the best of my knowledge, there are no detrimental influences. Inspection date—May 10, 1968.
Other Buildings —	None

28. *COST APPROACH*

Replacement cost new from Cost Index

Pages 306–307. Three- and one-story brick and granite building.
Average Type—Base 5—3,000 square feet.
Base Index @ 100—$9.68 Ground Floor Rate.
Excess area 1,941 square feet—Adjustment factor 917
917×9.68—Adjusted 100 index rate=$8.88
Local cost factor for April 1967—365.5
365.5×$8.88—Cost new, Ground Floor Area—$32.45

Ground Floor store area—4,941 @ $32.45 (Say)=	$160,300.
Depreciation—25% (called)	40,100.
Depreciated Value of Stores	$120,200.

Replacement cost new for upper section
—$10.81 per square foot.

Area 5,759 square feet @ $10.81 (say)	$62,300.	
Depreciation: 43% (say)	$26,800.	
Depreciated value of upper section		$ 35,500.
Depreciated value of structure		$155,700.
Estimated land value		$ 65,000.
Indicated value by Cost Approach		$220,700.

29. *EXPLANATION OF DEPRECIATION*

The owners occupy one store and the basement for their business and have made extensive alterations to this portion and the other store. This part of the building is newer than the upper section, so I have applied a different depreciation for each section as follows:

Stores—	Effective Age	15 years
	Economic Remaining Life	45 years
	Total	60 years
	Depreciation 15/60ths or 25%	
Upper Section—	Effective Age	30 years
	Economic Remaining Life	40 years
	Total	70 years
	Depreciation 30/70ths—say 43%	

The above represents depreciation from all causes.

30. *SUMMARY OF COST APPROACH*

Building Value	$155,700.
Land Value (Paragraph #26)	$ 65,000.
Indicated Value by Cost Approach	$220,700.

31. *MARKET DATA APPROACH*

I could find no recent sales of downtown properties with a sufficient degree of similarity to be termed comparable. For this reason I did not use this approach to value.

32. *SALES ANALYSIS, ADJUSTMENT AND CONCLUSION*

Not applicable.

33. *ESTIMATED VALUE BY MARKET DATA APPROACH*

Not applicable.

34. *INCOME APPROACH*

Rent Schedule

Appliance Store—3,300 sq. ft. @

$4.50 (estimated) (Including sales basement and air-conditioning)		$14,850.
Finance Company—800 sq. ft. (actual)		5,100.
Six offices (actual rents)		4,500.
Three apartments (actual rents)		2,880.
Gross annual rental income		$27,330.
Vacancy Loss—		
Stores	None	
Second and third floors—5%	$369. (say)	
Total		$ 369.
Effective Annual Gross Rental Income		$26,961.
Estimated Annual Expenses:		
Real estate taxes	$4,239.	
Fire Insurance	450.	
Liability insurance	250.	
Steam boiler insurance	50.	
Water	176.	
Electricity	200.	
Fuel	1,000.	
Supplies & Maintenance	300.	
Reserves for repairs and replacements	300.	
Management—5%	1,348.	
Total		$ 8,313.
Net income from property		$18,648.
Net income $18,648 capitalized at an overall rate of 8½% indicates a value of—		$219,388.
Indicated Value by Income Approach—		$219,500.

35. *EXPLANATION OF ADJUSTED INCOME*

Estimated rentals taken from my office records of other downtown buildings of a similar nature.

36. *EXPLANATION OF ADJUSTED EXPENSES*

There were no adjusted expenses. They were taken from an average of the past five years, furnished by the owner.

37. *EXPLANATION OF CAPITALIZATION RATE*

Most prudent buyers of downtown investment properties use an overall rate of capitalization when purchasing this type of property. It generally ranges from 8 to 10% depending upon the physical attributes and condition of the premises, types of occupancy, leases and risk inherent in the property.

I have applied the rate most applicable to the subject property.

38. *CALCULATIONS*

Annual Gross Income	$27,330.
Vacancy allowance—5% of second and third floor rentals (5% of $7,380)	$ 369.
Annual Effective Gross Income	$26,961.
Less Expenses	$ 8,313.
Net Income to land and buildings	$18,648.

Net income $18,648 capitalized at an overall rate of 8½% indicates a value of $219,388.

Indicated Value by Income Approach, Say—$219,500.

39. *INCOME APPROACH* (Other than the Approach used)

Not applicable.

40. *AFTER VALUE*

This is a total take. There is no after value.

41. *ANALYSIS, CORRELATION AND CONCLUSION*

Para. #30—Cost Approach	—	$220,700.
Para. #33—Market Data Approach	—	Not applicable.
Para. #38—Income Approach	—	$219,500.

The buyer rarely considers a cost approach to value when purchasing this type of property. It generally reflects the upper limit of value. He is interested in a monetary return on his investment. I could find no comparable sales which would enable us to employ the market data approach.

For these reasons, I have relied upon the income approach as the indicator of market value, but have rounded out my final estimate to an even figure.

42. *TABLE OF BEFORE AND AFTER CONCLUSIONS*

This is a total take; therefore, there are no after values.

Final Market Value as of May 10, 1968—$220,000.00

43. *ESTIMATED MARKET VALUE OF AREA BEYOND MINIMUM RIGHT-OF-WAY LINE*

None

44. *LIMITING CONDITIONS*

I assume all information furnished me by others to be substantially correct, and that the facts and figures contained in this report are also correct, to the best of my knowledge and belief. The information contained in this report was gathered from reliable sources, but is in no sense guaranteed.

It is assumed that the title to the property is good and marketable, and that there are no encumbrances which cannot be cleared through regular processes.

I have made no survey of the property, but believe that all dimensions given are substantially accurate.

This report is not to be used in full, or in part, for publication nor for any other purpose than for that which it was made, except by the applicant, without the written consent of the appraiser or applicant.

45. *LIST OF SALVABLE ITEMS*

(x) Air Condition Units	( ) Fencing	( ) Porch Screens
( ) Air Tower	( ) Floodlights	( ) Radiators
(x) Baths (3) pcs.	(x) Furnaces (x) Oil	( ) Refrigeration
( ) Built-in Ovens	( ) Gas	( ) Scales
( ) Built-in Cabinets	( ) Garbage Disposal Unit	( ) Shelving
( ) Blowers	( ) Gas Pumps	( ) Signs
( ) Business Fixtures	( ) Hoists	( ) Storage Tanks
( ) Canopies	( ) Hot Water Heaters	( ) Storm Windows
( ) Cook Tops	( ) Hot Water Tanks	( ) Storm & Screen Doors
( ) Compressors	( ) Jalousies	( ) Shutters
( ) Conveyors	(x) Lighting Fixtures	( ) Special Elec. Wiring
( ) Cranes	( ) Lube Cases	( ) Special Hoppers
( ) Dish Washers	( ) Laundry Trays	( ) Special Plumbing
( ) Dust collectors	( ) Laundry ( ) pcs.	( ) Stall Shower
( ) Elevators	( ) Medicine Cabinets	( ) Venetian Blinds
( ) Electroliers	( ) Noon Lights	( ) Wall-to-wall Carpet
( ) Electrical Service	(x) Oil Burners	( ) Water Pumps
( ) Exhaust Fans	(x) Oil Storage Tanks	( ) Yard Lights
	(x) Plumbing Fixtures	( ) Misc.

Plumbing Fixtures (as listed)
   3 bathtubs, 3 toilets and 3 sinks in apartments
   5 toilets and 5 sinks in other areas

Special Plumbing
   1 oil-fired furnace—1 oil storage tank
   13 radiators

Other Special Equipment
   Two 5-ton York Air-conditioning units

Misc. Items
   46 lighting fixtures

Plumbing Fixtures (as listed)
- 3 bathtubs, 3 toilets and 3 sinks in apartments
- 5 toilets and 5 sinks in other areas

Special Plumbing
- 1 oil-fired furnace—1 oil storage tank
- 13 radiators

Other Special Equipment
- Two 5-ton York Air-conditioning units

Miscellaneous Items
- 46 lighting fixtures

46. *NON-COMPENSABLE ITEMS*

In estimating our value, herein reported, we have not included any items considered by the United States federal government to be non-compensable.

47. *AFFIDAVIT OF APPRAISER*

State of ________________		Name: Appliances, Inc.
	S.S.	Address: 95–103 Blank Avenue
County of ______________		Town: City
		Project: 595–1040

____________________________, being duly sworn deposes and says:

1. That I have personally inspected the property herein appraised on May 10, 1968.

2. That, to the best of my knowledge and belief, the statements contained in the appraisal hereinabove set forth are true, and the information upon which the opinions expressed therein are based is correct, subject to the limiting conditions therein set forth.

3. That I understand that such appraisal is to be used in connection with the acquisition of lands for open spaces as provided for in the Open Space Grant-In-Aid Assistance Program, and that such appraisal has been made in conformity with the appropriate state laws, regulations, and policies and procedures applicable to appraisals for such purposes and that, to the best of my knowledge, no portion of the value assigned to such property consists of items which are non-compensable under the established law.

4. That neither my employment nor my compensation for making this appraisal and report are in any way contingent upon the values reported herein.

5. That I have no direct or indirect present or contemplated future personal interest in such property or in any benefit from the acquisition of such property appraised.

6. That I will not reveal the findings and results of such appraisal to anyone other than the proper officials of the town, state or federal government, or until I am required to do so by due process of law, or until I am released from this obligation by said proper officials.

7. That I have given consideration to the damages and benefits to the remainder land, if any.

8. That in my opinion, as of May 10, 1968, the within described premises have an estimated market value of $220,000. prior to the taking; an estimated market value of $None after the taking; resulting in damages in the amount of $220,000.

IN WITNESS WHEREOF, the said (Appraiser) has hereunto set his hand and seal.

Subscribed and sworn to before me this 14th day of May, 1968.

Notary Public

48. *PHOTOGRAPH OF SUBJECT PROPERTY*

49. *AREA MAP AND ADDENDA*
Showing Five Comparable Land Sales
in Vicinity of Subject Location:

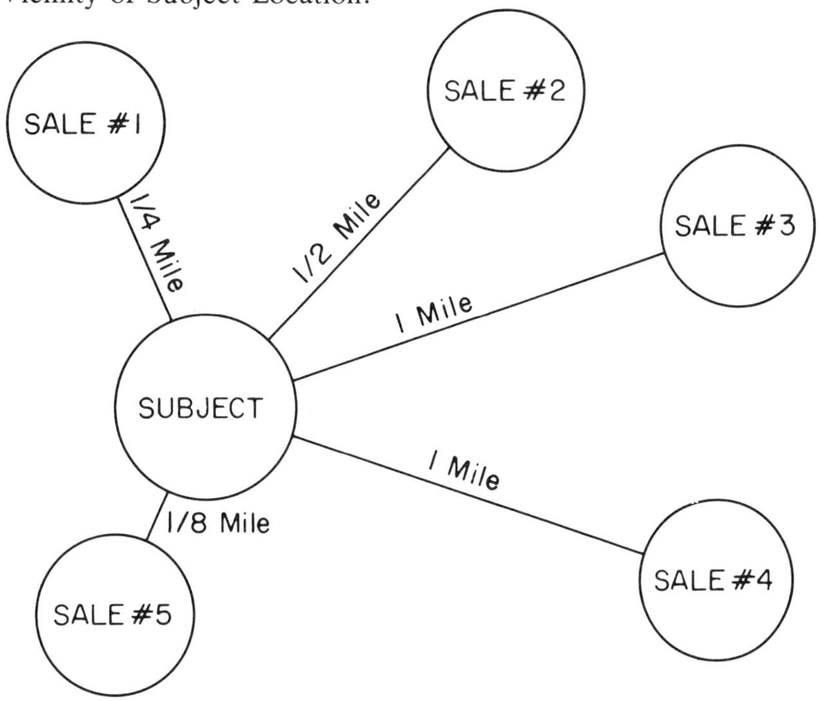

Note: In this instance, the court awarded the owner of the condemned property the sum of $300,000, as "just compensation," although conceding that Fair Market Value was approximately $220,000. The difference of $80,000 was the court's discretion in allowing for the owner's dislocation in business, and the cost of moving his equipment and stock and setting it up in a new location, in all called "just compensation."

XV

Appraising for a Tax Function

The Model Appraisal at the end of this chapter returns to narrative style, as though written for an owner's attorney, on the basis of his appeal to his local Tax Board of Review for a lower assessment on his land and buildings, owing to economic deterioration of the property's locale. It is a typical *ad valorem* appeal, and it is presented as the most common type of appraisal for tax function.

Introduction

Tax function market value appraisals are made frequently to settle disputed claims pertaining to Income Tax, Estate and Inheritance Taxes, Gift Taxes and Special Assessments, but a far greater number, involving astronomical sums and thousands of properties daily, are made for real estate assessment (or *ad valorem*) values.

On one side of the fence in real estate assessment-appraising are the armies of municipal and county assessors, often aided by professional appraisers retained to support their calculations. On the other side, there may be overburdened lessors or lessees paying exorbitant levies on properties gone into decline, unnoticed by civic officials looking only for greater revenues with which to pay for public services. This chapter will pose the question of fairness to both sides in such a situation.

Dominant Requirements in Appraisal for Ad Valorem *Appeal*

Familiarity with the assessment pattern of a city, and of variations within parts of that city, are dominant requirements for the appraiser who sets out to prove a lower market value for real estate than that long established by the city's assessors on the Grand List.

If, for 50 years past, the assessment for land value in a given downtown locale has been borne out in numerous appraisals for the Probate Court, the Internal Revenue Service, and for the renewal of major chain leases, as $20. per square foot, it is difficult to prove that within a year or two it has become less than half that value, unless the change indications in the environment are dramatically exposed.

The *purpose* of any appraisal to establish a new tax base is to estimate *fair market value* and to prove beyond a doubt that the economic climate which produced the estimate is a matter of some permanence. The data documenting this atmosphere will be of prime importance to the judge or jury reviewing the evidence. The power to tax is the power to destroy. It is also true that when you pay taxes you buy a degree of civilization. The evidence furnished by the appraiser must show which way his subject's fate lies.

Data Requirements

Depending upon classification of the subject property, such as retail use, office building, apartment house, or other, the appraisal for tax re-assessment must be bound up in the same data that a *fair market value* report for any other function would embrace. Market data as to land sales, improved properties, comparable rentals, and income and construction data will bear heavily on the consensus required to re-assess subject property's tax base.

Commencing the Appraisal for Tax Re-assessment

The *first step* the appraiser must take in evaluating commercial property for tax re-assessment is to process its actual or hypothetical income. If there is no income, as might be found in the case of vacant land, or an empty retail store building, income must be hypothecated on the basis of the property's highest and best use, as compared to similar occupied, income-bearing properties.

The appraiser makes up his mind about valuation technique and capitalization method after he has processed the subject's actual or hypothecated income stream, reaching a rate based on the quantity and quality of the income that he finds peculiar to the subject, or similar income properties.

It is the earnings or Income Approach, adequately supported, that will prove market value to the Tax Board or the court attempting to settle an assessment dispute. The tax function appraisal must concentrate on earnings when it is concerned purely with income or investment property, as the Model Appraisal at the end of this chapter will demonstrate. If decline of the neighborhood has caused a sharp slump in subject property's earning power, obviously the neighborhood's tax base must be altered.

Subject property may be well-designed, properly maintained and functionally apt for its use, but if it has permanently lost patronage in a backwater left by new economic tides in its area, it is a fitting subject for tax re-assessment.

Market Survey and Property Analysis

The *second step* the appraiser takes in evaluating a property for *ad valorem* appeal is to gather and correlate data which exposes the questionable aspects of the tax burden on the subject property in its specific locale. He relates this information to his analysis of the subject property in this manner:

Macro-market Study

1. *Prospects.* Trends of area economic situations, measured against the demand for use of the subject. In measuring area and municipal economic conditions, the following factors must be scrutinized:

a) Type of city government and its effectiveness politically and economically.

b) Population of the city itself and of suburbs within a 15-mile radius.

c) Principal industries within the city, their growth patterns, and public utilities that serve them.

d) The tax policies and municipal ordinances affecting the property and its district must be set forth, along with the planning and zone code.

e) Where is the demand, outside the neighborhood, for stated use coming from? State the scope and intensity of this demand, or lack of it.

Micro-market Study

2. *Market Analysis of the Commercial District and Block.* Data concerning the immediate vicinity of the property should be elucidated as follows:

a) Assuming that highest and best use of the site is the stated use, with public transportation and automobile parking at hand, where will the tenants for the property come from? State the rent per square foot in competing buildings nearby. *Note number of vacancies.* (See list in Model Appraisal.)

b) Describe trends in the district and block. Is the district growing or decaying? Is redevelopment underway? Is the block the best one in the district? How far away is city hall, the public library, hospitals, medical clinics, the newspaper plant, public utility offices? Is the district served by main highways and a sensible traffic pattern? Is it readily accessible to other important districts within the city?

3. *Property Analysis and History.* Specific details of the property under appraisement must be clearly delineated: (a) Recitation of the title, including metes and bounds, assessments and tax levy; (b) Zone requirements; (c) Description of the site topography and subsoil conditions, plottage and shape of the land area, together with list of utilities on site or available; (d) The type of construction, use and condition of the property, together with site improvements, planned or existing, such as paved parking, fencing, outdoor floodlighting; (e) Each floor of the building must be measured and described; (f) A summary of the development of the property, if existing, with a five-to-ten year history of income and expense, and type of management and maintenance attending the property; (g) The anticipated useful life of the property must be estimated and allowances made for depreciation and obsolescence.

4. *Comparable Land Sales and Leases.* The appraiser must list in detail verified data concerning land sales and leases of space in buildings similar to the subject property, in the locale of the subject property. These comparables should be inspected and similarities or differences described, as compared to subject land or office space, summing up the property analysis.

THE APPROACHES TO VALUE

The appraiser's *third step* in tax function evaluation rests in selection of Approaches.

If his subject is different from any other in terms of location, tenant mix and income flow, not to mention age, style and services, and its character tends to make it distinct and difficult to compare with sales of other buildings, the Market Data Approach may be inapplicable, *except for purposes of estimating land value and gauging the office rental market.* If, however, similar buildings of like use are nearby, the Market Data Approach should be employed as support to the Income Approach.

In appraising for *ad valorem* adjustment, the *Market Data Approach* may lend better support to the Income Approach than the Cost Approach, particularly in the case of older retail buildings, which would not be reproduced in like style today. It is beside the point to reconstruct the columns, high ceilings, terra cotta tile facades, and solid brick walls of 1920 vintage, when the replacement facility, rebuilt today, would be dissimilar in every aspect of construction. The current market for such buildings is the proof of the pudding.

The *Income Approach* is the chief guide to value and is the proper test of an income property's ability to throw off a worthwhile investment yield over a long period of time.

Since the market value of an investment property depends to a great extent upon the *present worth of its future earnings,* the appraiser must rationally anticipate such earnings and estimate how long they will endure, if he is to calculate their present worth in money.

Capitalization rates on office buildings will vary with circumstances. Yield percentages will differ. Choice of capitalization rate and method is the appraiser's critical *fourth step* in evaluating an income property in an assessment appeal.

Capitalization Methods. Depending upon the *quality and durability* of income flowing from the property you are appraising, you can elect to follow either of the following courses of capitalization:

1. Use the straight-line depreciation plus capitalization-rate method of capitalization when you anticipate that the net income before depreciation *may decline* regularly each year in the future or if at least it is not assured over the long term.

2. But if the net income before depreciation is expected to be level or better and is *of a contract nature,* say with a bank on the ground floor; if the financial stability of the other tenants is substantial and the leases extend over a period of at least *fifteen years,* then the Inwood premise may be used. This premise is used only on prime office buildings with rated corporations as tenants on long-term leases. (See Chapter V, Page 56.)

TECHNIQUES FOR ESTIMATING VALUE OF LAND AND IMPROVEMENTS IN *AD VALOREM* APPRAISAL

Procedure for Estimating a Separate Land Value Under the Building

As the *fifth step* in tax function evaluations, a separate land value must be estimated, since the land will be assessed separately from the improvements.

On occasion Market Data on land may be scarce, but the appraiser may know from the outset the value of the building, particularly if the structure is new or recent, and the builder's costs are competitive and at hand. In that case, the appraiser would set up his Cost Approach first and find his land value using the Land Residual Technique.

Methods of evaluating land. Land value may be estimated by: (1) Recent sales of nearby vacant land; (2) Recently executed land leases; (3) The Land Residual Technique. This chapter will emphasize the first method, recent sales of nearby vacant land, with adjustments of comparables.

Procedure for Estimating Value of the Improvements in Ad Valorem *Appraisals*

Residual Techniques Under the Income Approach. An older property may be leased for rentals that, capitalized, prove investment or market value greater than Depreciated Reproduction Cost could show, which is contrary to the fact that on new or recent buildings, the Cost Approach is usually the upper limit of value.

Therefore, we will turn to other means of finding the value of the improvements, when the value of the land is already known through Market Data. These means are provided by the Building Residual Technique under the Income Approach. This is *the sixth and final step* in the appraiser's road to valuation.

In the following Model Appraisal of older, two-story retail store buildings, the *Building Residual Technique* is employed as stronger proof of value than the Cost Approach could show. Available Market Data on similar improved facilities is included as an index of support to the Income Approach.

MODEL APPRAISAL OF TWO BLOCK-FRONT RETAIL BUILDINGS: USING MARKET DATA APPROACH IN SUPPORT OF THE BUILDING RESIDUAL TECHNIQUE UNDER THE INCOME APPROACH

The following is an appraisal of a pair of two-story retail buildings occupying a downtown block which was formerly near the 100% corner of a city in the Northeast. The structure has, as prime tenant, a prominent national chain tenant on the ground floor with basement selling space, but the commercial district has been adversely affected with competition from new major retail facilities with ample parking in the urban renewal project nearby. Nevertheless, highest and best use of Main Street land remains retail, because the chain tenant and others will renew their leases if rentals are not increased and an overflow patronage for the locale continues to exist.

Owner of Property

Estate of John Doe
c/o Attorneys-at-Law
100 Main Street, City

Type of Title on which Market Value Is Estimated

In Fee Simple.

Purpose and Function of the Appraisal

Fair Market Value for *ad valorem* adjustment by the Court of Common Pleas.

Valuation Premise

City population is 283,000, surrounded by easy-access suburbs within 15-mile radius aggregating a trade area of 450,000. Location is readily accessible from belt parkway and in-town avenues. It is, however, inhibited by lack of nearby parking.

Market Survey and Property Analysis (Macro-market)

City and area economic prospects are uptrend, toward employment increase in the area, and expanded commercial and industrial activity in the city, stemming from outburst of growth in local firms, banks, insurance and utility companies. Retail demand from downtown and perimeter residential areas, largely apartment houses, and trade area extending to growing suburbs, suggest the location will survive as *secondary* retail use. If property for municipal parking could be made available, further decline in value might be forestalled.

Government is by Mayor and City Council. Elected officials are progressives who pioneered redevelopment in this part of the nation as leaders of a growing cultural and industrial city with a large university and engineering school at its center. Retail sales in the trade area exceeded $409,000,000 in 1969, an increase of 6% over 1968. However, sales in the principal store of subject property fell from $750,000 to $600,000, a decrease of 20% in the same year. Also several store vacancies appeared in the neighborhood.

City unemployment is less than 3% of the adult population. Defense contracts account for less than 15% of the total annual industrial output, locally.

Market Analysis of the District and Block (Micro-market)

The district, block and subject site were formerly the prime downtown retail service core of the city. In the next block, immediately to the east of subject, another national chain store occupies the former 100% corner, now dislocated by the Redevelopment Agency's recent creation of a new shopping area with ample parking at the Expressway clover-leaf.

Six blocks to the east, this regional shopping center—with 80-store mall connecting two major department stores—linked to the municipal parking garage, has left subject district, block and site a secondary retail area, and the demand for retail goods at subject site has declined sharply as compared to earlier years. Lack of nearby parking makes recovery of lost trade impossible.

An inspection of the neighborhood on March 21, 1970 disclosed the following nearby vacancies:

The Professional Pharmacy, 88 Bill Street, moved out last week.

Junior Jane Stores, 917 Main Street, vacated last month.

Double-discount, 819 Main Street, vacated six months ago.

Zane Starbuck's Property, a store burned down about a year ago, was not rebuilt at 1116 Main Street.

Numbers 713, 815 and 1017 Main Street have been vacant stores for two years.

Property Analysis and History

Following a recitation of grantor, grantee, date of transfer with volume and page from the land records, and type of deed with metes and bounds, tax information, and zone and zone requirements, the property may be analyzed as follows:

The Site

The subject site enjoys frontages on three streets in the downtown shopping area. Almost square in shape, the site is 13,716 square feet in area. It is on the westside of Main Street, one block from city hall and one short block from the Oldtime Hotel. It is diagonally across Sill Street from the Superior Courthouse, the medical building and the main office of the national bank, and is one block from the U.S. post office, and two blocks from the railroad station. The site was formerly within one block of the 100% corner, which has now shifted six blocks eastward due to redevelopment.

The site is within three blocks of entrance and exit ramps at junction of interstate highways.

Improvements

The land is improved with two, two-story and basement, brick-on-steel buildings, both subleased to National Shops which occupy the ground floor and basement of Building No. 1 and sublease the second story of that structure together with Building No. 2 to others. Both buildings are faced with terra cotta tile and are of sound construction, but the total age is 39 years. As a retail store this location is handicapped by lack of adequate adjacent parking space and modern canopy coverage between parking and store interior. This latter functional inadequacy is a highly depreciating factor. The improvement covers the entire land area and is not equipped with elevators.

Lessees

The XYZ Company, a Delaware corporation, owners and operators of National Shops, New York, New York 10010.

Description of Property

Building No. 1 (Lot A)

The first part of subject property is a two-story and basement, brick-on-steel building used for retail store purposes. It is located at the northwest corner of Oak Street and Main Street. The ground floor and basement is subleased to National Shops. The second floor, a walk-up with entrance at 2 Oak Street, is subleased by National to the Photography Studio.

The building was put up in 1930. It fronts 50.31 feet on Main Street and 119.65 feet on Oak Street, then runs 116.05 feet along its westerly boundary to Sill Street where it enjoys a frontage of 46.57 feet. The total area of the building, including basement retail and storage space, is 27,400 square feet. The building was modernized in 1954, but is old, functionally inadequate and has much deferred maintenance. There is no elevator.

Building No. 2 (Lot B)

The second structure was built in 1931. It is also a two-story and basement, brick-on steel building used for retail purposes.

The building is located at the southwest corner of Main Street and Sill Street, with the ground floor subleased by National Shops to three retail stores.

Hamburger House—563 Main Street (at the corner)
Clothing and Uniform Company—557 Main Street
The Shoe Shop—555 Main Street

The second floor, with walk-up entrance from 143 Sill Street, is subleased by National Shops to:

The ABC Finance Corporation
Adele's Beauty Salon (vacant)

The effective age of each is estimated at 30 years. The Remaining Economic Life is estimated at 30 years.

Present Use

The subject property, Buildings No. 1 and No. 2, are presently used for retail store purposes.

Highest and Best Use

Continuation of the present use after renovation, restoration and modernization.

Utilities

There are bituminous concrete paved streets, cement sidewalks, city sewers and storm drains, fire hydrants, gas, electricity and water on the premises.

Topography

The land is level over the entire area and at road grade on all street frontages.

Justification of Land Values

The valuation estimate for raw land contained in the subject property has been based upon an analysis of the following sales of comparable land parcels located within the general area of the subject.

There is a scarcity of comparable land sales for this property and after a thorough search of the records and amongst brokers, I have been able to find two sales only, submitted herewith:

Sale No. 1:

Location:	816 Main Street running through to South Street, City
Grantor:	William Roe, *et al.*
Grantee:	John Smith
Recorded:	Volume—1287, Page—329, L/R Town of City
Date:	December 31, 1968
Conveyance Tax:	$44.00
Sale Price:	$40,000
Area:	4,000 square feet—North, 177.85′; East, 22.91′, Middle Street; South, 177.76′; West, 22.66′ Main Street
Price Per Square Foot:	$10.00
Zone:	Business No. 1

Analysis of Sale No. 1

This sale has frontage on Main Street and South Street. It is a small parcel. Small parcels usually command a higher unit market price than larger ones. The double exposure location on South Street gives the sale a superior location. This parcel is vacant and the basement has been excavated to an approximate depth of 8 feet. The cost of this work will be attributed to site preparation and construction, and will be adjusted by deduction from the sale price.

The adjustments are as follows:

Size	−25% or $2.50 per square foot
Double street exposure	−7.5% or 75¢ per square foot
Flexibility	+10% or $1.00 per square foot
Time	+5% or 50¢ per square foot
Net Adjustment	$1.75 per square foot

Indicated sale price of subject by comparison = $8.25 p.s.f.

Then,

4,000 square feet @ $8.25 per square foot =	$33,000.00
Deduct Cost of Excavation, 1,200 cubic yards @ $1.00 per cubic yard =	1,200.00
Total	$31,800.00

$31,800.00 + 4,000 square feet = $7.90

The Subject, 13,716 square feet @ $7.90 per square foot = $108,356.

Estimated Market Value of Subject Land by Comparison = $108,356.00

(The other land sale would follow here.)

Conclusion

The two sales submitted are the only ones made recently that I considered as having comparability. I have selected Sale No. 1 as the best comparable. Sale No. 1 is located about a block and a half from the subject.

Estimated Market Value of the Subject Land

One Hundred Eight Thousand Three Hundred Fifty-six Dollars
($108,356.00)

General Description of Construction

Building No. 1 (Lot A)

Exterior:

Foundation:	Concrete and brick, 16 inches.
Walls:	Brick and concrete, 12 inch on steel frame. The sheathing of brick veneer and terra cotta tile.
Sills:	Concrete coping—Terra-cotta and concrete.

Windows	Plate glass in aluminum steel casements on the westerly elevation, on the first floor. On the second floor, steel casement and glass block facing south on Oak Street.
Doors:	Aluminum and glass entrance doors.
Roof:	Framing, wood rafters and sheathing on steel beams with built-up tar and gravel composition covering. Drains are cast iron interior.
Interior:	
Basement:	Walls are plaster and the ceiling is acoustical tile on plaster. The total area is 90% retail selling space for National Shops. Terrazzo floor, carpet on cement in part, terrazzo-on-steel stairwell, locker rooms, toilets, boiler room and utility room.
First Floor:	The first floor is used entirely by National. It is attractively decorated with plaster walls, acoustical ceiling, carpeted floors and is air-conditioned.
Second Floor:	The second floor is used entirely by the Photography Studio. The walls are plaster and the ceiling plaster on wire lath. The floor is double hardwood.
Plumbing:	The plumbing consists of piping, brass and copper, with the heating pipes covered by asbestos. There are steam radiators. There are also men's and women's toilets and lavatories on each floor.
Wiring:	Bx and conduit with fluorescent fixtures.

Building No. 2 (Lot B)

This is a two-story and basement, brick-on-steel building partially sheathed in glazed tile. It is on the corner of Main and Sill Streets.

This building is 49.76′ × 90.38′ × 54.76′ × 86.06′, or 4,572 square feet gross, including walls on base.

Three levels @ 4,572 square feet = 13,716 gross square footage (including the outside walls, stairwells, utility areas, etc.)

Exterior:	
Foundations:	Concrete and brick, 16 inches.
Walls:	Brick and concrete, 12 inch on steel frame. Sheathing of brick veneer and glazed tile.
Sills:	Concrete coping.

Windows:	Plate glass in aluminum steel casements in three stores on the ground floor. On the second floor there are steel casements with leaded panes in the offices.
Doors:	Aluminum, stainless steel and glass entrance doors.
Roof:	Framing, wood rafters and sheathing on steel beams with built-up tar and gravel composition covering. The drains are cast iron interior.
Interior:	
Basement:	Unfinished storage and utility areas with concrete floors.
First Floor:	The first floor is occupied by three stores. The stores have modern fixtures and are attractively decorated. There are plaster walls, acoustical ceilings, fluorescent lighting and asphalt tile flooring.
Plumbing:	Copper and brass with asbestos-covered heating pipes. There are steam radiators, and men's and women's toilets on each floor with a janitor's supply closet and slop sink.
Wiring:	Bx and conduit fluorescent fixtures.
Heating and Air-conditioning:	Steam, heated, oil-fired. Air-conditioning on the first floor.

COST APPROACH

As a result of the changes in materials and design and the estimates of depreciation, the difficulties of estimating the cost of reproduction new and the applicable depreciation, physical, functional and economic, in a building such as the subject (built in 1931), would be so speculative and conjectural as to render this approach of questionable worth in reaching a value conclusion.

MARKET DATA APPROACH

Redevelopment, and the construction of Route 2, a limited access highway bisecting the city from south to north, and the consequent development of the new shopping plaza, have caused a competitive condition that has an adverse influence on the subject.

I have made a thorough search of the records of Main Street properties between State Street and Sill Street for recent comparable sales, and was able to find two. Of these, I have chosen Sale #1 as most comparable. A plus adjustment has been made for the second story. The sale is a corner parcel at Main and Bank Streets, two blocks east of subject.

Sale No. 1:

Location:	900 Main Street, City
Grantor:	Darby Day
Grantee:	Joseph James
Recorded:	Volume—1286, Page—605, L/R of City
Date of Sale:	December 5, 1968
Sale Price:	$100,000.00
Building Area:	7,313 square feet (Basement and one story)
Land Area:	81.75′ ×47.99′ × 81.69′ ×48.06′ =3,922 square feet
Sale Price Per Square Foot:	$13.67
Adjustments:	
Second story	$4.60 per square foot
Time	.70 per square foot
Sale Price	$18.97 —say, $19.00

Indicated Sale Price of the subject by comparison = $19.00 per square foot.

Then, 13,716 square feet @ $19.00 = $260,604.00

Estimated Market Value of the Subject by Market Data Approach

Two Hundred Sixty Thousand Six Hundred Dollars
($260,600.)

INCOME APPROACH

Properties of this type are usually held for the net return on the investment.

A Synopsis of the Lease is as follows:

Term: Twenty-five (25) years and six (6) months.

Date: From July 1, 1945 to December 31, 1970.

Rental: Annually $31,500.00, payable in quarterly payments of $7,875.00 each, in advance on the first day of July, October, January and April.

Taxes: All taxes and assessments levied by city, county, state, federal or other governmental agency, 1944 to 1969 inclusive, and 25% of the taxes on 1970 list, to be paid by the Lessee.

Utilities, repairs, maintenance, fire, boiler, plate glass and liability insurance premiums, and all claims to be assumed and paid by the Lessee, in other words, net, net.

Option to Purchase: Until the expiration of the Lease on December 31, 1970, on 30 days notice to the Lessor, the Lessee has an option to purchase for Five Hundred and Fifty Thousand Dollars ($550,000.00). This option will not be exercised according to information supplied by the Executors.

I hereby submit the following rental comparables:

Rental Comparable No. 1

Location:	956 Main Street, City (JKL Company)
First Floor:	5,500 square feet
Second and Third Floors:	10,500 square feet
Rent:	$16,000.00 or $1.00 per square foot

Rental Comparable No. 2

Location:	1170-1201 Main Street, City (National Bank & Trust)
Basement:	4,000 square feet
First Floor:	4,000 square feet
Rent:	$16,000.00 or $2.00 per square foot

Rental Comparable No. 3

Location:	1085 Main Street, City (department store)
Four Floors:	44,940 square feet
Rent:	$51,330.00 or $1.14 per square foot

Rental Comparable. No. 4

Location:	1154-56 Main Street, City
Grantor:	The Safe Estate, c/o National Bank & Trust
Grantee:	John and Kate Safe
Area:	45.04′ ± × 92.64′ ±
Rent:	$12,500.00 per annum or $1.00 per square foot
Lease:	Executed in 1941 for 30 years

The present lessees are negotiating to renew the lease at the subject property at an annual rental of $32,500.00 and the executors advise me that there are very good reasons to believe that this offer will be accepted. The terms will be net, net, as was the original lease executed in 1945.

Capitalization Rate

The Capitalization Interest Rate is developed by the application of the Band of Investment Theory. The Rate is a rated average of the mortgage and equity positions or band of investment, as follows:

Percentage of First Mortgage available, 65% @ 8% =	5.20%
Equity Prospect, 35% @ 10% =	3.50%
Total=	8.70%

Recapture

The Remaining Economic Life of the improvements is estimated at 17.5 years, or a Recapture Rate of the investment at the Rate of 5.7% per annum. This rate reflects the functional and economic depreciation of the improvement. Interest and Recapture=14.40%.

Calculations

After a study and analysis of the rentals and leases available, it is the opinion of this appraiser that a lease of the subject property at an annual rental of $32,500.00, the Lessee to assume all taxes, utilities, repairs, maintenance and fire, boiler, plate glass and liability insurance premiums, is the Economic Rental for the property.

Therefore, a value conclusion will be processed by the use of the Building Residual Method of Appraisal.

Effective Gross Rental Income=	$32,500.
Management, 5%=	1,625.
Net Income=	$30,875.

Expenses: (The lease is net, net)

Income Imputable to Land and Improvements=	$30,875.	
Income to Land—$108,356. × 8.70%=	9,427.	
	$21,448.	
Income to Improvements, 21,448 ÷ 14.40%=	$148,900.	
Add Land=	108,356.	
Total=	$257,256.	
	Rounded to	$257,000.

Estimated Market Value of Subject by Building Residual Technique:

Two Hundred Fifty-seven Thousand One Hundred Fifty Dollars
($257,150.)

Analysis, Correlation and Conclusions

Because subject structures would not be rebuilt today in the manner of 40 years past, and because depreciation factors applied to this type of remodelled facility would undoubtedly be misleading as value factors, I have eliminated the Depreciated Cost Approach from this report. I have selected the Income Approach here as best indicator of investment value, or the market price which a sophisticated investor would pay for the property. The Market Data Approach furnishes close support to this evaluation.

Estimated Market Value by Market Data Approach $261,000.00
Estimated Value By Income Approach (Building Res.) 257,000.00

Estimated Market Value of the Property

Two Hundred Fifty-seven Thousand Dollars
($257,000.00)

XVI

The Appraisal Report and The Appraiser in Court

The Written Report

Information contained in your appraisal report is invaluable to those negotiating in real estate transactions. It is the basis of "just compensation" when condemnation must be employed. It is supporting evidence for mortgage financing, in tax accounting, for investment analysis, and for insurability. Your information may set the basis for a corporate merger, or for a long-term lease or sale of major properties. Your report may carry the germ of a new airport, a new seaport, a new church, a new university, a new hospital, indeed a new city. It should be a vehicle of opinion loaded with ideas as well as fact, because an appraisal conjures up the future as well as confronting the present on the tracks of the past.

Your appraisal assignment may be only a vacant corner parcel. Your report of this possible keystone to a block, a neighborhood or a district is important to everyone involved, and your choice of highest and best use here may influence the community for a century or more.

Your appraisal report must be a comprehensive account of the appraisal process employed by you. The premises and conditions under which the appraisal was made must be stated, and an adequate description of the physical property must be included. Reasonable discussions and analyses of the approaches employed in the appraisal process must be elucidated. These things, along with others, should give convincing evidence of the soundness and reasonableness of your appraisal process and of your valuation conclusion.

Your appraisal report should be sufficiently documented to enable a reader, unfamiliar with the appraised property, to obtain a good mental picture of it, to understand the appraisal process employed and the analyses leading to your conclusion of value.

As a minimum standard of acceptability, each narrative appraisal report involving property of substantial value will contain adequate coverage of the following items:

1. Address of property appraised.
2. Owner's name and address.
3. Signed certificate of valuation substantially as follows:

   This is to certify that I have personally inspected the property described herein, that the facts and data used herein are, to the best of my knowledge and belief, true and correct, and that the appraised value represents my best and unbiased judgment of the fair market value of the property. I have no present or intended future interest in the property. A statement of my qualifications as appraiser is included in this report.
4. Purpose of appraisal (and function, if given).
5. Date of valuation.
6. Estate appraised, i.e. Fee Simple, or otherwise.
7. All assumptions and limitations. (Concluding valuation premise.)
8. Adaptability, including highest and best use.
9. Market Survey and Property Analysis:
   a) Comparable transactions.
   b) Income.
   c) Trend of values.
   d) Adequate analysis, including physical characteristics and condition.
   e) History of the property and its surroundings.
10. Summary of controlling factors of value.
11. Value conclusion.
12. Maps, photographs, etc.
13. Qualifications of appraiser.

The Importance of Your Appraisal

The appraisal of real estate is a recognized profession governed by strict ethics as represented in codes adopted by the American Institute of Real Estate Appraisers, the American Society of Appraisers, and the Society of Real Estate Appraisers.

The culmination of any real estate transaction is irrevocably concerned with the question of its fair market value. The marrow of the real estate deal is, therefore, the appraisal and fair market value estimate.

This places the transfer of real estate on a more complicated plane than exchanges concerned with expendable commodities where the field of duplication is practically unlimited and supply or production is capable of seasonal control to meet demand. The importance of sound appraisals cannot be exaggerated, not only because the courts have established basic rules controlling the power of eminent domain, but because of the obligation of the federal government, and of the states, municipalities and utility companies to protect the common welfare in paying just compensation, under the fifth amendment of the Constitution, for the taking of private property for public benefit.

Responsibilities of the Appraiser

In accepting an appraisal assignment, it is your duty to familiarize yourself with all the particulars of real estate performance for which your appraisal is to be made; first, of course, is the purpose of the appraisal. While most appraisals are made for the purpose of fair market value, with the function of evaluating certain permanent rights in property, it is sometimes necessary to estimate value for a variety of temporary uses. Second is the estate to be appraised. In some cases a fee simple estate is to be appraised; in others, surface rights only, easements, rights-of-way, leaseholds, or other unique interests. Third, date of valuation is vital. Fourth is the application of complete and verified data.

In order that an owner may understand that the appraiser is taking all these things into consideration in making the appraisal, the property owner or his attorney should accompany the appraiser on his inspection tour, where such questions can be settled on the spot.

Court Testimony As an Expert Witness

Condemnation is often considered a severe action, but usually owners are advised, in a friendly manner, that the condemnor will institute a friendly suit under its right and power of eminent domain, in the appropriate court, so that the court may vest title and decide the question of "just compensation." When such actions are filed, the appraised values of the properties are deposited to the owner's account as *estimated* "just compensation."

Condemnation proceedings are instituted and processed through to completion by the condemnor acting through local field attorneys. It is necessary for the appraiser, if called upon, to cooperate fully with his client's attorneys in preparing cases for trial and to act as expert witness.

It is your duty as the appraiser, under such circumstances, to make available to the court all of the information at your command; to present your reasoning in arriving at your estimate of the amount of values or damages; and in general to do anything that you can to assist the court in *determining* the "just compensation" to be paid to the property owner.

You will be expected to present and support only your own conclusions. However, you must make your presentation in cooperation with your client's attorney. It is therefore important that your client's attorney have full knowledge of all the facts about the property, of your reasoning, and of your conclusions, so that you may best present the material to the court. The plan of the attorney for presenting the evidence and the exhibits must be fresh in your mind before you go to the witness stand to state your opinion of value.

Since it is your duty to present the facts to the court for its consideration, it is especially important that you be fully and completely informed yourself. On the witness stand you should present a favorable personal appearance. In all your answers, you should be frank and truthful. You should speak distinctly so that the court and jury may hear and understand your answers. You must be courteous and respectful at all times. You must not only tell the truth but readily admit the truth and any errors or lack of information.

Direct Examination

Since as expert witness you are permitted to testify as to your considered judgment of the value of the subject property, you must be truly neutral in the presentation of your evidence. That is to say, you must be interested in the truth and only in the truth, and by your conduct convince those in the courtroom of your sincerity. *You cannot become an advocate of your own opinion.*

In general, in direct examination the client's attorney will pose his questions so that the expert witness shows what he did in forming his opinion. Thus the expert witness states his opinion and has an opportunity to reveal the reasons for it. It is essential that the court be fully acquainted with the qualifications of the appraiser, and learn just how the appraisal was made, and how the value conclusions were reached. Close teamwork between the client's attorney and the appraiser should result in the presentation of the facts to the court in a fair and proper light, so that the court will be assisted in its judicial determinations rather than hampered because of lack of factual, truthfully given information.

Cross-examination

After direct examination, it is customary for the witness to be examined by the opposing counsel. This is known as cross-examination. Opposing counsel on cross-examination may inquire into your qualifications, the rationale of your value concepts, the scope of your investigation, the valuation premise used, the correctness of your computations, the relevance of your sales data, your fairness, and the basis of your employment. The purpose of this inquiry is generally to discredit or reduce the value of the testimony that you have given. This period of cross-examination is an opportunity to better explain the facts considered by you in the making of your appraisal and in your conclusion as to the just compensation to be paid. Although the cross-examining attorney is in opposition to the witness, he should be courteously answered and courteously treated at all times. Clear-cut, truthful, complete answers based upon careful work in the appraisal can go a long way toward making the period of cross-examination a time of opportunity for the testifying appraiser.

Summation

As an expert witness, you are generally considered to have the right to explain your answers. Since you are permitted to give opinion evidence, you are also permitted to explain how you arrived at your opinion. Although every attempt must be made to conserve the time of the court, you should under no circumstances answer a question without answering it fully, fairly, and honorably. You have the right to explain any conclusion that you have reached, and you are doing less than your duty when you fail to fulfill your obligation to explain in full.

The diligent appraiser's most salient service is his documented judgment. To reap the harvest of his labor, he must maintain objectivity in his deliberations. He believes in equal treatment and justice for everyone. He will not sell his honor or lower his standards for personal gain. He is dedicated to ethical rules of conduct in his relations with the public. His most profitable and worthwhile asset is his reputation for these virtues. If your appraisals are prepared in the true spirit of these high standards of personal service, the fulfillment of your important responsibilities will be assured.

The future of the appraisal profession will depend on the capacities of highly educated appraisers to counsel their clients, not only on valuation but on the overall property problem, from land-use through total development. Tomorrow's appraiser will be competing with computers, and he will only meet the challenge by equipping himself as a full-fledged real estate economist, and master of the intelligence to be fed to the computers. If this book has brought the reader a step along the road to such an education, it has achieved its purpose.

Index

C

D

E

F

G

H

I

J

L

S

T

U

V

W

Z